Sonia W. Soltero

Schoolwide Approaches to Educating ELLs

Creating Linguistically and Culturally Responsive K–12 Schools

HEINEMANN
Portsmouth, NH

To the memory of my brother Scott.

Contents

CHAPTER 2: SCHOOL STRUCTURES: SCHOOLWIDE RESPONSE FOR ELL EDUCATION

CHAPTER 3: PROGRAMMATIC AND CURRICULAR DESIGN

CHAPTER 4: PRINCIPLES OF EFFECTIVE TEACHING AND LEARNING FOR ELLS

CHAPTER 5: LEADERSHIP, ADVOCACY, AND ENGAGEMENT

ACKNOWLEDGMENTS

||||||||||||||||||||||||||||||||||||||||||||||||||||||||||||||||||||||||||||||||||||||||||||||||||||||||||||||||||||

My deepest appreciation to all who supported me in making *Schoolwide Approaches to Educating ELLs* a reality.

I have infinite gratitude to Yvonne and David Freeman for their invaluable guidance in writing this book. Their insightful direction and unwavering support was instrumental in helping me complete a volume that is accessible to educators both in and outside the field of English language learner education.

I am also very grateful to Sharon Spellman for having given me intelligent, intuitive, and witty advice throughout the writing process. I thank Sister Frances Ryan for her continual and steadfast encouragement. Thanks to my parents who gave me the opportunity to attend the best bilingual schools in Latin America. Thanks to my bilingual education, I know first-hand what an advantage it is to be bilingual and biliterate.

The most heartfelt thank you to Jose who has always supported, encouraged, and motivated me to keep writing.

And a special thank you to all the teachers, school leaders, and parents who not only informed much of the content in this book but more importantly inspired me to write it.

INTRODUCTION: CHALLENGES AND OPPORTUNITIES

Imagine the non-English speaking child's introduction to American education ... he comes to school, not only without a word of English but without the environmental experience upon which school life is based. He cannot speak to the teacher and is unable to understand what goes on about him in the classroom. He finally submits to rote learning, parroting words and processes in his own self-defense. To him, school life is artificial. He submits to it during class hours, only partially digesting the information which the teacher has tried to impart. Of course, he learns English and the school subjects imperfectly!

(Sanchez 1940, as cited in García 1991, p. 261)

The quote above, which was made almost three-quarters of a century ago, still resonates with many students who enter schools in the United States not yet proficient in the English language. Despite important advances over the past several decades in meeting the needs of linguistically diverse students, educational changes and reforms have not been entirely successful in improving the underachievement of many English language learners (ELLs). Adding to this challenge are the changes in demographics over the past twenty years that have resulted in an increasingly diversified student population. This, in turn, has intensified the need to reevaluate existing education practices and policies that affect culturally diverse students, especially students from non-English-language backgrounds. This reality has made school leaders and teachers focus more attention on how to provide improved academic opportunities for ELLs.

A CALL TO ACTION

The urgency to address the academic needs of PreK–12 students from non-English-speaking backgrounds has been recognized by teachers, education leaders, and policymakers. Educators and researchers continue to look for better understandings of the link between language, academic attainment, and educational practices, and the broader historical, sociocultural, political, and policy circumstances of students. Reforming ELL education calls for all teachers and school leaders to develop core knowledge related to the linguistic, academic, policy, and programmatic factors that result in effective learning opportunities for ELLs. The large body of research on language-minority education points to key classroom-based and school-based approaches that show promise in improving academic outcomes for ELLs. Moving toward implementation of these recommendations has the potential to reform ELL policy and instruction as well as align practice to current research and theories in the field.

Colleges and universities that prepare teachers and administrators must also respond by providing appropriate teacher preparation programs that address future teachers' diverse classroom needs. Especially important is the need to increase the number of qualified teachers who speak the home language of their students. Adding to the difficult practical issues that schools face in teaching ELLs are the scarce numbers of teachers and school leaders with the necessary knowledge and skills to address effectively the academic needs of ELLs and their families. As a professional developer and university professor, I frequently hear from classroom teachers, school administrators, and college students about the need to increase their knowledge base and understanding about ELLs and how to best address their linguistic, academic, and socio-emotional needs. In my own university, the first-of-its-kind early childhood teacher preparation program in the state requires that all its undergraduate students take all the courses for the ESL or bilingual endorsement. A worthy goal would be for all our teacher preparation programs to include at least one required ELL course.

Recently, the National Association of School Boards of Education (NASBE 2007) published a report on language and learning, *E Pluribus Unum: English, Language Education, and America's Future*. The report examines current research on the education of elementary and secondary ELLs, explores policy issues, and provides a set of evidence-based recommendations for school districts across the nation. The NASBE Study Group on Language and Learning based their recommendations on current research findings that recognize long-standing principles related to the education of ELLs (4–5):

NASBE Study Group on Language and Learning Findings (2007)

* Language acquisition is a long-term process; numerous factors affect how long it takes any individual student to become proficient in English. Arbitrary timelines are not in students' best interest.

* There is an important distinction between "social English" and "academic English." Many groups of students, not just ELLs, have trouble learning academic English.

* A large body of credible research is conclusive that strengthening native-language literacy skills improves students' ability to become proficient in English. The "best practice" literature suggests that most ELLs should be helped to maintain and develop high levels of proficiency in their native language at the same time they are mastering English.

* Schools with high concentrations of ELLs face difficulties filling teaching vacancies, are more likely to hire unqualified teachers, and are almost twice as likely to rely on substitute teachers.

Although most of what an ELL teacher needs to know is similar to other teachers, teaching ESL requires proficiency with a specialized body of knowledge and skills.

Advancing ELLs' academic achievement requires that educators think about the broader contexts and the many factors that affect the quality of education for this population. NASBE recognizes the urgency to address

> the unprecedented challenge for today's education leaders
> to simultaneously improve the quality of public education
> while accommodating the largest number of ELLs the nation
> has ever seen … [there is] widespread recognition that ELLs
> have long been marginalized and too often segregated into
> programs that suffer from inadequate attention. (p. 8)

A multipronged and multilevel approach is needed to create sustainable solutions to the education challenges faced by ELLs and their teachers. One promising response is to adopt a schoolwide approach to educating ELLs. As a former classroom teacher I experienced firsthand the isolation of teaching in traditional bilingual education programs, where ELLs and their bilingual teachers are often disconnected from the rest of the school. I was also lucky to have experienced teaching in an inclusive schoolwide dual-language program, where not only bilingual and general classroom teachers collaborated daily but where ELLs and native-English-speaking students learned and played together every day. Schoolwide approaches that fully incorporate ELLs as well as their ESL and bilingual teachers into the school community have a greater potential for improving their education outcomes.

DEMOGRAPHIC PATTERNS AND DIVERSITY

The makeup of students in PreK–12 classrooms across the United States has become increasingly more diverse, and teachers are now much more likely to have linguistically diverse children in their classrooms, even in schools with traditionally white, middle-class, and English-speaking families. At the university where I teach in Chicago, for example, a significant number of students enrolled in teacher certification programs will end up in suburban schools that, unlike fifteen years ago, now have ELLs. Except for students enrolled in our Bilingual-Bicultural Education Program, these teacher candidates have limited knowledge and understanding of a population of children that they will very likely have in their classrooms and schools. The reality of the current demographics is especially important to understand so that education leaders and teachers are not taken by surprise when suddenly they become responsible for providing quality education to ELLs.

The demographic changes in the last several decades have created both complex challenges and unique opportunities for educators who want to address the academic needs of children that come from non-English-speaking backgrounds.

Projections show that the number of school-age children will increase by 5.4 million from 2005 to 2020 and that the main growth will come from children of immigrant families (Fry 2008). Children and youth of diverse backgrounds with English-language learning needs represent a large and growing share of the PreK–12 student population.

According to the U.S. Census, the total K–12 enrollment grew 12 percent, from 45,443,389 in 1993 to 49,619,090 in 2003. In contrast, ELLs' enrollment increased by 65 percent, from 3,037,922 students to 5,013,539 between 1993 and 2003. Of the 53.2 million children enrolled in K–12 classrooms, nearly 5 million children are not proficient in English. Between 1979 and 2004, the number of school-aged children (ages five–seventeen) who spoke a language other than English at home increased from 3.8 to 9.9 million (9–19 percent). Approximately 80 percent of ELLs are from Spanish-speaking homes and are more likely to come from lower economic and educational backgrounds. The majority of ELLs were born in the United States (65.3 percent), while of the 34.7 percent foreign-born ELLs the largest proportion was born in Mexico (18.6 percent); the subsequent largest foreign-born ELLs are from China (1.2 percent), El Salvador (1 percent), Korea (1 percent), Philippines (.09 percent), Dominican Republic (.08 percent), and Vietnam (.08 percent) (EPE Research Center 2009).

In 2004, almost 70 percent of ELLs lived in California (1,591,525), Texas (615,466), Florida (299,346), New York (203,583), Illinois (192,764), and Arizona (155,789) (NCELA National and Regional Data and Demographics 2004). Recent trends indicate that ELL enrollment has increased significantly in states that traditionally did not have immigration (see Figure I-1). Between 1995 and 2005 states that experienced the largest growth rates in ELLs included South Carolina (714 percent), Kentucky (417 percent), Indiana (408 percent), North Carolina (372 percent), and Tennessee (370 percent) (Kohler and Lazarín 2007). The nationwide challenge represented by insufficient second language education, bilingual programs, and culturally responsive curriculum are especially felt in urban areas. Suburban and rural areas have also experienced great increases of recently immigrated populations that have created unique regional challenges for addressing the educational needs of school-age ELLs.

It is important to understand that the ELL population is the most vulnerable group of PreK–12 students and has the highest risk for poor academic and future life outcomes. The median income for families of ELLs is $36,691 in comparison to

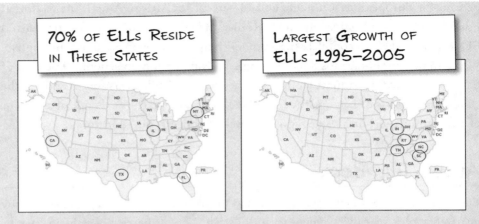

Figure I-1 ELLs in the United States

$60,280 for non-ELL families. Nearly 24 percent of immigrants from Mexico and Central America are below the poverty level, compared to 9–14 percent of immigrants from other regions of the world and compared to 11.5 percent of the U.S.-born population. Less than half of Central American and Mexican immigrants, about 40 percent, have the equivalent of a high school diploma, compared to 87.5 percent of the U.S.-born population and 80–90 percent of other immigrants (Capps et al. 2005). According to the report *Perspectives on a Population: English Language Learners in American Schools* (2009), a significant percentage of ELL families come from low-income backgrounds. In 2000 nearly 66 percent of ELLs lived in low-income families in comparison with 36.9 percent of non-ELL families (Capps et al. 2005).

Because nearly four-fifths (79 percent) of ELLs are of Latino origin and represent almost half of all Latino children (45 percent) in schools, this group has special relevance in any discussion about the academic achievement of students who are not yet proficient in English. Many factors, such as poverty, lack of English proficiency, and lack of access to social support systems, place Latino children at higher risk of academic underachievement than other groups (Suárez-Orozco, Suárez-Orozco, and Todorova 2008). Latino students have the largest high school dropout rate in the United States and have experienced an alarming rate of school failure. According to census data, Latino immigrants' graduation rates are well below that of native-born groups such as African Americans and European descendants. For example, only 34 percent of Mexican immigrants have a high school diploma, compared to 90 percent for European descendants and 74 percent for African Americans (National Education Longitudinal Study 2002). Kohler and Lazarín (2007) report that Latino ELLs are less likely to complete high school than Latinos who are fluent in English. While 15 percent of Latinos fluent in English drop out of high school, 59 percent of Latino ELLs do not graduate from secondary school. While measures to address the educational needs of Latino students have been adopted, the academic attainment of this group continues to be a great source of concern for educators.

About This Book

The ideas and recommendations presented in the following chapters are shaped by my twenty-plus-year involvement with ELLs. The book is based not only on current literature in the field and my own research findings, but also on the broad experiences I have been fortunate to have as a teacher, school leader, researcher, and professional developer. These experiences have given me an invaluable "insider" perspective and understanding about the challenges of educating ELLs in the United States.

The primary objective of this book is to provide comprehensive schoolwide frameworks for developing transformative educational opportunities and programs for ELLs that are based on the latest theory and research. In the book I address questions on how to create schools that best meet the needs of ELLs and their families by understanding their linguistic, cultural, academic, and demographic contexts. The purpose of developing these understandings among all educators, not just bilingual and English as a second language (ESL) teachers, is to create a basis for informed decision making about the instructional, curricular, evaluative, and programmatic elements of effective educational practices for ELLs. A starting point of discussion is to identify the many challenges that school districts across the United States face related to the education of ELLs and to rethink how we address these dilemmas in light of current research (see Figure I-2).

The topics presented in this book are intended for school leaders, teachers, and other educators who serve or will be serving linguistically and culturally diverse students, including recent immigrants, nonstandard English speakers, Native Americans, and other nonimmigrant groups. The content of the book is intended both for "specialists" (bilingual and ESL-trained educators) and for mainstream education practitioners, special education teachers, and school administrators who must attend to the education of all students, including those who are learning English as a new

- Rapid growth in the numbers of ELLs in PreK–12 schools, particularly in suburban and rural areas as well as regions not traditionally populated by recent immigrants
- Shortage of qualified teachers and administrators specifically trained to address the needs of ELLs
- Lack of adequate course offerings related to ELLs in most higher education teacher preparation programs
- Insufficient opportunities for professional development related to ELLs
- Inadequate funding and financial commitment by school districts and states
- Invalid accountability systems and unrealistic expectations stemming from NCLB mandates
- Structural obstacles in reaching out to the families and communities of ELLs

Figure I-2 Critical Dilemmas

language. This text is especially relevant because it provides a strong knowledge base for educators trying to transform traditional ways of addressing the needs of ELLs, or for those educators who suddenly find themselves faced with the new challenge of educating linguistically diverse learners. The distinguishing feature of this book is that it frames the education of ELLs within a broader district- and schoolwide agenda, calling for the need to view their education as the responsibility of the entire school and district. In the book I emphasize the importance of the interconnectedness of school structures that enhance the educational experiences and academic outcomes of ELLs.

In organizing the book in these categories, the issues that affect ELLs are seen as interrelated and not in isolation from the classroom setting alone, but rather as interconnected and as a shared responsibility. In each chapter I present real-life examples of students, parents, teachers, school leaders, and community organizers that illustrate the schoolwide challenges and successes of educating ELLs. All names have been changed to maintain confidentiality. At the end of each chapter is an Applications section that provides exercises to engage readers, as well as a list of Suggestions for Further Reading that includes professional development books for teachers and school leaders.

In Chapter 1 I discuss the fundamental theories of second language acquisition and explain the critical importance that this knowledge has on all education decisions affecting the academic achievement of ELLs. Educators and policymakers who have a clear understanding of the basic concepts of second language acquisition and fundamentals of language-minority education are able to make better and more-informed decisions about the education of ELLs.

In Chapter 2 I present programmatic schoolwide frameworks that support the academic achievement of all students and, in particular, ELLs. This chapter provides a broader view of the education of ELLs within the school context, placing responsibility for their success on all aspects of the school organization rather than only on the traditionally marginalized bilingual and ESL programs within a school.

In Chapter 3 I describe bilingual and English-only models of language education programs for ELLs and the types of conditions needed for effective implementation. I also provide a set of recommendations for conducting schoolwide needs assessments, identifying criteria for program selection, coordinating ELL program/s with other school programs, forming implementation plans, and creating program evaluation systems. In this chapter I give special attention to the key role that preschool has on preparing ELLs to enter kindergarten as an important foundation for later school success.

Chapter 4 begins with a discussion of effective classroom instructional practices that are situated in constructivist principles of teaching and learning, which subscribe to learner-centered active engagement and authentic learning constructs. In this section I present the types of classroom contexts for effective language and literacy development and describe approaches and activities that lead to successful student outcomes. A main focus is the development and importance of oral language (both native and second language) and the relationship between increased levels of academic language and literacy.

In Chapter 5 I bring together the remaining essential components of effective schoolwide efforts that support and enhance the academic and linguistic success of ELLs: leadership, advocacy, and community-family engagement. Here I describe the critical role of school and district leaders and offer a number of ideas on how administrators and other leaders can create sustainable and comprehensive improvements for ELLs' education. In the next section of this chapter I discuss the role of advocacy as a fundamental aspect of school improvement efforts. In the final section

I describe the types of family and community participation and involvement that best support students' learning and positive academic outcomes.

The quote at the beginning of this introduction describes the confusion and isolation that many ELLs still experience as they enter school for the first time. ELLs' introduction to U.S. education does not have to be a painful and confusing experience. School and classroom practices that support the learning and socio-emotional needs of children not yet proficient in English help them to be engaged in school from the moment they walk through the classroom door. This book offers a comprehensive and integrated approach that best addresses the academic, linguistic, and sociocultural needs of ELLs.

(Credits continued from p. ii)

Naperville Community Unit School District 203 *Diversity Statement.* Used by permission of Naperville Community Unit School District 203, Naperville, Illinois.

Joint Statement on the Teacher English Fluency Initiative in Arizona issued as a press release on May 14, 2010 by TESOL and AZ-TESOL. Reprinted by permission of TESOL.

NCTE Speaks Out on Arizona Department of Education Ruling on Teacher Speech issued as a press release on June 7, 2010. Reprinted by permission of NCTE.

Schoolwide Approaches to Educating ELLs

Chapter 1

Critical Issues in Second Language Acquisition

Sometimes in education, there are great divides between evidence concerning the effectiveness of one or another instructional strategy and public perceptions and even public policy. Bilingualism is an example of such a divide.

(Lagemann, Bilingual Benefits Interdisciplinary Perspectives Conference 2004)

As the chapter opening quote suggests, educating English Language Learners (ELLs) is not a simple undertaking. Everything to do with ELLs is open to debate by both educators and the public alike: from whether ELLs should receive instruction in the native language or not, to whether they should even receive any education services at all if they are undocumented. Many of these debates are grounded on common but incorrect assumptions about language acquisition. This chapter clarifies these mistaken beliefs and explains basic principles about second language acquisition and ELLs.

Across the United States there is growing recognition that proficiency in more than one language benefits both the individual and society, an idea supported by extensive research findings. Studies show that individuals who are proficient in more than one language experience both cognitive and academic advantages, interact better with others, have more employment opportunities, and earn more money (Caldas and Boudreaux 1999; Thomas, Collier, and Abbott 1993). For a society, multilingual and multiliterate citizens are better able to interact with others, whether they are different or alike. Increasing this type of cross-cultural knowledge and understanding can improve intergroup relations, strengthen a nation's political and security stability, and enhance economic competitiveness abroad. By developing understandings of the customs, languages, and values of other cultures we are more likely to reduce intergroup conflict and to build stronger collaborations among diverse groups.

The position of the United States as a political global leader requires that its citizens have knowledge of the world, a deep understanding of other cultures, and the ability to speak languages other than English. In addition, there is an urgent need in the United States for bilingual and biliterate people who can read and write in multiple languages, for business and social services as well as for national security and diplomacy. This "linguistic capital"—the advantages that come with being literate in two languages—offers benefits both to society and to individuals who are bilingual and biliterate. Schools are where biliteracy can best be developed.

In this chapter, I present key topics related to second language acquisition that focus both on linguistic and cognitive processes as well as sociocultural and sociolinguistic factors. The first section of the chapter presents a summary of the many internal (individual) and external (societal) factors that can shape the academic outcomes of ELLs as well as theories of second language acquisition. This is followed by a discussion of the most common misconceptions related to the acquisition of English as a second language. The main purpose of this chapter is to offer a general background on the sociolinguistic aspects of second language acquisition as a foundation for contextualized programmatic and curricular decision making for ELLs.

FACTORS THAT AFFECT SECOND LANGUAGE ACQUISITION

Aadesh spent his early childhood on the north side of Chicago in a culturally and linguistically rich and lively community made up of mostly Indian, Pakistani, and Bangladeshi descent, where he felt at home surrounded by familiar sounds, smells, and sights. Now a young adult, he remembers being happy and thriving during those years. When he turned six, however, the family moved to a mostly white suburb because of his father's new job. It was not long before Aadesh began to be teased by his new suburban classmates for the way he looked, the lunch food he brought to school, his name, his heavy accent and broken English, and many other things that made him feel rejected by his new school and ashamed of his background. Beyond having to put up with his peers' teasing, he had to deal with teachers who, although well meaning, were full of stereotypes and unrealistic expectations. He remembers teachers commenting on how "all Indians speak English" and how "Indian kids are really smart, so he does not need ESL." He also painfully remembers that he never had much to share in class because his experiences and stories were so very different from those of the other students. To cope, he ended up inventing stories about his summer vacations and what gifts he got for Christmas, which his family did not celebrate. Aadesh quickly adopted the American English way of speaking from his peers in an effort to fit in and be accepted by his classmates. Unfortunately, his quick acquisition of conversational skills led teachers to believe that he was fully proficient in English and capable of tackling academic subjects at the same level as his English-speaking peers. Aadesh remembers struggling with academic subjects, especially in literacy and social studies, not having sufficient background with academic English or American history and culture.

Aadesh's experiences illustrate how several factors interact to influence the academic success or failure of ELLs. These factors are both internal and external and have a direct impact on the academic achievement and overall school success of

ELLs. Internal factors that influence second language acquisition include personality traits, age, motivation, attitude, self-esteem, learning style, and level of proficiency in the native language. For Aadesh, what once was a very healthy self-esteem quickly turned to insecurity and a negative self-image when his family enrolled him in a school that had little understanding of his background. On the other hand, external factors that affect the acquisition of a second language involve social conditions and structures related to the learner, including quality of second language instruction, access to speakers of the second language, teacher expectations, education policies and instructional practice related to ELLs, and society's attitudes toward ELLs' backgrounds (see Figure 1-1). In the case of Aadesh, the lack of second language instruction, teachers' misguided expectations, and his classmates' negative attitudes about his culture all contributed to lower academic outcomes and slower English proficiency acquisition.

Internal Factors That Affect Language Acquisition

Personality traits and individual preferences can explain why some learners acquire a second language more easily and more quickly than others. Children and adults who are outgoing risk-takers and have few inhibitions tend to acquire second languages faster and more easily than those who are shy, reserved, and easily embarrassed. Learners who are perfectionists also stumble more in language learning

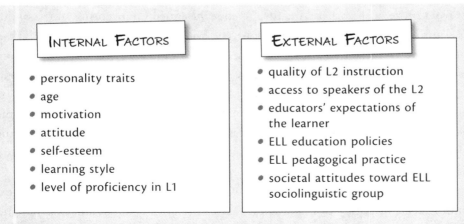

INTERNAL FACTORS	EXTERNAL FACTORS
• personality traits • age • motivation • attitude • self-esteem • learning style • level of proficiency in L1	• quality of L2 instruction • access to speakers of the L2 • educators' expectations of the learner • ELL education policies • ELL pedagogical practice • societal attitudes toward ELL sociolinguistic group

Figure 1-1 Factors That Influence Second Language Acquisition

because the process requires engaging in trial and error, especially with grammar and pronunciation. The age of learners also affects how well and how quickly they acquire a second language. Adolescents and adults tend to learn languages faster and more efficiently than younger learners because they often have a more developed native language and also more world knowledge. In general, motivation for acquiring a second language can be linked to higher levels of proficiency. However, individuals with high motivation sometimes fail to reach proficiency in a second language because of other factors that interfere with their learning, such as lack of access to native speakers or low-quality instruction. Positive attitudes toward the language and its speakers—enjoyment, admiration, affection—can result in better proficiency, while negative attitudes—resentment, envy—can get in the way of successfully acquiring the second language. Other internal factors that play a role in how well and how quickly students acquire a second language include learners' self-esteem and their learning styles.

Those who maintain that language minorities refuse to learn English often overlook the types of factors that can slow down the acquisition of English for certain groups. Income and education have a major impact on the rate and level of acquisition of English. The more schooling students have in their native countries, the higher likelihood they will have the necessary background knowledge and skills to ease their transfer into English academic learning. Also, higher income levels allow families to have access to more educational resources, more access to English speakers, and better knowledge about dealing with the legal, social, and cultural aspects of society (Suárez-Orozco, Suárez-Orozco, and Todorova 2008).

External Factors That Affect Language Acquisition

In general, external factors that affect language acquisition are beyond the control of ELLs and their families. A society's expectations of and attitudes toward a particular language group influence their education experiences and outcomes. Negative attitudes toward a minority language and its speakers make their acquisition of English much more difficult, as illustrated in the case of Aadesh. Because of these negative attitudes and expectations, education often comes in the form of remedial rote-learning types of instruction. In addition, negative attitudes toward the home languages of ELLs often result in policies that give preference to English-only programs. The quality of instruction and the types of education practices have a direct effect on how well and how quickly ELLs master proficiency in academic

" env. safe, secure, community oriented; academically rigerous.

English. For ELLs, access to native English speakers is not always readily available, either because they are physically isolated—living in ethnic communities where there are few English native speakers—or they are economically isolated—living in communities where they are divided by income levels (Suárez-Orozco, Suárez-Orozco, and Todorova 2008).

Many external and internal variables affect the speed of acquisition of academic second language proficiency. For example, ELLs who have grade-level literacy in their native language, have motivation and self-worth, and have talent for language learning are more likely to develop English in a shorter time. On the other hand, ELLs who are not literate in their first language, have had interrupted or no schooling in their native language, have a low self-concept, and are disengaged from schooling may take up to ten years to acquire academic English (Collier 1995). García (2000) expands on factors within the individual, such as whether one is foreign or U.S. born or one's level of education in the home country, that shed light on the length of time it may take to learn a second language.

Foreign-Born ELLs

Only about one-third of all ELLs are born outside the United States. The age of ELLs at time of their first enrollment in a U.S. school often affects the length of time they are able to receive specialized services in the form of ESL or bilingual education. For example, elementary school-age students take much longer to catch up to their English-speaking peers than secondary school-age students. Age also affects the level of difficulty of the curriculum and the academic demands with which ELLs must deal. Foreign-born students who are refugees face special psychological and social adjustments because of their traumatic life experiences in addition to academic and language challenges. Finally, foreign-born students include those who come from families with undocumented status, which is often a source of added anxiety and stress (García 2000).

Level of Education in the Home Country

ELLs come with different educational experiences and academic levels from their home countries. These students' experiences range from no schooling at all, interrupted schooling, and low levels of academic performance, to high academic achievement in their home countries. It is important to note that even students who arrive in U.S. schools with high academic background levels may face difficulties not only with the English language but also with a different curriculum and school culture than that of their home countries (García 2000).

U.S.-Born ELLs

About two-thirds of all ELLs are born in the United States, and except for the case of Native Americans, Puerto Ricans, and those from other U.S. territories, their parents immigrated to this country. Second-generation ELLs enter school with a range of proficiencies in English. In some cases, these students are no longer proficient in the native language and have become monolingual speakers of a different social dialect of English, such as Chicano English or Indian English. The mismatch between the academic Standard English used at school and the sociocultural dialect of English used by these groups can lead to problems in identifying their needs and in providing adequate support services. García (2000) maintains that these students can be considered limited English proficient but not in the same way or degree as those considered by teachers as traditional ELLs.

Negative attitudes toward a non-English language may cause ELLs to undervalue their own language, reject it, and even keep their own children from learning it. Low expectations on the part of educators toward ELLs also have a major impact on their academic success. The interaction of schooling factors such as curriculum, instructional methods, school policies, and educational theories, and the sociocultural factors such as student knowledge, self-image, and motivation, combined with society's attitudes and policies toward immigrants and languages, leads to more comprehensive explanations for ELLs' success or failure.

THEORIES OF SECOND LANGUAGE ACQUISITION

Krashen's (1981) *interactive pedagogy principle* proposes that language is acquired subconsciously and without much effort only when it is comprehensible. The important element in Krashen's model is *comprehensible input*—messages in the second language that make sense when modified and helped by visual aids and context. Krashen maintains that second language learners acquire language by understanding messages that are slightly above their current language level (Input+1). We acquire grammar structures in their natural order when enough high-quality input is present. The principle of comprehensible input is based on the idea that the main purpose of language is for meaningful communication. Meaningful language use at all stages in the acquisition of second language skills has become recognized as important for the successful development of a second language and the maintenance of the first language.

The *comprehensible output hypothesis* (Swain 1985) suggests that output is also important in the development of a second language. That is, learners acquire language when they try to communicate verbally but fail, leading them to try again and refine their message. Long (1996) contends that comprehensible input alone is not sufficient to attain proficiency in a second language. He argues that to acquire the new language, learners must interact with speakers of the target language through social interaction and by checking for understanding, asking for clarification, and by requesting explanations of unfamiliar words. Students must have opportunities both for receiving comprehensible input (listening and reading) and for having opportunities to practice expressive language through output (speaking and writing).

How Long Does It Take to Acquire a Second Language?

Decades of research have shown that the acquisition of *academic language* for ELLs generally takes between four to nine years in comparison to the length of time to develop *social language*, which can take from one to two years (Cummins 2000). According to Cummins (2008, p. 73), the distinction between academic and social language is framed within

> a range of cognitive demands and contextual support involved in particular language tasks or activities (context-embedded—context-reduced, cognitively undemanding—cognitively demanding). Internal and external dimensions of context were distinguished to reflect the fact that "context" is constituted both by what we bring to a task (e.g., our prior knowledge, interests, and motivation) and the range of supports that may be incorporated in the task itself (e.g., visual supports such as graphic organizers).

Cummins' language quadrant sets ranges of language demands (from cognitive-undemanding to cognitive-demanding) as well as ranges of context supports (from context-embedded to context-reduced) to illustrate the types of activities and language use that helps second language learners develop academic language (see Figure 1-2). Although the major focus should be on engaging students in learning opportunities that fall under quadrant B (context-embedded and cognitively demanding), as students progress in their second language their academic participation should also include many opportunities to use language in quadrant D (context-reduced and cognitively demanding). Cummins warns that these language dimensions are not fixed because of the differences that learners have in aptitude, motivation, interest, and prior knowledge. For example, an accountant would find reading the tax code as more context-embedded and less cognitively demanding than a nurse, whereas a nurse would find reading a medical article context-embedded but an accountant would not. Walqui (2000) points out that for high school students, inappropriate assessment of their second language proficiency often leads to partially mainstreaming them into English in certain content areas, like math and science, because these are thought of as subjects that are more context-embedded. However, math and science also require higher-order thinking and problem solving that uses complex language and subject-specific word knowledge.

Cummins argues that the development of academic language is mostly dependent on context-embedded instruction. In addition, teachers support students' academic development by providing opportunities that value their backgrounds,

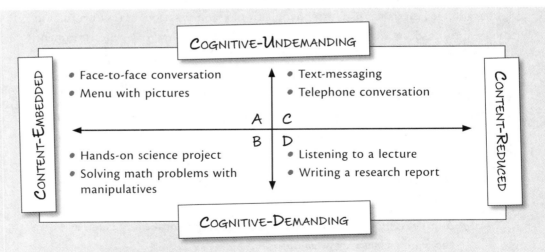

Figure 1-2 Cummins Language Quadrant

encourage sharing, and expand on their prior experiences. This approach is effective for several reasons:

* ELLs' anxiety levels are lowered because the content is familiar and relevant.

* ELLs take on active roles by engaging in real communicative activities about their life while learning about others' experiences.

* ELLs take ownership of the processes involved in learning language in the context of their own experiences.

An additional obstacle for ELLs is the stress of being in an unfamiliar culture, not able to understand its language, and constantly afraid of not being wanted or accepted. For Aadesh, these same stressors are what made schooling for him painful and difficult. Britton (1992) offers a fitting description of what school life might be like for many ELLs:

> It is an act of faith for a small child to address an adult he does
> not know; to do so across the silence of thirty other children
> can only magnify the difficulty; add to that the fear of rejection
> of what he offers and the picture is complete. (p. 181)

What makes the length of time of acquisition different between conversational and academic language? The faster acquisition of conversational language, as was the case for Aadesh, is connected to greater motivation—for play, entertainment, social bonding, completing a task, etc.—less need for knowledge of complex language structures and vocabulary, and support by context, gestures, and pictures, as well as prior knowledge. For example, "You have a nice car! Is it new?" would have a lot of context support because the speaker is pointing to the person's car, the intonation of excitement, and the use of high-frequency words and simple phrases. The acquisition of academic language on the other hand is slower because it depends on:

* Wide knowledge of abstract linguistic structures (such as passive voice or subordinate clauses)

* A large number of complex and sophisticated vocabulary (such as the words *democracy* or *endeavor*)

* Understanding content-specific vocabulary (such as *math table* versus *geological table*)

You have a nice car!! Is it new?

Fragments accumulate onto collapsed ridges that trigger further destruction.

SOCIAL LANGUAGE

- used for everyday social conversations
- easily understood and spoken
- not cognitively undemanding
- assisted by facial expressions, gestures, tone of voice, context, pictures acquired at home
- made up of high frequency, monosyllabic, familiar words
- made up of mostly Anglo-Saxon words
- has short simple sentence structures

ACADEMIC LANGUAGE

- used for learning school subjects
- abstract and complex
- cognitively demanding
- used by teachers, textbooks, literary works
- learned at school
- made up of low frequency, multisyllabic, and specialized words
- has complex sentence structures, such as passive voice and embedded clauses

Figure 1-3 Social vs. Academic Language

* ELLs having to catch up to their native-English-speaking peers who are continually progressing in their academic skills in their native language

For example, getting at the meaning of "Fragments accumulate onto collapsed ridges that trigger further destruction" cannot be helped by facial expressions or intonation and is much more decontextualized than "You have a nice car! Is it new?" (see Figure 1-3). What makes the first statement more difficult to understand are the longer and more abstract academic words (*fragments, trigger, further*) and the complex sentence structure.

SECOND LANGUAGE MYTHS

Misinformation about how children and adults acquire a second language has serious implications for policy and instructional decision making at all levels: classrooms, schools, districts, states, and federal government. Dispelling these misconceptions is a critical first step toward having a better understanding of the complexities involved in the education of ELLs and learning a second language. The following section outlines several "myths" that have direct impact on ELLs' education (Soltero 2003).

◆ The Myth That ELLs Don't Need Specialized Support

Immigrants and other linguistic minorities realize that learning English is a necessity, not a luxury. For many parents and families, the only means to accomplish this task is through school. Understandably, many non-English-speaking parents look for the quickest path to English proficiency, academic achievement, and economic success for their children, so they sometimes refuse support services like ESL or bilingual education. However, for most ELLs, the absence of specialized language support has negative academic results. Students that don't receive specialized support are submersed in English and expected to learn it and the academic content at the same pace and level as their native-English-speaking peers, who do not have the added burden of learning a second language. While their English-speaking peers are learning academic content and progressing in literacy acquisition, ELLs fall behind academically.

Such was Mirka's case. When Mirka's mother took her to school for the first time in the United States she enrolled her in a mainstream English second-grade classroom, declining both the bilingual Polish program and ESL pullout services for her daughter. Later in the year when Mirka's teacher approached the mother with concerns about her daughter's struggles with English literacy and academic subjects, Mirka's mother disclosed that other Polish parents had warned her not to put Mirka in the bilingual program because this would delay her development of English. This advice, the other parents told her, had come from several teachers in the school. The other Polish parents had also told her that the ESL program was for students with learning disabilities. Instead of being promoted to third grade, Mirka was retained in second grade. For most ELLs like Mirka, the results of English immersion are often low academic performance, loss of the native language, and marginalization from both the mainstream society and the home culture. Students who are left to sink or swim in English-only classrooms, with little or no help in understanding the language of instruction and of textbooks, end up learning little English and little academic content. Students who are in classrooms where the native language is used for instruction to make the academic content meaningful as they receive specialized language instruction to acquire English are better served linguistically, culturally, socially, and academically (August and Hakuta 1997).

The Grandfather Myth

The argument most often heard against bilingual education goes something like this: "My grandfather came to this country and did very well without bilingual education." This statement seems reasonable until it is examined more closely. The argument against this common belief is twofold. In the first place, how well past immigrants "succeeded" depended greatly on their educational, economic, migratory, and political conditions before immigrating, and on the levels of literacy and academic English proficiency needed for employment in the United States. Second, there exists the mistaken view that past immigrants did not participate in bilingual education.

Until recently, not all children went to school, regardless of the language of instruction. During the last great wave of immigration to the United States, between 1880 and 1915, very few succeeded in school, native or foreign born. Half of all Americans aged fourteen to seventeen either did not reach high school or dropped out before graduating. Rothstein (1998) presents data on the federal immigration commission of 1911, which points to southern Italian immigrants as having the least success in school: 58 percent of southern Italian children in the seventh grade stayed in school another year, while 80 percent of native-born white children, 62 percent of Polish children, and 74 percent of Russian Jewish children did so. In New York 54 percent of native-born children went on to high school while only 34 percent of foreign-born did so. In 1931, only 11 percent of Italians graduated from high school compared to a 40 percent graduation rate for all students. In the first part of the 1900s, immigrants had access to jobs that did not require proficiency in reading and writing or even in the English language. Today, jobs require more skills in reading and writing as well as proficiency in English.

As Rothstein (1998) points out, recent immigrants are not the first to want bilingual education for their children. In the nineteenth and early twentieth centuries, European immigrants fought for and won the right to educate their children in two languages in public school. In New York, the first bilingual school was established in 1837 to provide German-speaking children instruction in the native language as they acquired English. In 1866 the Chicago Board of Education created German-language schools to address the educational and linguistic needs of German-speaking children, who made up one-fourth of the city's enrollment. In San Francisco, Chinese-language schools were established in 1885. From 1880 to 1930, Polish immigrants in New York had a preference for bilingual instruction as a way of maintaining their cultural traditions through parochial schools. Interestingly, researchers found that the bilingual instruction the Polish children received helped them progress more rapidly than Polish and Italian children who attended monolingual English public schools. However, as is the case today, language minorities were divided on whether it is best to be bicultural and bilingual or to become entirely assimilated to the majority language and culture. Today as it was then, language-diverse families prefer either bilingual or English-only instruction depending on their views toward assimilation or maintenance of the home language and culture.

Suárez-Orozco and Suárez-Orozco (2001) report on fourth-generation English monolingual parents in Massachusetts who send their children to after-school classes to learn Yiddish and Lithuanian so that they can relearn their heritage language. In Chicago, the Ramallah Arabic School, Latvian Childcare and Preschool, Matejko Saturday Polish School, North Chinese School, and Aristotle Greek as a Second Language School, among many other language schools for ethnic language communities, show the desire of these groups to reconnect with and maintain their rich linguistic and cultural heritage.

◆ The Myth That Immigrants Refuse to Learn English

> Tragically, many immigrants these days refuse to learn English!
> They never become productive members of American society.
> They remain stuck in a linguistic and economic ghetto, many living
> off welfare and costing Americans millions of tax dollars each
> year.
>
> *Statement from U.S. English, as quoted in Crawford 1992, p.xi*

Another common belief is that immigrants resist learning English and cling to their native language and culture at the expense of assimilating into the mainstream society. The reality is that the strong pull toward the "language of status"—English—and the loss of the native language is increasing among immigrant groups. Immigrants now shift to the majority language by the second generation. A few decades ago this used to happen in the third generations. According to Crawford (2001), after fifteen years in the United States about three in four Latino immigrants speak English on a daily basis, while 70 percent of their children become dominant or monolingual in English. By contrast, for earlier immigrants it was their *grandchildren*, not their children, who became entirely monolingual in English. However, the idea that immigrants resist learning English is still a common belief. In 2007 former House Speaker Newt Gingrich made these remarks at the National Federation of Republican Women: "We should replace bilingual education with immersion in English so people learn the common language of the country and they learn the language of prosperity, not the language of living in a ghetto." On the issue of "language ghettos," Tse (2001) points to a recent survey of immigrants in the United States from four Spanish-speaking populations—Colombian, Dominican, Guatemalan, and Salvadoran—concentrated in major cities. Tse found that on average about 70 percent of respondents said they understood English well or very well.

In the United States, English is a basic tool for students to achieve academically and to succeed in society. However, the loss of the home language and culture is often seen as necessary to achieve in English. When they lose their first language, ELLs not only experience a loss of personal identity and emotional bond with their communities, but also often experience rejection from the mainstream society. Ada (1995, p. 237) stresses that "[d]espite its widespread acceptance, the subtractive model of bilingualism, in which mastery of the second language is achieved at the expense of proficiency in the first, need not be the framework on which bilingual education rests. Additive bilingualism, in which a second language is acquired while maintaining and continuing to develop the first, is a healthy and viable alternative to subtractive bilingualism." Bartolomé (1994) points to the contradictions in the status of non-English languages in the United States: "... while we discourage the maintenance of linguistic minority students' native language throughout their education, we require English-speaking students to study a foreign language as a prerequisite for college ..." (p. 207).

Claudia's own early experience with language loss illustrates Bartolomé's point. Claudia, the second of four children, came to the United States from Mexico at age six with her family. No one in her family was proficient in English, although her father had taken English as a foreign language in high school in his country of origin. Claudia was placed in a bilingual first-grade class but was transitioned out to a mainstream English class in second grade because the teachers thought she was progressing well in English. Upon reaching school age, her two younger siblings were placed in mainstream English classrooms since they had had more time in the country and the added benefit of having two older sisters speak to them in English at home. By the time Claudia graduated from high school she no longer spoke Spanish. Soon after beginning her university studies, her classmates and professors questioned her about why she was not proficient in Spanish, and why she was taking French for her foreign-language requirements. These kinds of questions were repeated throughout her university years. She felt both embarrassed about not knowing Spanish and envious of her white classmates who in high school had acquired Spanish as a foreign language and were continuing to improve their second language skills in college. Now an ESL teacher, Claudia recounts her unhappiness and frustration: "It is almost as if my language was stolen from me and I didn't even know it. It's sad that when I was growing up I was ashamed of speaking Spanish, and now I am ashamed of not speaking it." She goes on to say, "I am dark skinned, I look like a Latina, I have a Spanish last name, I was even born in Latin America. But I can't speak Spanish. That is pathetic!" Up until college Claudia had not thought about her "language shift" from her first to her second language and her eventual loss of Spanish. Only then did she realize that she had chosen to take French because she was ashamed that she did not know Spanish. Even though cases like Claudia's are commonplace, the education system has the capacity to end the loss of linguistic capital, which should be considered a valuable asset and resource, by implementing more additive bilingual education for all students.

Access to adult language classes is also a major problem for those who want to become proficient in English. The demand for adult ESL classes is increasing as their funding and availability decrease. In addition to the shortage of ESL instruction, other obstacles to learning English reflect the inequality that results from poverty. Because community- and state-sponsored ESL adult classes are often full and have long waiting lists, the only other options are programs that are too expensive for low-income families. This is especially difficult for migrant workers and their families, who are constantly on the move and have little time to participate in English language programs—even less time if they are working two or three jobs.

The circumstances under which Mr. and Mrs. Wu, parents of four school-age children, find themselves illustrate the challenges of many recently immigrated families. Mr. Wu works fourteen-hour shifts six days a week between two local restaurants in Chinatown while Mrs. Wu works five days a week in a small women's garment factory. They have been in the United States for eight years, and two of their four children were born here. They think of themselves as beginners in their English proficiency, although Mrs. Wu considers herself more proficient than her husband because her children now mostly speak English at home and she has taken ESL classes on and off at her children's school. Her husband, on the other hand, is surrounded by Cantonese speakers at his job and has little opportunity to use English. A few years ago Mr. Wu enrolled in an ESL class in a local community college but had difficulty keeping up with the homework assignments due to his long work hours and other responsibilities at home. When asked about his experiences learning English in the ESL class he said through a translator, "The class is very hard because we study a lot of rules and we have to write a lot. The teacher has too many students and can't give us individual time for questions. If I had more time to do the sheets they give us I could keep up." He was forced to drop out after the evening ESL course he was taking was moved to an earlier time slot due to city and state budget cuts. Mrs. Wu also took ESL classes at her children's school, but they were often canceled because the parents' ESL instructor was also the assistant principal and was frequently called to do other duties. Even though both Mr. and Mrs. Wu clearly recognize the importance of learning English, their work and family circumstances—as well as the inadequate English instruction offered—keep them from reaching their goal of becoming proficient in English.

◆ The Home-Learning Myth

Parents of ELLs feel ever more pressure to assimilate their families into the American culture and speak English. They believe this to be the only way for their children to succeed in this country. Understandably, parents want to protect their children from the prejudice and discrimination of speaking imperfect English. For some parents, who themselves have experienced discrimination because of their lack of proficiency in English, instruction solely in English is an attractive and promising alternative to native-language instruction. Often, these same parents go even further by making the painful decision to speak only English at home, even when they are not proficient in the language and in spite of experiencing communication problems with their children (Tse 2001). Wong Fillmore (2005) shows how childrens' shift from the native language to English has many negative consequences, including the breakdown of the family unity, interference with the parent-child emotional bond, and the loss of parental authority over their children. This type of family strain is illustrated by Wong Fillmore's case of a mother's relationship with her son: "The mother reported that her seventeen-year-old son is having problems in school. He is often truant and in danger of dropping out. She has tried to influence him but can't because he doesn't understand her. A recent attempt at discussion ended in physical violence, with mother and son coming to blows when words failed them" (p. 305). This type of tense mother-son relationship begins early on, as in the case of Miguel, a six-year-old kindergartener born in the United States to parents who had immigrated from Mexico. Based on the parents' best intentions to help speed up Miguel's English learning, they decided to enroll him in an all-English classroom because, they said, "le vamos a enseñar español en casa" [we will teach him Spanish at home]. Below is a conversation between Miguel and his mother about the Mexican Day of the Dead celebration.

Miguel: Ma ¿qué es el Día de Muertos? mis amigos ni saben que es.

Mother: English ... speak English ... teacher say.

Miguel: [rolls his eyes] ¡Noooo mamá! ¡tu no sabes inglés!

Mother: Yes, English ... English ... say English.

Miguel: Ay no ma ... ¡no me gusta en inglés contigo!

Mother: What? English ... English ...

Miguel: [walks away]

On another occasion Miguel asks his mother about his aunt who is in the hospital in Mexico.

Mother: Mi'jo tía Tere ... in hospital.

Miguel: ¿Qué le pasó a la tía Tere? ¿Porqué esta en el hospital?

Mother: English ... speak English!

Miguel: ¡Ahhh mami! ... ¿Why she in hospital?

Mother: He ... hospital go ... he, he ... ¿cómo se dice? he, he ...

Miguel: [sighs and turns on the television]

In Miguel's case, the mother's decision to use her imperfect English to speak with her son came from Miguel's teacher. Though their intentions are often good, teachers who are not knowledgeable about second language acquisition tell parents who are not yet proficient in English to speak English at home so that their children can acquire the language more quickly. The push by teachers to encourage non-English-speaking parents to shift to English at home is not only a bad idea because these parents are not good English-language models for their children, but also because parents and their children can no longer have meaningful communication. For linguistically diverse families, the rejection of the home language and culture carries a high price: a language gap between parent-child and between grandparent-grandchild, disconnect from the heritage community, break from cultural norms and customs, loss of identity, and social isolation.

When teachers tell non-English-proficient parents to speak English at home:

* There is a break in family harmony.

* Emotional attachments are at risk.

* Important values/norms are not transferred from parent to child.

* Parents' authority is weakened.

* Children develop self-shame about their origins.

Unlike Mirka's mother, who turned down specialized language services for her daughter because of misinformation and fears about bilingual education and ESL programs, Esteban's parents' decision to place him in a mainstream English classroom came from their desire to speed up his English learning and the belief that they could teach him to read and write in Spanish at home. Esteban's mother had been a first-grade teacher in Colombia and was well qualified to teach him literacy and academic subjects in Spanish at home. This plan turned out to be more complicated than the parents had anticipated. After only six months of try-ing to teach Esteban to read and write in Spanish at home, his mother gave up. She admitted that her son seldom wanted to participate in her daily after-school Spanish classes. His complaints ranged from being too tired, to needing to do his English homework, which he told her "es más importante" [is more important], to wanting to watch television or play outside with his friends. His parents also noticed a gradual but troubling change in Esteban. He not only refused to speak Spanish at home, but also insisted in only eating "American" food, and generally rejected anything "Colombian."

ELL families who decline bilingual schooling for their children believe they can maintain the language by using it at home. This is not an easy task, as illus-trated in the case of Esteban's well-meaning parents. On one hand, the influence of English-speaking peers and media makes children shift more quickly to English and resist the use of the native language. Children's resistance together with parents' insistence in using the native language often results in confrontational and stressful home situations, eventually leading the parents to give up trying to maintain the native language at home. The literate language proficiency needed for future professional occupations, such as knowledge of sophisticated writing styles and extensive vocabulary, is reached only through formal schooling. Even very educated bilingual professionals find it difficult to take on the responsibility to educate their children at home in the native language. This task becomes much harder for parents who have limited education and/or have multiple jobs.

Contributing to parents' mistaken ideas about bilingual education are several key points: the social shame often linked to minority languages; the belief that bilingualism is a problem; and the fear of *linguicism* (prejudice based on language or dialect). When parents understand the benefits of bilingualism and biliteracy, the fundamentals of what makes a good bilingual program, and the underlying reasons for wanting to eliminate bilingual education, then they can make informed decisions about language choices and rights. Other common misconceptions that influence policy, instructional trends, and assessment practices include perceived advantages of young over older language learners, assumptions about time-on-task and maximum-exposure, distinctions between academic and conversational language, how languages are learned or acquired, perceptions about error correction, and explanations for ELLs' low academic achievement. The following section addresses each of these myths.

The Myth That Young Children Learn Languages More Easily

It may seem that younger children acquire a second language faster and more easily than older students because the language demands are much lower for younger children than for older learners. Older school-age students have to deal with increasingly sophisticated and abstract language as they go up the grades, particularly after fourth or fifth grade. Also, younger children tend to have more motivation and incentives for acquiring the second language (such as playing, communicating with friends, television, Internet, etc.), while teenagers and young adults may be forced to learn the second language for graduation requirements or a job. Older students also have the advantage of cognitive maturity. That is, abstract thinking at the formal operational stage in human development allows students to understand explanations and use deductive reasoning, helping second language acquisition. Older students also have higher cognitive awareness; they are conscious of their acquisition and progress in the second language, which may lead them to use linguistic and cognitive devices to support their learning (Goldenberg and Coleman 2010). Development of native-like pronunciation and accent is the one linguistic area where younger learners have an advantage over adolescents or adults. Younger second language learners pick up the sound system of the second language more easily than adults given that after puberty neurophysiological patterns fossilize in the first language, thus becoming more difficult to change in the second language (McLaughlin 1992).

The Myth That More English Is Better

One of many claims used against the use of native-language instruction is that ELLs can develop English in one year with intensive English-language instruction. Those that support the *time-on-task* or *maximum exposure hypothesis* maintain that ELLs must be exposed to great amounts of English to become proficient in the language. From this perspective, instruction in the native language interferes with the acquisition of English. Research evidence rejects this claim and instead suggests that ELLs who receive instruction in the native language develop the second language more efficiently than children who are immersed in the second language (García 2009; Genesee et al. 2006). However, researchers caution that the negative or positive effects of instruction in the first or the second language depend greatly on the context in which it takes place (Cummins 2000). In other words, what is more important is how each language is used and for what purposes, instead of the language itself. For example, a bilingual classroom that uses the native language of the students but follows rote learning, direct instruction, teacher-centered, and remedial approaches with no use of students' culture and prior knowledge is less effective than an English-only classroom that uses student-centered, active and authentic learning, and hands-on instruction while valuing ELLs' backgrounds.

Hornberger (1994) also suggests that context factors, such as development in the first language, parent support, and status of each language, are much stronger determinants in the outcome of initial first or second language instruction. Cummins' (2000) *interdependence principle* points to an underlying cognitive and academic proficiency that is common across all languages regardless of their distinct surface features (sounds and grammar structures). Cummins maintains that first and second language academic skills depend on each other and that there is no relationship between the amount of instructional time spent in the second language and academic achievement. According to Cummins, the *common underlying proficiency* helps with the transfer of literacy-related skills between languages.

◆ The Myth That Speaking Equals Proficiency ←

A common idea is that once ELLs are able to speak in English they are proficient in it and are able to function in the classrooms at the same level as their native-English peers. Extensive research in second language acquisition disproves this. Cummins (2008) cites Vincent's 1996 ethnographic study of second-generation Salvadorans who developed conversational skills in English in two or three years and were considered by teachers to have native-like proficiency. Vincent points out that this oral fluency is misleading. Students seem to be fully proficient because they have no accent and are able to use language for everyday social interactions on familiar topics. On the other hand, the decontextualized and cognitively demanding language needed for thinking, speaking, and writing about academic subjects (Cognitive Academic Language Proficiency—CALP) is not yet developed in these same students. Misconceptions about second language proficiency often lead teachers to exit ELLs too early into mainstream classes based on their English conversational skills alone (Basic Interpersonal Communicative Skill—BICS). These reclassified "former" ELLs no longer receive specialized academic or language support in the form of ESL or bilingual services even though they continue to struggle with the demands of academic English. As a result, these students often lag behind their native-English-speaking peers in their academic performance.

◆ The Myth That Learning Two Languages Causes Confusion

One of the most persistent misconceptions in the United States is that growing up with two languages causes confusion or even cognitive problems and therefore children must be exposed to and taught in only one language. On the contrary, studies have found that bilinguals show a greater understanding of linguistic meanings and seem to be more flexible in their thinking than monolinguals. For example, in Cummins' (2000) *additive bilingual enrichment principle*, "the development of additive bilingual and biliteracy skills entails no negative consequences for children's academic, linguistic or intellectual development ... the evidence points in the direction of subtle metalinguistic and intellectual benefits for bilingual children" (p. 21).

Through the effort of having to handle two languages, bilinguals must interpret much more linguistic input than monolinguals that have to deal with only one language system. Cognitive skills are developed best through the primary language and then transferred to the second language. The use of the home language helps ELLs develop critical-thinking abilities and cognitive skills. The way ELLs think is shaped by their linguistic knowledge as well as by cultural knowledge and the context in which that knowledge is developed.

The Myth That Errors Should Be Corrected Immediately

Although errors can at times block communication, they are a natural part of second language acquisition. All learning processes involve making mistakes that slowly go away, and this is also true for ELLs as they become more proficient. The question is: Which is more important for second language development—fluency or accuracy? Researchers and language teachers agree that there is a delay between fluency and accuracy. ELLs are able to pinpoint and self-correct their own errors only when they have become fairly proficient in the second language. Corder (1967) states that there is an important difference between a *mistake*, which is a random and short-term breakdown that the learner can self-correct when it is pointed out, and an *error*, which is a deviation that happens often and which the learner cannot self-correct even when it is pointed out (see Figure 1-4).

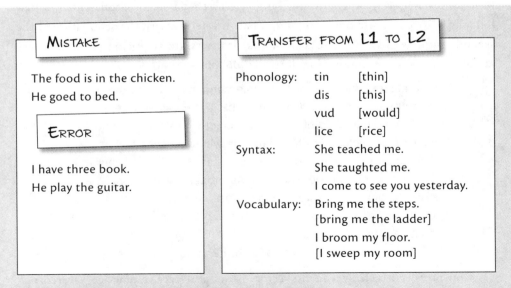

MISTAKE		TRANSFER FROM L1 TO L2		
The food is in the chicken.		Phonology:	tin	[thin]
He goed to bed.			dis	[this]
			vud	[would]
ERROR			lice	[rice]
		Syntax:	She teached me.	
I have three book.			She taughted me.	
He play the guitar.			I come to see you yesterday.	
		Vocabulary:	Bring me the steps.	
			[bring me the ladder]	
			I broom my floor.	
			[I sweep my room]	

Figure 1-4 Errors vs. Mistakes and Transfer Between L1 and L2

Learning from errors and using those errors to get feedback from other speakers helps ELLs develop greater fluency and accuracy. This feedback assists ELLs to self-correct and to try again until they reach native-like language use (Corder 1967). Also, the errors that ELLs make give teachers valuable information about students' progress and help to guide their instruction. Figure 1-5 shows an example of error and mistake and also how students may transfer structures from their first language into a second language. In this sample, a second-grade Spanish-speaking ELL writes "I broom the floor." Not knowing the verb "sweep," she uses the next familiar word and substitutes it for the noun "broom." She is aware that this is not quite the right word but overgeneralizes by trying to make a noun into a verb. This mistake is later corrected as she learns the appropriate word for sweeping. At the end of the sample, the student transfers a Spanish word-order construction into English: "and she does not let me clean *all* the house," which in Spanish would be "y no me deja limpiar *toda* la casa."

The best way to deal with ELL errors is to guide them in finding the right forms themselves and then have them test different ways of applying these forms. Because it is common for ELLs to rely on their first language as a bridge to the second, many errors that ELLs make come from their native language. Much as we do with any other kind of learning, we build on our prior knowledge to help us gain new knowledge. This is also the case for the second language acquisition process: learners rely on the native language as they become proficient in a new language. Errors should not be thought of as interfering with the acquisition of the second language. Instead, errors show that learners are acquiring rules that they are overusing and/or underusing. Karra (2006) states that:

> Interference features will not become permanent unless the child does not have sufficient exposure to L2. If there is sufficient exposure, then instead of reaching a point where they can no longer be corrected (as often happens with phonetics features), interference features can be easily eliminated.... The teacher should know that a child who is in the process of acquiring a second language will subconsciously invent structures influenced by knowledge he already possesses. These hypotheses he forms may constitute errors. These errors, though, are completely natural; we should not expect the child to acquire L2 structures immediately.

Constantly correcting students' errors is not an effective practice. Overcorrection can be especially harmful because students often feel discouraged and end up

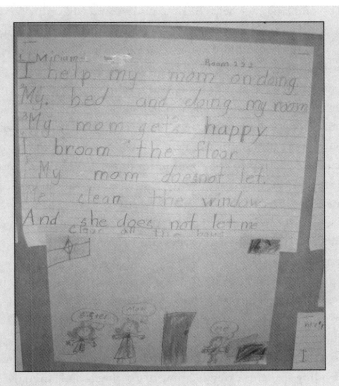

Figure 1-5 2nd-Grade Spanish-Speaking ELL

shutting down the learning process. Students who are corrected frequently can also become overly worried about using correct language and making mistakes. This worry can lower learners' motivation. Krashen's (1982) *affective filter hypothesis* points to how anxiety and low motivation can block the acquisition of the second language. Krashen identified three important elements that can influence learners' affective filter: motivation, self-confidence, and anxiety. The goal of a language teacher is to increase learners' motivation and self-esteem while lowering their anxiety. Overcorrecting errors and highlighting students' wrong use of language can do exactly the opposite: build anxiety, lower self-confidence, and reduce motivation.

A more helpful approach is for teachers to model and encourage ELLs to engage in self-correction. Teachers can use strategies that help students develop a deeper understanding of the correct language forms. Contrastive analysis, for example, is a strategy where the teacher guides students in making comparisons between their first language and English. Understanding the similarities and differences between the first and second language helps ELLs to understand what transfers and does not transfer between the two. For example, there is no plural form in Chinese nouns, so to indicate plural in a word like *book,* the speaker would have to include qualifiers like *many book* or *three book.* For Chinese ELLs, understanding the differences in how their native language and English deal with plurals can help them focus on learning to add the *s* to plural nouns in English.

Having ELLs participate in engaging language games and activities can help to lower their anxiety and motivate them to take more risks in language use. For example, games like "jump to the right, jump to the left," where students have to jump to the right if they think the sentence is wrong or to the left if they think it is right, is an engaging and nonthreatening activity. Other games like "guess the missing word," which can be an oral or written cloze activity, and "too many words," where students have to identify the extra word in a sentence, provide opportunities for engaging in self-correction.

Guided practice with meaning-focused activities is also helpful in expanding opportunities for students to use their expressive language skills (speaking and writing). For example, students can participate in story retelling and dramatization individually or in small groups according to their English proficiency level. Students can also follow a familiar storybook pattern to create a new context or storyline. Providing students extended time to use the second language for authentic purposes helps them to "practice" the language in a safe environment where they can get feedback from other peers and the teacher. An effective alternative to error correction is for the teacher to plan minilessons with small groups that focus on high-frequency errors and then have the students test out their new knowledge with each other.

OVERCOMING THE MYTHS

Assumptions about immigrants' experiences as well as unrealistic expectations about ELLs' academic progress in English often result in practices and policies that are more harmful than helpful. Acquiring English as a second language in order to function successfully in schools is not a straightforward task. While acquiring the dominant language of society—English—ELLs experience emotional, psychological, physical, and cognitive changes. ELLs must reconcile the native language and culture with a new language, new culture, and new ways of being. Educators need to think

- Recognize that ELLs are not all the same but may have different social and psychological backgrounds and experiences.
- Make conscious efforts to learn about ELLs' backgrounds, experiences, and preferences.
- Value, respect, and integrate students' native language and culture in the classroom and the school.
- Address parents, teachers, administrators, and community members' wrong ideas about second language acquisition and ELLs.
- Engage ELLs in rigorous academic experiences that are relevant to their lives rather than remedial rote-learning and decontextualized activities.
- Advocate for ELLs' rights to a quality education.
- Have high expectations and positive attitudes toward ELLs.

Figure 1-6 Guiding Principles for Educating ELLs

beyond language acquisition alone and consider the sociocultural and sociopolitical situations of ELLs. The principles outlined in Figure 1-6 are grounded on these social, cultural, and political circumstances.

The outlook of a teacher who "lives" these principles every day sheds light on how possible this can be. Alexa is a third-grade teacher proud to be part of a school that exemplifies these principles. This medium-sized (approximately 450 students) urban school is in a multilingual and multiethnic neighborhood. The children in this PreK–5 grade school are linguistically and culturally diverse, with 90 percent coming from families whose parents are foreign-born and where a language other than English is used at home. The other 10 percent are African American children, most of whom speak a nonstandard English dialect. Half the school personnel, including teachers and staff, come from some of the same backgrounds as the students while the other half are of white European descent. The principal is a white middle-aged woman who is married to a man from Thailand and whose children are now proud biracial adults. Alexa and the other teachers have great respect for the principal because she has set the tone for this school. The core philosophy of the school is promoting heritage pride and high academic achievement. Even though the staff members don't speak the twenty-eight languages represented in the student population, these languages are evident everywhere one turns: print in the halls, bilingual books in the classrooms, newsletters, intercom announcements, performances, parent meetings, and more. The school works closely with local social service organizations, religious institutions, and consulates that serve these language communities, recruiting their assistance with interpreters and translators. Many of the students' families have fled religious or political persecution while others migrated to seek better economic opportunities, only to find more hardships in the United States. Because of the high numbers of recently immigrated students in this school, teachers, staff, and school leaders have become well versed in issues related to immigrant rights and have established networks with several not-for-profit legal and medical organizations to help families navigate these systems. Their belief is that if students are sick, hungry, or afraid they will not be able to participate fully in the learning process.

Alexa was hired by the principal five years ago because of her noticeable passion for working with nonmainstream children from diverse populations. The school proudly boasts of having children from thirty-six different countries, including several countries from Latin America, Africa, Eastern Europe, and Asia. Alexa acknowledges that working at this school is not easy and that every day the school and teachers face challenges never experienced before. "The solutions to the problems that come up here on a daily basis can't be found in a book or by calling the district office," she says. "We call and they have no idea what to do or say. Every day we have to find solutions ourselves. It's very challenging, but it's also very fulfilling. Coming to this school is never boring!" Understanding that there are also tensions between the many different ethnic, racial, and religious groups represented by the student body, teachers and school leaders developed a core literacy program that uses multicultural children's books, not only to teach reading and writing but also cultural pluralism. They have also aligned their social sciences curriculum to engage students in comparative studies between the standard mandated topics of study and related transnational subjects. For example, the study of the City of Chicago in third grade takes place as a unit on large world cities that include Mexico City, Beijing, London, Moscow, New Delhi, and Cairo. Another curricular example that links the United States and topics related to the countries where some of the students' families originate is the third-/fourth-/fifth-grade social science Illinois standard (below) that provides the ideal foundation for a more substantive cross-cultural curriculum:

> Students who meet the standard can understand United States
> foreign policy as it relates to other nations and international issues.

1. Name an international organization of which the United States is a member (e.g., United Nations).

2. Identify the role of the president in making foreign-policy decisions.

3. Describe how the interests of the United States and other nations may or may not allow for international cooperation.

Educators such as the ones in Alexa's school, who understand that learning English as a new language is complex and multidimensional, are better prepared at creating learning communities that support ELLs' academic engagement and educational success. It is especially important for all teachers, support staff, and school leaders to become familiar with current literature in order to make the best decisions, create the best policies, and use the best practices related to the education of ELLs. The guiding principles for educating ELLs outlined in Figure 1-6 offer a broad but solid framework for improving ELLs' academic outcomes. Central to changing how educators address the needs of ELLs is the understanding that ELLs are not all the same because of their diverse backgrounds and experiences. Developing this understanding requires that teachers and school leaders learn about ELLs' backgrounds, experiences, and preferences. Knowledge about ELLs and their families allows educators to value, respect, and integrate their native language and culture in the classroom and the school. Adopting high expectations and positive attitudes toward ELLs, offering ELLs rigorous academic experiences that are relevant to their lives, and advocating for their rights to a quality education will promote higher academic achievement.

APPLICATIONS ||||||||||||||||||||||||||||||||||||||||||||||||||||||||||||||||||||||||||||||||||||

1. Create a list of possible reasons that explain why, in the United States, English-speaking students' learning a foreign language is celebrated but ELLs' maintenance of their native language is not.

2. What other individual and social factors, besides those presented in this chapter (see Figure 1-1), may delay ELLs' English acquisition? From this list, create possible solutions to these obstacles that educators and administrators can implement in their schools.

3. If the parents of an ELL decline to have their child in a bilingual classroom and say they will teach their child the native language at home, what would you say to them based on the discussion presented above?

4. Write down what a teacher or principal should say to non-English-speaking parents who do not want their ELL child to receive specialized services in the form of ESL or bilingual education.

5. Add two more myths about ELLs and second language acquisition to the list presented in this chapter and provide a rebuttal for each myth.

SUGGESTIONS FOR FURTHER READING |||||||||||||||||||||||||||||

August, Diane, and Timothy Shanahan. Eds. 2006. *Developing Literacy in Second-Language Learners: Report of the National Literacy Panel on Language-Minority Children and Youth*. Mahwah, NJ: Lawrence Erlbaum Associates.

Freeman, David E., and Yvonne S. Freeman. 2004. *Essential Linguistics: What You Need to Know to Teach Reading, ESL, Spelling, Phonics, and Grammar*. Portsmouth, NH: Heinemann.

Genesee, Fred, Kathryn Lindholm-Leary, William M. Saunders, and Donna Christian. 2006. *Educating English Language Learners: A Synthesis of Research Evidence*. New York: Cambridge University Press.

Chapter 2

School Structures: Schoolwide Response for ELL Education

Second language learners are second language learners of English all day long, not just during certain periods of the day. We can no longer afford to deceive ourselves that the ESL or bilingual teachers are single-handedly responsible for a child's academic success and it can't be "us and them." All teachers must be provided with, and expected to use, strategies to differentiate instruction to meet the various needs of their students.

(Commins and Miramontes 2005, p. 132)

Dimitar's school experiences capture Commins and Miramontes' point that schools can no longer view educating ELLs as the responsibility of ESL or bilingual teachers alone. Dimitar, whose family immigrated to the United States from Bulgaria when he was ten years old, struggled in fourth grade because of his limited knowledge of English. He was in a mainstream English classroom and at first received forty-five minutes a day of pullout ESL classes that had seven other beginner ESL students, from second through fourth grades. Because Dimitar and another student, Farah, were making slow progress in English, they were later pulled out for a second period and joined a group of beginner ESL students from kindergarten and first grade. This did not sit well with Dimitar, who started acting out in his fourth-grade class after his classmates began to tease him about being with the young first graders. Dimitar also felt that he was more and more disconnected from what was going on in his classroom as a result of his daily pullout sessions with the ESL teacher. For example, Dimitar was removed from a science group project because he was pulled out for ESL during the time that the rest of his group was working on it. Often when he returned from ESL sessions, he felt lost and unable to keep up with his classmates or the lessons that were going on. Dimitar's fourth-grade teacher was also unhappy with the situation because he did not know how to integrate Dimitar in the classroom and help him keep up with lessons he lost while he was in his daily ESL pullout sessions.

The school had been experiencing a steady increase in the numbers of ELLs and recently began to receive a few ELLs from less common language backgrounds, like Bulgarian, Latvian, and Persian speakers. Dimitar was the only Bulgarian-speaking student in his fourth-grade class, making him feel even more alone and anxious. The ESL teacher also found herself struggling. Under pressure to meet the needs of all her pullout students, she was forced to make decisions that she knew were not good practice, like having the two fourth graders, Dimitar and Farah, join the first-grade beginner ESL group. The ESL teacher felt she had few options because the principal and the general classroom teachers relied on her for anything having to do with ELLs. They expected her to have all the answers and resolve all the issues. In the end, Dimitar, his classroom teacher, and his ESL teacher all felt frustrated and unhappy. In this school, Dimitar's was one of many cases where both students and teachers experienced the same frustrations. This example clearly shows how all teachers and administrators need to work together to create teaching partnerships and better understandings about ELLs, and how best to address their academic, language, and emotional needs.

The number of ELLs has outpaced the overall growth in school enrollments, creating even more challenges for schools to meet the demands for adequate culturally responsive education, bilingual programs, and ESL services. The education needs of ELLs, such as those of Dimitar, have attracted more attention since the passage of the No Child Left Behind (NCLB) Act, which has more rigorous requirements and accountability measures for educating ELLs than any previous federal policy. NCLB requires that states and districts follow ELLs' academic progress over time, that ELLs be an integral part of each state and district's accountability system, and that each state develops standards for English language proficiency linked to the Academic Content Standards set by the state. These requirements have important implications for every teacher and school administrator across the country because ELLs are almost certain to be part of nearly every classroom and school.

To better address the academic need of ELLs, schools, districts, and teacher preparation programs must make a shift from a narrow perspective that views the responsibility of the education of ELLs as entirely that of bilingual and ESL teachers, to a broader, more inclusive recognition that the education of ELLs is a schoolwide responsibility. This shift can happen only when current practices, structures, and policies of schools and districts are changed. For this change to have positive impact, it must integrate and consider the many complex elements surrounding the education of children not yet proficient in English. The Education Alliance's handbook for improving education for ELLs through comprehensive school reform (2003) states: "Comprehensive reform strives to improve schooling for all children through integrated, well-aligned, schoolwide changes in instruction, assessment, curriculum, classroom management, school governance, professional development, technical assistance and community participation" (p. 1).

In this chapter I present a number of issues and ideas for creating comprehensive schoolwide approaches in addressing the needs of ELLs and their families. These approaches help to build unified structures of connectedness among all stakeholders within the school community. The chapter begins with a discussion of several elements that are needed for creating a supportive, culturally and linguistically responsive school. These elements include:

* Positive schoolwide culture and climate for all students, including ELLs
* School vision and mission that reflect inclusion of ELLs and a common shared value of their linguistic and cultural capital

* Culturally responsive and language-inclusive classrooms and schoolwide practices

School Climate and Schoolwide Practices

To create a school culture and climate that promotes ELLs' academic success, teachers and school leaders must have positive and well-informed views and attitudes toward these students and their families. Commins and Miramontes (2005) argue that "the responsibility of educators is to maximize the academic achievement of every child who arrives at school, whatever it takes" (p. 123), and they point out that a major challenge for teachers and administrators is to overcome commonly held beliefs that students who are not yet proficient in English are somehow broken, making the teacher responsible for "fixing" them. The authors argue that "this can result in a climate where professionals are pitted against each other in a finger pointing blame game of whose job it is to 'fix' students" (p. 123). Two false assumptions that create divisions among educators need to be dispelled: one is the notion that non-English-proficient students have "an illness that needs to be cured" (Nieto 2010, p. 87), and second is the idea that a few specialized teachers in the school have the sole responsibility of educating ELLs.

A two-step approach to dispel these common assumptions is first to recognize that the education of ELLs must be a schoolwide effort, and then to develop core knowledge among all teachers and administrators on what it takes to acquire a second language as well as to understand the many sociopolitical factors that are linked to learning English in the United States. Promoting education equity and academic excellence for ELLs must be viewed as a schoolwide effort, requiring commitment and dedication from all teachers, administrators, and support staff. Building a responsive, cohesive, and sustainable school climate that results in positive academic outcomes for ELLs requires that teachers and school leaders recognize the elements presented in Figure 2-1.

The last three points listed in Figure 2-1 deserve special attention, since many educators see the academic needs of ELLs solely based on language. Findings from research on language and culture point to the positive impact on academic success associated with maintaining the home culture and language as well as the interconnectedness between language and culture in relation to school achievement (Nieto 2010). When students' culture, language, and class are viewed by the school and society as "inadequate and negative," the academic underachievement of language-minority students is better explained (Nieto and Bode 2008). Delgado-Gaitan and Trueba (1991)

SCHOOLWIDE APPROACH	The education of ELLs is the responsibility of the entire school.
SCHOOL VISION & MISSION	The school affirms the value of the languages and cultures of all students and integrates ELLs in all school goals.
BUILD KNOWLEDGE	All teachers and administrators must be knowledgeable about second language acquisition and topics related to the schooling of ELLs.
SPECIALIZED INSTRUCTION	ELLs require specialized instruction by specially prepared teachers.
CONTINUED LANGUAGE SUPPORT	Language support is necessary for ELLs in the mainstream classroom and immediately after they are reclassified as English proficient.
HOME LANGUAGE & CULTURE	ELLs' home language and culture are assets that provide bridges to English and academic success.
LEADERSHIP & ADVOCACY	Schoolwide and community advocacy coupled with strong and collaborative leadership ensures sustainable, high-quality education for ELLs.
UNDERSTAND ELLs' CIRCUMSTANCES	Many ELLs and their families live with significant stressors, such as prejudice, poverty, violent environments, poor health, etc.

Figure 2-1 Premises for Building a Responsive School Climate for ELLs

argue that the conflict between the largely white mainstream teachers and principals and the culturally diverse body of students and parents can result in problems with communication, misinterpretation, a clash of cultural values, and the eventual academic underachievement of these students. This "interethnic" conflict is based on cultural differences that often lead to deficit models for explaining ELL academic achievement. Such models are guided by the belief that language-minority students, especially those from poor families, have serious handicaps and limitations that make it almost impossible for the education system to teach them successfully.

Educators who show respect and caring toward students and their families are in the best position to create a positive school climate. Relationships between students and their teachers need to be based on mutual respect, understanding, and trust. Based on findings from her study on schooling orientation and academic achievement among Mexican youth, Valenzuela (1999) concluded that high school students oppose and resist school practices that disrespect them. She adds that schools are organized "formally and informally in ways that fracture students' cultural and ethnic identities, creating social, linguistic, and cultural divisions among the students and between the students and the staff" (p. 5). As a result of these divisions, she argues, relationships between students and educators are "often fragile, incomplete, or nonexistent." In Valenzuela's view, "subtractive schooling"—educational systems and practices that devalue students' backgrounds and aim to assimilate them into the mainstream culture and language—contribute significantly to ELLs' academic performance. According to Delgado-Gaitan and Trueba (1991) "... antagonistic conditions determined by social institutions such as schools, force minority children to abandon their native values and adopt mainstream norms ... creating cultural alienation" (p. 26). The idea that those who come from culturally diverse backgrounds must become assimilated to function in society places great demands on immigrant groups to make major changes when they enter school.

Mercedes and her family share many characteristics of those who may be considered "at-risk." When she was four years old, Mercedes and her mother arrived in the United States from a rural area of Ecuador, joining her aunt and two young cousins in an entry-port neighborhood of Chicago. Mercedes' father had stayed in Ecuador and her mother was in the midst of divorce proceedings. Even though Mercedes liked kindergarten at first, it did not take her long to become withdrawn and apathetic toward school. She did not speak English and had little contact with English speakers outside school. Not having attended preschool, Mercedes' low academic performance was compounded by her mother's limited time to prepare her for school because she was working two jobs. Being the oldest child in the household, Mercedes had to help with her younger brother and cousins. To complicate matters for Mercedes, her mother had to enroll her in three schools within a span of two years due to job loss and continual raises in their rent. Even at a young age, Mercedes understood the tensions of coming from a poor family with undocumented status, often expressing anxiety about being separated from her mother. The family, school, economic, and social circumstances that Mercedes had to negotiate every day typify the realities of many ELLs who struggle in school.

Nieto and Bode (2008) point to how teachers and administrators must take into account the "personal, cultural, familial, interactive, political, relational and societal issues" in addressing ELLs' academic needs. The authors speak to the "ethic of care," suggesting that teachers can make a critical difference in their students' achievement that translates into high but achievable expectations and a real concern for the well-being of their students. Cummins and Nieto, among other scholars in the field, argue that a major reason reforms have proven unsuccessful is that the relationships between students and teachers, and between school systems and the communities they serve, have remained the same. They suggest that beyond legislative and policy reforms, there is an urgent need for teachers and principals to redefine their roles with respect to culturally and linguistically diverse students and communities. A starting point in redefining these relationships within the school is to revisit the school vision and mission statements.

School Vision and Mission

Because a school's vision and mission guide it toward common goals and also establish its philosophical base, its position statements must reflect a positive valuation of linguistic and cultural diversity as well as embrace the education of every student, including the specific academic, linguistic, and sociocultural needs of ELLs. Vision and mission statements are best developed by involving all stakeholders, but it is especially important to include all educators within the school to formulate what the learning community is trying to achieve. Even though this can be a sensitive process because the beliefs of the staff are often not identical, it can be achieved by first understanding what vision and mission statements are and then by brainstorming concepts and ideas related to the collective shared philosophy of the school.

What Are Vision and Mission Statements?

The *vision* is a statement of a view of the world that a school is working toward based on a shared understanding of a set of goals to be achieved. The vision presents the overall and comprehensive goals and aspirations of the school, which may include intellectual, academic, linguistic, cultural, social, emotional, aesthetic, physical, and technological dimensions of learning. The vision may also include the roles of staff, students, parents, and community in relation to the school's goals and objectives. The *mission statement* includes the ways in which the stated vision will be accomplished. Elements of the mission may include the commitments that the school makes in terms of school climate and culture, instruction and curriculum, assessment, community involvement, funding, etc.

Possible Concepts for Inclusion

Schools that show the most successful outcomes for ELLs are the ones that include the value of diversity in their vision and mission statements. The diversity in language and culture represented by students and their families is seen as a valuable resource that can strengthen students' perceptions about themselves, increasing their potential for academic success. School visions and mission statements that highlight the inclusion of all students' learning needs and stress collaboration have more effective results. The shared philosophy that a school follows should also include the importance of social responsibility in helping to create a safe and welcoming learning environment in and outside the school walls. A critical component of any school vision and mission is academic excellence, the aim of which is to engage students in critical thinking and problem solving through a rigorous and challenging curriculum. The extent to which ELLs' needs and backgrounds are reflected in a school's vision and mission statement shows how much or how little they are part of the school's education agenda. The following example of a charter school's vision and mission is reflective of the school's attitude to language, culture, and diversity.

Vision

Erie Elementary Charter School provides Chicago children with a high-quality bilingual education that values their unique life experience, language, and culture. The Erie Elementary Charter School strategy is centered on an innovative curriculum, high expectations, outstanding educators, strong governance, and enriching partnerships. With the value-driven culture at Erie Elementary Charter School, we can foster leadership, create stronger communities, and most importantly, provide our students with self-confidence and prepare them for a bright academic and personal future.

Mission

The mission of Erie Elementary Charter School is to nurture and empower students to successfully and productively engage in the

local community and broader society. Erie Elementary Charter
School is a community where students, parents, and educators work
together to develop children who are confident in their culture and
ethnic origin, biliterate in Spanish and English, achieve academic
excellence, and are firmly placed on a path to higher education.

The school vision and mission should be accessible to all members of that learning community, and if possible, written in all the languages spoken by the students
and posted in prominent places around the school as well as on the school's website.
Schools with students who speak languages not spoken by anyone on the staff can tap
those students' families for help with translations, or they can work with local community organizations that serve these language groups. Well thought-out, inclusive
vision statements can inspire and provide a sense of purpose and direction for the
entire school community. The vision statement from Amistad Dual Language School
in Manhattan clearly reflects this:

Amistad Dual Language School is a community of learners that embraces
the unique path of each individual. Together we foster a sense of
communal responsibility
and solidarity through the
celebration of culture, language,
and diversity. Our children will
move forward ready to meet
the academic, social, and
human demands of the larger
community, taking with them
the magic of discovery and
the power of two languages.

Another example of a vision and
mission is from a New York City public
school in the Bronx that implements
a very successful schoolwide dual-language program (see Figure 2-2). The values and beliefs of the school are clearly
reflected in their statement and in the
fact that it is displayed at the entrance
of the school in both languages.

Figure 2-2 Vision and Mission from PS 218 Rafael
Hernandez Dual-Language Magnet School

Vision and mission statements that reflect the value of promoting diversity are not limited to schools with large populations of ELLs. Some districts have taken the bold step to expand their vision and mission statements to include the value of diversity in guiding their policies related to students, families, and staff. Such is the case of the Diversity Policy in Naperville Community Unit School District 203 in Illinois (to see the entire diversity policy, goals, and action plans go to www.naperville203.org/about/Diversity.asp).

> In support of quality education for the benefit of all students, the Board of Education embraces human diversity as an important value of the District. The District seeks to recruit and to retain employees who reflect a culturally rich and diverse perspective. Diversity is reflected by infusing an inclusive focus into curriculum content and a multicultural perspective into instructional strategies. Staff shall receive training with the objective of increasing knowledge, skills and sensitivity in the area of diversity. The District shall communicate the benefits of diversity in education to parents and the community. The Superintendent shall include these areas of diversity in the annual plan and report to the Board of Education.

> The Diversity Action Plan must:
> * support employment opportunities that correspond to student demographics
> * initiate a staff development program to increase awareness, understanding, and acceptance
> * develop curricular opportunities for students to experience the richness of our diverse community
> * address public awareness to support building relationships across groups (citizen, public and private)
> * communicate initiatives that foster the cultural diversity of the school district

Considerations for Building a Culturally Responsive Climate

An inclusive, culturally responsive school climate creates spaces where all students, parents, educators, and other school staff feel valued, accepted, and secure. Schools that promote mutual respect among teachers, administrators, students, and parents help to open communication, build trust, and increase a shared common vision. In creating learning environments that support improved academic outcomes for ELLs, several considerations must be taken into account. Establishing safe and inclusive school environments helps to foster mutual respect and understanding among students, families, teachers, and school leaders. This is especially important in schools that have students from different languages, cultures, and religions. For example, schools with students from both Muslim and Jewish backgrounds may reduce possible tensions by offering opportunities for cross-cultural activities, integrating culturally relevant topics to the curriculum, and creating shared family and community projects. Valuing and using the linguistic and cultural capital of all students helps to reduce misunderstandings among different cultural groups in the school, has the potential for creating strong cross-cultural bonds, and helps to build understanding between teachers, students, and their families. Engaging families and the community by providing many opportunities for school partici-pation through ongoing two-way communication also helps to increase a sense of shared responsibility for the education of all children.

One of the most important elements is to ensure that ELLs are included in mainstream school activities and academic programs and also receive appropriate specialized language support. ELLs are often isolated from the rest of the students, creating disconnects between them and the rest of the school. One of the most effective ways to integrate ELLs and their English-speaking peers is to implement dual-language education programs that benefit both groups. Because dual-language programs are not always possible to implement, other options like offering ESL sup-port within the mainstream classroom and creating opportunities for joint projects between ELLs and their native-English-speaking peers are also recommended.

The school staff plays a critical role in creating a supportive learning environ-ment that embraces positive attitudes toward ELLs. Schools that recruit and retain experienced, qualified, and well-prepared teachers and school leaders with expertise in ELL education are in a stronger position to understand the needs of ELLs and promote policies and practices that foster their success of ELLs' academic develop-ment. Schools should increase professional development requirements and offerings for all teachers that specifically address the needs of ELLs and implement high-quality, meaning-centered programs rather than remedial, transmission-oriented instructional models.

The following section provides examples of the types of practices, routines, and policies that can be implemented in schools to increase positive academic outcomes for ELLs. The last three considerations—culturally relevant curriculum, transactional instructional practices, and parent involvement—will be further expanded on in the remaining chapters of the book.

Safe and Inclusive School Environments

Creating a safe school climate supports students' healthy development, helps reduce antisocial behavior and discipline problems, contributes to higher morale, promotes positive interpersonal relationships, and allows students to learn at the most favorable levels (Marshall 2003). A "safe" school is normally understood to include physical safety, but just as important is the psychological and emotional safety of all members of a school, especially that of students and families from different cultures and language backgrounds. For ELLs and their families it is especially important to create safe and welcoming school environments, because not only do they often lack the needed English proficiency to communicate effectively with school personnel but also tend to be unfamiliar with U.S. school norms and expectations. In addition, schools must recognize how the difficult conditions under which many ELLs live may affect their interactions with schools. Continual opposition in the media and society toward immigrants, fear of deportation for undocumented families, and prejudice based on language and ethnicity make ELLs and their families live under constant stress. This can result in students' being unable to connect with their teachers and can force parents to maintain a certain distance from the school.

To offset this type of disconnect, schools must organize themselves in ways that do away with segregation and isolation of ELLs and instead integrate them into mainstream school activities and academic programs. The key to success in integrating ELLs is that they receive specialized support and that teachers have appropriate expectations regarding academic and second language progress. A cautionary note is that integrating ELLs does not mean submersion (also known as sink or swim), where they are placed in mainstream classes with no specialized support. In addition, ELLs often find themselves isolated in self-contained bilingual/ESL classrooms or ESL pullout programs that are often viewed by the learning community as separate and disconnected from the rest of the school. Although bilingual education is clearly a preferred alternative to English-only instruction (Genesee et al. 2006), schools need to make greater efforts in facilitating collaboration between bilingual education and mainstream teachers as well as cross-partnerships between bilingual and mainstream English classrooms.

Team-Teaching and Collaborative Planning

Coltrane (2002) reports on Viers Mill Elementary School in Maryland, where collaborative teaching has become a critical part of their instructional organization:

> For the last 7 years ESOL and mainstream teachers have
> implemented a model of instruction for K–2 students based entirely
> on collaborative team teaching. Rather than pulling intermediate- and
> advanced-level English language learners out of their classrooms
> for separate instruction, the ESOL and mainstream teachers work
> together to develop lessons and activities that are effective for all
> students, then co-teach these lessons within the context of the
> regular classroom. Like other educators who have implemented
> this model to serve English language learners, the teachers at
> Viers Mill have found team teaching to be extremely effective in
> spite of the challenges inherent in any team-based effort. (p. 6)

For team-teaching structures to be effective, administrators should:

* provide adequate time for teachers to plan
* create schedules (lunch and specials) that facilitate interaction/ exchanges between the two classrooms
* be flexible in the time distribution of required curriculum, such as language arts and content areas
* supply team-teachers with appropriate and sufficient instructional materials

In the case of Viers Mill, Coltrane reports, "The model began on a voluntary basis; teachers could choose whether or not to participate. As teachers and administrators began to see the positive results of team teaching, they decided to implement this model in all primary classrooms" (p. 7).

   This type of cross-program partnership proved to be very valuable for two teachers in a suburban elementary school. Susana and Caroline are second-grade teachers in a midsize school that has, in the past fifteen years, experienced a large influx of working-class Latinos in a community that was predominantly white and middle class. Susana teaches in the bilingual second-grade classroom, and Caroline teaches the English general program second grade. They decided to try team-teaching after a student from Russia and an Arabic-speaking student from

Iraq were enrolled in Caroline's class because they could not be placed in Susana's bilingual Spanish-English classroom. The school did not have a pullout ESL teacher, and Caroline found herself struggling to meet the needs of the two new ELLs in her class. Susana offered to take the two students during her daily forty-five-minute ESL class, but both teachers soon realized that, much like an ESL pullout program, removing the two ELLs from Caroline's class created disruption in their learning and widened the disconnect to their English-speaking classmates. Through several conversations and reflections, they also realized that Susana's Spanish-speaking ELLs would benefit from having access to and working with Caroline's native-English students. They decided to team-teach in the content areas and differentiate instruction for students, whether ELL or struggling native-English speakers. They also infused a peer-mediated approach in which heterogeneous groupings of students from various second language proficiency levels and academic levels collaborated in group projects in the different content areas as well as in literacy. Susana and Caroline also decided to have flexible groupings during language arts in order to include a systematic ESL component for all ELLs.

Both teachers reported that in the first few months of team-teaching, they invested a lot of time in planning and coordinating curricular and instructional content. However, by the start of the second semester both teachers felt comfortable with the schedule and time distribution, various student groupings, collaboration on developing lesson plans, and sharing both groups of students. Parents and students were also very happy with this team-teaching approach. While parents of native-English speakers began requesting Spanish classes for their children, parents of ELLs told the teachers they were pleased their children were interacting with English-speaking children in school. A chain reaction was unleashed, ending up with the school choosing to become a dual-language school!

The Importance of Access to English-Speaking Peers

An unintended consequence of transitional bilingual education programs is the tracking of students who are segregated for several years from their English-speaking peers based on their language proficiency.

For ELLs, access to native-English-speaking peers in the context of academic activities is especially important for the acquisition of academic English. Based on research findings of their study on segregation of Latinos and ELLs in California schools, Gifford and Valdés (2006) argue that the hypersegregation of Hispanic students, and particularly Spanish-speaking ELLs, suggests that little or no attention has been given to the consequences of linguistic isolation for a population whose future depends on the acquisition of English. Unfortunately, segregation of ELLs from both their white and black English-speaking peers has profound consequences for their acquisition of English. For ELLs, interaction with ordinary English-speaking peers is essential to their English language development and consequently to their acquisition of academic English. (pp. 146–147)

Drawing On and Celebrating Students' Language and Culture

In order to make the most of students' linguistic and cultural capital—the knowledge of their native language and sociocultural practices seen as valuable resources—educators must first recognize that these are valuable assets and are the foundation for successful learning. Teachers agree that learning is most effective when it is built on students' background knowledge and prior experiences (Marzano 2004). However, this principle is not often applied in the case of ELLs' cultural and language backgrounds because their experiences and knowledge tend to have less social worth than those of other groups (Nieto 2010). Teachers of ELLs with incomplete knowledge and preparation in ELL education often work under mistaken beliefs about students' language and culture. For example, Ballantyne, Sanderman, and Levy (2008) report on several studies that show teachers' knowledge gaps related to second language acquisition:

> Reeves (2006) found that 71.1 percent of teachers surveyed believed that ELLs should be able to learn English within two years. In a survey of 729 teachers in a school district in which almost one-third of students were ELLs, Karabenick and Clemens Noda (2004) found that a majority (52 percent) believed that speaking one's first language at home inhibited English language development. Nearly one-third (32 percent) thought that if students are not able to produce fluent English, they are also unable to comprehend it. The authors also reported that many mainstream teachers do not distinguish between oral communication proficiencies and cognitive academic language capabilities. (p. 10)

Professional development, university coursework, book study groups, and promoting schoolwide understanding of students' language and culture are a few ways in which teachers and school leaders can gain better understandings about their students.

Many educators recognize that making the most appropriate and effective instructional decisions for ELLs requires that they develop better understandings of ELL education. For Sharon, a new ESL high school teacher in a large city, this type of wrong judgment was exposed by the actions and unwritten policies of her new principal. Sharon, a young, hardworking white teacher, had been teaching for two years at this high school, which had predominantly Latino and African American students. She was the only ESL teacher. At the end of Sharon's first year, the principal retired and in the second year the district assigned a new interim principal to the school. Sharon's first encounter with the principal's uninformed and biased position regarding students' language came when her very upset ESL students approached her about how the principal had told them in the hall, "In this school, English is what we use. You are not to speak Spanish in the halls anymore." The students were dismayed that they were not allowed to speak Spanish as they were walking from one class to another. "Nosotros entendemos que no nos dejen hablar en Español en el salón pero no entendemos por que no nos dejan hablar en nuestro idioma en el pasillo [we understand why we are not allowed to speak Spanish in the classroom but don't understand why we can't speak our language in the hall]," they explained. As weeks went by, more students complained to Sharon as well as a few of her colleagues, whose Latino students were English-proficient but nonetheless found the new "no Spanish rule" offensive and demeaning. Not long after these incidents, the principal told the Spanish foreign-language teacher that she too was not allowed to speak Spanish in the halls because this was an "English-only school."

Because Sharon did not yet have tenure and was unsure about what to do, she looked for advice from her network of colleagues involved in ELL education (ESL teachers in other schools as well as her graduate-school classmates and professors), who recommended that she call the district's legal office to report the incidents while requesting anonymity because of fear of retaliation. As a result, the district departments made sure that the new principal understood that prohibiting students and teachers from speaking Spanish in the halls is unconstitutional and illegal. These incidents also resulted in positive learning experiences for Sharon and her

ESL students as they embarked on a study of the U.S. Constitution and the First Amendment. They studied several U.S. Supreme Court cases that protect the rights of people to speak in any language, such as the *Meyer* v. *Nebraska* case (1923) where the Supreme Court ruled that "the protection of the constitution extends to all. To those who speak other languages as well as those born with English on the tongue," and *Tinker* v. *Des Moines Independent Community School District* (1969), where the Court stated that "schools may not prohibit student speech because of undifferentiated fear or apprehension of disturbance" and further argued that "students do not shed their constitutional rights of freedom of speech or expression at the schoolhouse gate." Both students and teachers turned these negative events into valuable learning experiences and found convincing arguments that they could use in the future to oppose discriminatory practices.

Research suggests that assimilation slows down academic achievement and that students who keep a strong bond with their linguistic and cultural heritage are more likely to succeed in school than those who assimilate to the dominant language and culture (García 2001; Nieto 2010; Trueba 1999). The types of prejudiced assumptions and uninformed practices that Sharon's students experienced require that teachers and principals develop deeper understandings of language and culture related to "bilingualism and biculturalism, the process of acculturation and bicultural identity development, and the sociopolitical context of teaching ELLs" (Ballantyne, Sanderman, and Levy 2008, p. 24). The experiences, prior knowledge, and abilities that ELLs bring to school should not only be affirmed and celebrated, but also intentionally and systematically used as bridges for developing English, academic competence, and strong bicultural identities. These cross-cultural identities develop when minority students are able to negotiate between the home and the mainstream culture and languages. Schools are in the best position to support students' bicultural identities by promoting practices that celebrate both cultures and languages instead of assimilation approaches that try to get rid of students' heritage. It is important to note that acculturation is not a simple or trouble-free process. The crossing of two cultures may create conflict and friction for students if both cultures have opposite norms and beliefs. For example, gender roles and expectations vary greatly across cultures: some cultures promote girls' active participation and self-assertiveness while others insist on passivity and obedience. Reconciling these types of opposing views is not an easy task for ELLs as they negotiate their way between home, school, and society.

For teachers and school leaders to make the most appropriate instructional and policy choices as they relate to ELLs, understanding each student's background is essential. Consider, for example, students whose formal schooling has been interrupted due to economic crisis, natural disaster, or war in their home country and how they must not only adjust to a new school culture, but likely need to overcome major traumas. The experiences and needs of refugee ELLs are quite different from the needs of working-class urban ELLs, for example. Even though many ELLs share common characteristics, teachers and administrators should also recognize the diversity among ELLs, including differences in:

* race and ethnicity: black, white, indigenous, biracial, etc.

* social class: middle class, working class, poor, etc.

* geographic origin: urban, suburban, rural, refugee settlements, etc.

* cultural background: depending on country or region of origin, ethnicity, class, etc.

* education background: high- to mid-education levels, interrupted or no schooling

Becker (2003) emphasizes:

> Equity doesn't imply that the instructional strategies that work best for one individual or group work for all. Students come to us with different backgrounds and different language proficiencies and with different educational histories. We need to differentiate instruction based upon students' prior knowledge of language, literacy, and content. The specific needs and strengths of the ELLs in a particular school need to be taken into account in designing that school's reforms. (p. 2)

Teachers and school leaders can implement several strategies to support ELLs' language and culture in the school. Using students' languages in printed material displayed throughout the school and in communications to parents, as well as using their language for instruction, sends the message to students that their language is valued. One way to accomplish this is to display students' work in the classroom and halls in multiple languages and on topics related to cultural diversity. Students' home language can also be used in assemblies and award ceremonies and their cultures represented in performances and school events. Schools' websites should also reflect the linguistic and cultural diversity of the families by including links to student and parent resources in their native language. Schools can also create "multilingual and multicultural school zones" that celebrate all the cultures and languages represented in the community. Classroom libraries and instructional materials should include multicultural and bilingual books, films, multimedia, reference books, and periodicals (see Figure 2-3). School libraries can increase their holdings by allotting a certain percentage of the library budget to purchase bilingual, multicultural, and native-language books and multimedia. Schools can invite speakers and organize events that relate to students' language and culture. Family literacy nights where parents and children share stories, books, poetry, and songs from the ancestral country and/or native cultures in both English and the home language are often very successful and build a sense of community.

Becoming Culturally and Linguistically Responsive

Demographic trends show that general program teachers are more and more likely to have ELLs in their classrooms. However, the increase of ELLs is not matched by the number of teachers with specialized training to address their academic and

Figure 2-3 Bilingual and Culturally Responsive Classroom Libraries

language needs. In 2003, only 18 percent of teachers who taught ELLs reported having an ESL certificate or endorsement, and only 11 percent reported having a bilingual certificate or endorsement. A comparison across a span of ten years shows even bleaker conditions for ELLs: in 2003 only 41 percent of all ELLs received some instruction in their native language compared to nearly 75 percent in 1992. Additionally, in 2003 only 52 percent of ELLs received specially designed curriculum for second language learners compared to nearly 75 percent in 1992 (Zehler et al. 2003). A recent report from the U.S. Government Accountability Office (GAO 2009) reported that in 2004–2005, students with disabilities made up 9 percent of the total K–12 population while ELLs were about 10 percent of K–12 students, and that many of these students spent a majority of their time in mainstream classrooms. The GAO found that

> programs at institutions of higher education nationwide required at least some training for prospective general classroom teachers on instructing students with disabilities and English language learners. While the majority of programs required at least one course entirely focused on students with disabilities, no more than 20 percent of programs required at least one course entirely focused on English language learners. Additionally, more than half the programs required field experience with students with disabilities, while less than a third did so for English language learners. Despite recent steps by the majority of programs to better prepare teachers for instructing both of these student subgroups, many programs faced challenges in providing this training. (14)

Especially relevant is the need for all teachers and administrators to participate in training on theoretical and instructional approaches related to second language acquisition and linguistically diverse student education. Few teacher preparation programs in the United States require that all preservice teachers take courses related to the education of ELLs. A nationwide survey of 417 universities conducted in 2001 by the National Clearinghouse of Bilingual Education reported that only a small number of them offered programs to prepare bilingual education teachers, and "fewer than 1/6 of the higher education institutions studied require preparation for mainstream teachers regarding the education of ELLs" (Menken and Antuñez 2001, p. 4). According to Ballantyne, Sanderman, and Levy (2008) it is likely that half of all teachers can expect to teach an ELL during their career. Because students who are considered "at risk" typically underperform academically, they require access to qualified teachers and quality language programs to address their language and academic needs (Nieto 2007).

Of the teachers who teach ELLs, fewer than 13 percent are certified or endorsed in ESL or bilingual education, even though NCLB requires that all teachers be qualified to teach in their area of professional practice. According to Gándara (2008) the shortage of bilingual teachers, in particular, is the single greatest obstacle to the improvement of instructional programs for ELLs. Researchers in the field agree that bilingual teachers are essential in the education of ELLs (Bartolomé 2000; Commins and Miramontes 2005; Darder 1997; Nieto 2000). Gándara and Maxwell-Jolly (2005) point to the value of well-prepared qualified bilingual teachers who go beyond providing instruction in students' mother tongue. Teachers who speak the language of their students are more likely to understand a number of issues that may not be so apparent to mainstream teachers (see Figure 2-4), such as having a better understanding about the processes of acquiring a second language because they are bilingual themselves.

In its recent report, the National Comprehensive Center for Teacher Quality and Public Agenda (2008) concluded that "more of the same knowledge is insufficient for preparing future teachers to deal with student diversity in schools and classrooms today" (p. 11). Survey results confirm that new teachers' biggest concern is that they are likely to finish their preparation programs not well prepared to meet the needs of a growing and multicultural student population. One student teacher in

- Understand and appreciate the complexities and challenges of acquiring an L2.
- Have the ability to assess ELLs' academic understanding through students' L1.
- Can recognize the difference between language difficulties and learning disabilities.
- Better understand ELLs' sociocultural contexts.
- Can raise the status of students' L1 in the classroom and school.
- Communicate effectively with parents in their L1.

Figure 2-4 Bilingual Teachers' Knowledge

a traditionally white neighborhood reported that in his school there are children from over twenty language backgrounds. The report further states, "Contrary to the popular view that suburban schools are not racially integrated, suburban teachers in focus groups mentioned that they increasingly find themselves with a wide range of populations from cultures from Asia, Latin America, the Asian subcontinent, Eastern Europe and the Middle East" (p. 12). The challenges of this new demographic shift in many suburban schools are expressed by my own graduate students, who increasingly speak about their frustration at the poor responses to the needs of ELLs by their suburban districts. I routinely ask students in my courses how many of them work in schools where all their students are of white European descent and monolingual in English. Eleven years ago more than a third of my students raised their hands. For the past four years no hands have been raised in response to this question. Almost two-thirds of my graduate students teach in suburban districts and report that not only do their schools have more student diversity in terms of economic, racial, and ethnic student background, but also students who are not yet proficient in English.

Teacher preparation programs and school districts can establish a number of practices that can help all educators become better acquainted with ELLs' language and cultural contexts. Teacher preparation programs in universities and colleges should require coursework on ELLs for preservice and inservice teachers that includes field experiences with ELLs. In Illinois, a new statewide law that requires bilingual education and/or ESL for all early childhood ELLs has prompted DePaul University to require all undergraduate early childhood students to take the courses for ESL and bilingual endorsement. School district officials, especially those with large numbers of ELLs, should communicate to teacher education programs the need for all teachers to have knowledge and skills to work with ELLs. Local universities, school districts, and state agencies can collaborate in creating and supporting "grow your own" programs that help bilingual teacher assistants to become certified and endorsed. State boards of education can set aside funding—full or partial—for mainstream teachers to get ESL endorsements.

Professional Development and Support Services

Knowledge of second language acquisition and language-instructional approaches has become a necessity for all school personnel, both for schools with high concentrations of ELLs and for districts that are just beginning to work with this population. Ballantyne, Sanderman, and Levy (2008) highlight how few professional development opportunities are related to ELL education: "ELL education was the least likely topic of focus. While 80 percent of those surveyed had participated in staff development that related to their state or district curriculum, only 26 percent had staff development relating to ELLs" (p. 10). A constant challenge in preparing school personnel to provide the most appropriate and effective education services for ELLs is to get rid of long-lasting misconceptions about second language acquisition, ELLs, and bilingual education. Ongoing professional development opportunities that bring together bilingual and ESL teachers with general program and content-area teachers can facilitate much-needed conversations between these traditionally divided groups. A model of professional development that is participatory and collaborative can support schoolwide efforts to address the needs of all students and create a collective sense of responsibility by all stakeholders (Meskill 2005). The Training All Teachers Project, a federally funded initiative (2005), recommends teacher preparation and professional development that emphasize key areas in relation to the education of ELLs (see Figure 2-5).

Other areas for ELL-related professional development include content-area teaching and learning in a second language, developing literacy in the first and second language, assessment and evaluation, student integration, second language learners, and special education issues. Improving language and cultural competencies for teachers requires that they have access to broad professional development opportunities.

The types of comprehensive, focused, and ongoing ELL professional development are exemplified in an urban PreK–8 school headed by a visionary and committed principal. Justyna, who has been the principal at this school for six years, views language and cultural diversity as assets, not as problems. "We have the great fortune of having more than twenty-five languages and more than thirty-six countries represented in our school community, which makes us truly diverse and global," she says. "What great opportunities we have right here for learning about the world, with our students' and families' firsthand stories and experiences from so many parts of the world!" While the majority of students in Justyna's school come from immigrant families, many of the teachers come from white, middle-class, mainstream backgrounds. Because of this high concentration of students from linguistically and culturally diverse families, Justyna and her leadership team

LANGUAGE	the nature of language and its relation to society and culture
ACQUISITION	the processes of first and second language development, including best instructional strategies and accommodations
CULTURE	cross-cultural issues in schooling
REGULATIONS	roles/responsibilities of schools and school personnel regarding ELLs
COMMUNICATION	methods for communicating effectively with school personnel and parents about ELLs

Figure 2-5 Critical Factors in Educating ELLs

decided to institute several innovative activities and projects with interested faculty as part of their professional development.

One of these projects involved teachers, administrators, and other school staff in the creation of a "book club study group" committed to reading and discussing two professional and/or fiction books a year, one related to instructional approaches for ELL literacy and content instruction and the other related to language acquisition, culture, and the immigrant experience. The leadership team asked for suggestions from the school staff and created a list of books for selection. After briefly reviewing the books, the decision of which books to select was put to a vote. Groups were then formed according to teachers' preferences. The books were purchased with funds from the school budget designated for professional development, from fundraising by parents, and from grants. At first, the reaction to the book club study groups was mixed. About half of the teachers felt overburdened and thought this new initiative was one more task on their already overflowing plates. After a time, though, teachers began to see the book club as a fun opportunity to have interesting discussions with colleagues as they connected what they were reading to their everyday situations. A major reason they became more enthusiastic about this type of professional development activity was because the teachers themselves selected the books according to their interests and backgrounds. This made it easier to form smaller discussion groups. Teachers and administrators reported that the self-directed-group professional development approach was worthwhile and instructive. Teachers were especially eager to read and collectively explore immediate challenges in their classrooms related to cultural and linguistic issues that were unfamiliar to them.

Increasing the relevant knowledge among teachers and administrators, as well as growing the numbers of teachers and principals who come from underrepresented groups, greatly affects the academic success of ELLs. School districts, state boards of education, and universities should develop and adopt the critical knowledge and appropriate initiatives to address the needs of an ever-increasing population of ELLs. These practices could include having state boards of education create sound language education policies that recognize the need for universities to prepare *all* teacher candidates to work with ELLs. In addition, there should be an increase in coordination among school district offices (such as assessment and accountability, special education, early childhood education) to optimize services for all ELLs.

Additive Language Opportunities

Although education models that use the native language for instruction started as enrichment programs aimed at developing fluency in two languages and promoting cultural pluralism, the focus has shifted to remedial efforts designed to help *disadvantaged* children overcome their *handicap* of limited English proficiency. Bilingual education was offered in the United States as early as the 1600s. In 1839, Ohio became the first state to adopt a bilingual education law approving German-English instruction, and in 1847 Louisiana approved a similar provision for French-English education. The New Mexico Territory adopted a law to allow Spanish-English schooling in 1850 (Rothstein 1998). Pennsylvania, Colorado, New York, Illinois, Maryland, Iowa, Indiana, Kentucky, Nebraska, Wisconsin, and Minnesota followed suit, and bilingual instruction was offered in languages as diverse as Norwegian, Italian, Cherokee, Polish, Chinese, and Czech (Crawford 2001). San Francisco established Chinese-language schools beginning in the mid-1880s, and in the late nineteenth century Czech-language schools were offered in Texas. By the early twentieth century at least 600,000 students in public and parochial schools received instruction in German. However, anti-German and anti-immigrant sentiments after World War I prompted states to abolish bilingual education in most U.S. schools and enact English-only instruction laws (Rothstein 1998). The ban against bilingual schooling lasted until the early 1960s, when bilingual education programs were established by Cuban exiles in Dade County, Florida, in an effort to have their children become bilingual and biliterate (Baker 2006).

Bilingual education and ESL instruction have been typically implemented as remedial and subtractive programs that aim to assimilate ELLs into the mainstream culture and produce monolingual English speakers. The most harmful part of this subtractive education is not only the loss of the first language, but the resulting isolation from the home culture (García 2009). Cummins' (2000) idea of *coercive versus collaborative relations of power* considers how educators define their roles, expectations, and assumptions about ELLs. For ELLs, coercive relations of power are found in school practices that aim to assimilate them and make them give up their home culture and language. This is seen by many teachers and principals as necessary to succeed in the mainstream society. On the other hand, collaborative relations of power value and recognize the sources of knowledge that ELLs have even though they may be outside the dominant discourse of schools. For ELLs, the extent to which schools affirm and promote their language and cultural backgrounds supports either empowering or disabling educational approaches.

Children benefit cognitively from learning more than one language. For ELLs, transitioning from their first language to English before they have a solid foundation in their first language, usually by the end of third grade, can have long-lasting damaging academic and linguistic effects. ELLs who are taught in English-only classrooms or transitioned to English instruction before they can show well-developed oral language abilities in their own language often don't achieve high levels of English fluency and do not do as well as those who have the opportunity to learn in two languages (García 2009). ELLs who have extended learning opportunities in their home language from ages three to eight consistently outperform those who attend English-only programs on measures of academic achievement in English during the middle and high school years (Campos 1995).

Making additive bilingual and world language programs part of the standard curriculum and an integral element of PreK–12 education has not yet been embraced by educators. To achieve a multiculturally and multilingually competent society, educators and policymakers must make long-term commitments to expand opportunities for all students to become bilingual and biliterate. In 2003, former Secretary of Education Rod Paige gave the keynote address at the American Council on the Teaching of Foreign Languages Conference, in which he stressed the importance of language study:

> Foreign language instruction should be part of every child's
> education. A language is more than sounds and syntax: it is a culture,
> a way of thinking, and a perspective on the world. Each language
> is a precious resource that must be studied, used, and preserved
> precisely because a language opens the mind to new possibilities.
> The study of language is the study of life, literature, history, and
> thought. It is nothing less than the study of our world and ourselves.

Extensive research on language education points to key elements and approaches that show promise in improving academic outcomes for ELLs and expanded language opportunities for native English learners. Moving toward implementation of these recommendations will help to restructure policy and instruction and align practice with current research and theory. Recommendations to improve opportunities for all students to develop bilingual abilities build on important research findings on effective schools and language education.

APPLICATIONS ||||||||||||||||||||||||||||||||||||||||||||||||||||||||||||||||||||||||||||

1. Create a list of beliefs about ELLs that you have heard from the public or other educators. Are they correct or incorrect assumptions? Support your conclusions.

2. From the above list, create a "Frequently Asked Questions About ELLs" booklet with accurate information regarding these commonly held beliefs.

3. Investigate and compile a list of resources for teachers related to the education of ELLs (bibliography, research and education centers, online teaching, bilingual, policy links, etc.).

4. Develop a proposal to present to a teacher preparation program at a college or university. The proposal should include: a) rationale for requiring coursework related to ELLs for all teacher and administrator candidates; b) outcomes for teachers, administrators, and ELLs that may come from the inclusion of ELL-related teacher preparation coursework; c) sample courses that should be required for all teacher and administrator candidates.

5. Read the American Federation of Teachers Resolution below to guide you in creating a position statement about the education of ELLs.

In 2006 the American Federation of Teachers adopted the following resolution delineating a set of principles related to the education of ELLs and supported by extensive research and theoretical foundation of the field.

The American Federation of Teachers Resolution:

WHEREAS, bilingualism is an asset in our global economy, and it is our goal to improve the education of English language learners (ELLs); and

WHEREAS, 60 percent of all preK–12 educators nationwide currently have at least one ELL student in their classrooms, and this percentage is steadily increasing; and

WHEREAS, ELLs often have very low levels of academic achievement and educational attainment (only 57 percent of Latino ELLs graduate from high school), and ELLs often do not have access to rigorous college preparatory coursework or to high-quality career and technical education programs or appropriate guidance about postsecondary options; and

WHEREAS, school systems often place ELLs into English-only instruction before they are ready. Research indicates that it often takes ELLs up to seven years to become proficient and academically successful in a new language and frequently requires more than four years for ELLs to graduate from high school; and

WHEREAS, research on language acquisition supports native language literacy instruction as a helpful support for school language acquisition, we need more research—especially at the secondary school level—on how to raise the academic achievement and literacy rates of ELLs, ELLs with disabilities, and ELLs with limited or interrupted formal education; and

WHEREAS, current ELL testing practices often do not separate the assessment of content knowledge from the assessment of English language proficiency, and such practices often result in improper over and under-referrals to special education; and

WHEREAS, poor assessment practices that do not use linguistically modified assessments and other appropriate testing accommodations for ELLs often result in the misidentification of schools and school systems and lead to No Child Left Behind (NCLB) Act sanctions; and

WHEREAS, teacher education programs often do not expose preservice teachers to coursework and clinical training to support ELL achievement; and

WHEREAS, there is a nationwide shortage of teachers, paraprofessional and support staff (counselors, school psychologists, social workers, intake specialists, etc.) who have the requisite training/certification to work with ELLs, and it is common for ELLs to receive primary, direct instruction from paraprofessionals who are not under the direct supervision of a certified teacher; and

WHEREAS, there is often insufficient collaboration between the staff who work exclusively with ELLs and all other school staff; and

WHEREAS, most schools do not include ELLs in their comprehensive school reform plans, and they lack sufficient social service supports, parent education programs and outreach to families; and

WHEREAS, NCLB has insufficient funding, including those programs affecting ELLs:

RESOLVED, that the American Federation of Teachers and its affiliates:

* Raise awareness about the urgency of closing the achievement gap for ELLs.

* Continue providing members and leaders with publications, professional development, and union-sponsored resources on effective instruction and on ways to increase parent and community outreach for ELLs such as Colorín Colorado.

* Call on the federal government to:

    * fund and disseminate the findings from longitudinal, independent, rigorous, scientifically based research and on what works to enable academic success and literacy for ELLs of all language backgrounds, ELLs with limited or interrupted formal education, and ELLs with disabilities, especially at the secondary school level;

    * allocate resources for comprehensive school reform plans that address how all school staff can collaborate to improve the academic performance of ELLs and that include better recruitment, retention, mentoring and induction

programs of bilingual educators, teachers of ELLs and ELLs with disabilities, including a career pathway for paraprofessionals;

* allocate funds for professional development for educators who have not worked with ELLs to provide appropriate instruction to emerging ELL populations;

* devise assessment, accountability and school improvement systems that are fair, valid, reliable and appropriate;

* assess the impact of high-stakes assessment on the graduation rate of ELLs;

* assure that high school accountability systems permit late entry ELLs more than the standard four years to graduate from high school; and

* adopt the DREAM (Development, Relief, and Education for Alien Minors) Act or similar legislation that would allow undocumented students who fulfill the requisite criteria of the DREAM Act—as referred to in AFT's resolution of support adopted in 2005—to enroll in college and seek conditional residency status.

* Call on schools of education to incorporate courses and experiences that prepare teachers to meet the instructional needs of ELLs.

* Support the implementation of research-based instructional models for ELLs such as dual immersion, ESL and other programs that include:

* a school culture of high expectations for all students;

* prescreening and ongoing assessment programs that determine students' levels of English language proficiency separate from students' content knowledge and that have the appropriate tools to distinguish between lack of linguistic abilities in English and learning disabilities;

* reading instruction that emphasizes phonemic awareness, phonics, vocabulary-building and comprehension activities connected to meaningful literacy and writing instruction;

* frequent teacher-led, structured opportunities for ELLs to discuss topics that are directly relevant to their lives and for them to interact in the classroom with native English speakers; and

* native language instruction, where appropriate, to facilitate English language acquisition and content knowledge, delivered by teachers who are certified in the requisite content area(s) and paraprofessionals who work under the direct supervision of a teacher.

SUGGESTIONS FOR FURTHER READING |||||||||||||||||||||

Crawford, James, and Stephen Krashen. 2007. *English Learners in American Classrooms. 101 Questions 101 Answers*. New York: Scholastic.

Samway, Katharine D., and Denise McKeon. 1999. *Myths and Realities: Best Practices for Language Minority Students*. Portsmouth, NH: Heinemann.

Tse, Lucy. 2001. *Why Don't They Learn English? Separating Fact from Fallacy in the U.S. Language Debate*. New York: Teachers College Press.

Chapter 3

Programmatic and Curricular Design

… studies demonstrate consistently and conclusively that schools with high quality programs have a cohesive schoolwide vision, shared goals that define their expectations for achievement, a clear instructional focus on and commitment to achievement, and high expectations … research show[s] that students, be they mainstream or ELLs, are more academically successful when they attend schools that integrate rather than segregate students and that provide a challenging curriculum for all students.

(Lindholm-Leary and Bosarto 2006, p. 186)

Many teachers and school leaders recognize that the traditional one-size-fits-all approach to ELL education, whether through English-only or bilingual programs, falls short for many ELLs who continue to struggle in school. A more holistic and integrative approach is needed to improve their academic achievement. The quote above sums up extensive research on the characteristics of effective and successful schools: a cohesive and shared school vision, common goals and expectations for achievement, focused instruction, and a challenging curriculum. In addition to these core elements, several recent research reports have identified other important characteristics related to the education of ELLs. For example, the Mauricio Gaston Institute for Latino Community Development and Public Policy (2008) identified additional features of effective schools for Latinos and ELLs based on their findings at five Boston schools whose Latino students are succeeding academically. These features included:

* an open, nurturing, and safe school climate
* shared decision making and mutual respect between administrators and teachers
* a positive and empathetic view of the students and their families

Another recent report, by the Council of the Great City Schools (2009), which studied district-wide efforts to address the needs of ELLs, found that districts with higher ELL academic achievement had:

* sound plans for ELL instructional improvement
* collaboration and shared accountability
* strategic school staffing
* relevant professional development

The discussions I introduce in this chapter about schoolwide curricular planning and program design for ELLs are based on the effective school features mentioned above. In addition, I build on the key concepts presented in the two previous chapters: second language acquisition processes, inclusive and culturally responsive school culture and climate, and focused professional development and support services. I begin by exploring bilingual and English-only models of language-education programs and the conditions needed for their effective implementation. This is followed by a set of recommendations for conducting schoolwide needs assessment, indentifying criteria for program selection, forming implementation plans, and creating program evaluation systems. Special attention is given to the role that preschool education has in preparing ELLs to enter kindergarten. Because native-language instruction in preschools is so important, I also discuss ideas on how teachers and school leaders can support preschool children's mother tongue as a bridge to English. The next section offers suggestions on how to effectively coordinate and align school programs under a common shared vision that integrates ELLs in all aspects of the school. The final section presents several considerations for student assessment and program evaluation. For student assessment, a discussion on the limitations of standardized tests for ELLs is presented as well as the importance of using authentic and performance-based assessment. Finally, program evaluation is discussed as part of reflective practice to reach schoolwide cohesion, compatibility, and consistency in program implementation and cross-program alignment.

LANGUAGE PROGRAM MODELS

ELLs who are in mainstream English-only or English-immersion classrooms with no specialized support often have lower academic achievement and higher dropout rates than their peers who receive specialized language instruction through ESL or bilingual programs (Genesee et al. 2006). According to the 2001–2002 national school survey, about 60 percent of ELLs in K–12 received English-only education in the United States with different degrees of ESL instruction and no native-language support. Of these ELLs, 12 percent received no specialized services at all (Zehler et al. 2003). The remaining 40 percent of ELLs received different degrees of native-language support through bilingual education that ranged from a few hours a week of pullout services to full native-language instruction in self-contained bilingual classrooms with ESL instruction. The authors found that the degree, scope, and length of native-language support in bilingual education programs differed greatly across programs and districts.

The labels for the different types of second language models vary across schools and districts. However, there is major overlap and blending of program types for ELLs. For example, structured English immersion is sometimes considered a form of submersion, while others consider two-way bilingual education and dual language to be different programs (one for language-minority children and the other for majority-language students). The models presented in the next section provide general characteristics of the types of education programs offered to ELLs in the United States.

Additive and Subtractive Models

Education models for ELLs range from *additive* programs that promote bilingualism and include instruction in the native language for an extended time (*maintenance, developmental, heritage language, dual language*) to *subtractive* programs that use only English for instruction and move students toward monolingualism in English (*English structured immersion, ESL, newcomer programs*), to programs that temporarily include instruction in the native language and also have monolingualism in English as the main goal (*transitional bilingual*). Education programs for ELLs that offer limited or no first language instruction include *structured English immersion* and *ESL* programs. Programs that use the native language for some or most of the academic instruction are under the umbrella of bilingual education, which includes *transitional, maintenance, heritage language*, and *dual language* models. Figure 3-1 provides an overview of additive and subtractive programs.

ADDITIVE PROGRAMS	SUBTRACTIVE PROGRAMS
• Goal: bilingual and biliterate	• Goal: monolingual and monoliterate
• Cultural goal: multicultural	• Cultural goal: monocultural
• Maintenance approach	• Transitional approach
• Long-term	• Short-term
• Enrichment in nature	• Sometimes remedial in nature
• Add English to the native language	• Replace the native language with English
• Acculturation orientation	• Assimilation orientation
• For language minority and majority students	• For language minority students
• Models: *maintenance, developmental, enrichment bilingual, heritage language, dual language*	• Models: *transitional bilingual education, structured English immersion, newcomer programs, ESL*

Figure 3-1 Language Programs Paradigms

Second language education in the United States falls under three broad categories:

* bilingual education

* foreign or world language education

* English as a second language (ESL) education

Even though there is overlap between these categories (for example, ESL is a component of bilingual education; bilingual immersion can be classified both as a world language and bilingual education program), there are important differences in language goals, students, length of program, orientation, language of instruction, and academic content areas (see Figure 3-2). Because this book is focused on ELLs, the descriptions of the language programs will be limited to ESL and bilingual education programs. The following section describes program models that use bilingual instruction and those that use English only for instruction. Figure 3-2 provides an overview of the different programs.

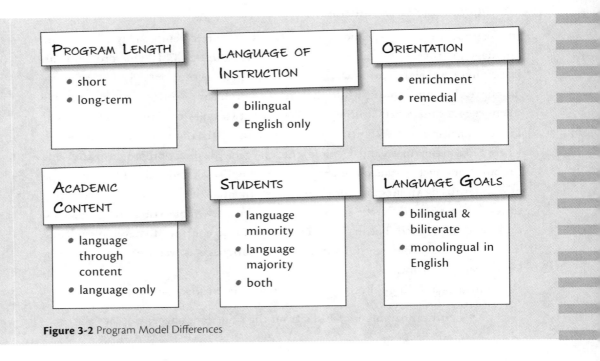

Figure 3-2 Program Model Differences

Programs with Native Language Instruction

In general terms, bilingual education is defined as any education program that uses two languages for instruction. Unlike foreign or world language education, where students study the target language and culture as a subject, bilingual education usually involves the study of literacy and/or content areas (math, science, and social studies) through two languages, the majority language—English—and another language, such as Spanish or Polish. The decision to offer bilingual education over English-only programs to ELLs depends on several factors:

* sufficient numbers of students from the same language group

* availability of certified bilingual teachers

* state and local policies

According to Baker and Jones (1998), "bilingual education is a simple label for a complex phenomenon" (p. 172). Recognizing that there are different ways for defining bilingual education and the models that fall under it, the following section describes *transitional*, *dual-language*, *maintenance*, *developmental*, and *heritage language* models.

Transitional Bilingual Education

In this model ELLs' academic development is supported temporarily with native-language instruction as students acquire English through ESL. This program can last from one to eight years. The main objective is to help students by means of the language they understand while they acquire proficiency in the second language to function academically in English. There are two types of transitional bilingual models, *early-exit* and *late-exit*. Early-exit programs are the most common model, where ELLs are mainstreamed (exited) into the general education program after one to four years once they achieve proficiency in English as determined by some type of standardized exit-language proficiency test. In late-exit programs, ELLs continue to receive instruction in the native language for a few more years after achieving proficiency in English. The main goal in late-exit is to continue to develop students' literacy and oral language skills in the native language as well as in English for a longer period of time.

Transitional bilingual programs are appropriate for schools that have:

* significant number of ELLs from the same language group at each grade level

* access to certified bilingual teachers

* access to quality instructional materials in the language other than English

* state policies that allow for native-language instruction

Dual Language Education

Also known as *two-way bilingual immersion*, this is the only bilingual education model that integrates native-English speakers and speakers of another language with the goal of developing bilingual, biliterate, and multicultural competencies among all students (Soltero 2004). Dual language education is a long-term additive bilingual and bicultural model that consistently uses two languages for instruction, learning, and communication. A balanced number of students from two language groups are integrated for instruction for all or at least half of the school day. The goals are for students to gain bilingual, biliterate, academic, and cross-cultural competencies. There are two models of dual-language programs, *total immersion* and *partial immersion.* In the *total immersion* model (also known as the 80-20 or 90-10 model), the amount of instruction in the minority language (such as Korean) is initially greater than in the majority language (English), usually 80 percent to 90 percent of the time in the primary grades, with English instruction increasing by each grade level until students receive equal amounts of majority- and minority-language instruction by the intermediate grades. In the *partial immersion* model (also known as the 50-50 model), the minority and majority languages are used equally for instruction at all grade levels. Total immersion programs require that teachers in the early grades be proficient in two languages because the majority of the instruction is conducted in the non-English language, whereas in the partial immersion model, monolingual English teachers can team-teach with bilingual teaching partners. The dual language program, regardless of model type, is offered for at least six to eight years.

Dual language programs are appropriate for schools that have:

* sufficient number of ELLs from the same language group as well as English native speakers at each grade level

* access to certified bilingual and ESL teachers

* access to quality instructional materials in the language other than English

* a desire for developing fully bilingual/biliterate and bicultural students

Maintenance Bilingual Education

This model is sometimes known as *developmental bilingual* or *enrichment bilingual*, where the goals are to develop students' bilingual and biliterate proficiencies, multicultural competencies, and academic achievement. In this model, ELLs maintain and develop their native language as they acquire English, usually through eighth grade or beyond. Maintenance bilingual programs are culturally responsive because they value and build on students' home cultural and linguistic knowledge.

Maintenance bilingual programs are appropriate for schools that have:

* significant number of ELLs from the same language group at each grade level
* access to certified bilingual teachers
* access to quality instructional materials in the language other than English
* state policies that allow for native-language instruction
* a desire for developing fully bilingual/biliterate and bicultural students

Heritage Language

This program model is designed for students who come from homes where a language other than English is or has been used, including children and grandchildren of immigrants as well as Native Americans and U.S. territories such as Puerto Rico and Guam. The goal of these programs is either to maintain the language and culture of the home or to revitalize the native language and culture, which is no longer used fluently by the younger generation of its speakers. Heritage language programs can be offered schoolwide, as a strand within a school, as an enrichment supplement, or as an after-school program.

Heritage language programs are appropriate for schools that have:

* significant number of students from the same heritage language group
* access to certified bilingual or world language teachers

* access to quality instructional materials in the heritage language
* a desire for developing the heritage language of students

Programs with English-Only Instruction

Also known as ESOL (English for Speakers of Other Languages) and ELD (English Language Development), ESL provides specialized instruction in English to students who are not yet proficient in the language. ESL programs are usually offered in schools where students come from multiple language backgrounds or where there are no bilingual teachers or programs. The most common programs are ESL and structured English immersions. Newcomer centers provide ESL instruction for a special population of students who are not able to cope with grade-level material in ESL or bilingual programs due to interrupted schooling in their home countries.

English as a Second Language

ESL programs are either *traditional grammar-based* or *content-based* and are offered either as pullout or push-in, or sometimes as self-contained ESL classrooms. In *traditional grammar-based ESL*, English is taught as a subject and the focus is on grammar, vocabulary, and error correction, usually through drill and practice. Traditional models of language instruction that focus on the language itself have proven to be ineffective for most ELLs (Corson 2001). By contrast, in *content-based ESL*, ELLs learn all or part of the content curriculum through the second language. Rather than learning the language as isolated skills, content-based ESL develops the second language as it is being acquired and used for meaningful purposes while learning academic content. Language is then taught as ELLs learn science, math, social studies, and other subjects. In the elementary grades, ESL programs are most often pullout, where ELLs are taken from their home classroom for a few periods a week in small groups. ELLs are often instructed in a type of *ESL Resource Center* where they are grouped by language proficiency level with students from several grades. A better alternative to pullout is the push-in model, where the ESL elementary teacher provides instruction in the ELLs' home classroom. In middle school and high school, students receive ESL during a regular class period, grouped according to their language-level proficiency—ESL 1, ESL 2, ESL 3. In elementary and middle school, self-contained ESL classrooms are also known as *sheltered English programs*, where all students are ELLs and receive ESL and sheltered English instruction throughout the day.

Specially Designed Academic Instruction in English (SDAIE) is an approach that uses special teaching techniques to help students understand English curricular content. Although this approach was designed to provide comprehensible input in the academic areas for English language learners, the techniques can be easily applied to other second language learners, such as in the case of students learning the target language in dual language programs. Thus, the primary focus in sheltered instruction is to acquire and develop the academic curriculum through comprehensible input in the second language. In contrast to SDAIE, *English Language Development* (ELD) has a primary focus on language development through content for beginner second language learners who may not be at grade level academically. In sheltered classrooms, instruction is given in a controlled or sheltered format. Linguistic modifications characterize the language used by teachers, such as modified syntactic structures, controlled vocabulary, and shortened sentences.

ESL programs are appropriate for schools that have:

* ELLs from multiple language backgrounds
* no access to certified bilingual teachers
* access to qualified ESL teachers
* access to quality ESL instructional materials
* state policies that restrict the use of bilingual education

Structured English Immersion

This model provides specialized instruction in English to ELLs through ESL with limited or no native-language support. Students receive all or most of their instruction in English, using specialized ESL instructional methods and approaches, such as *Sheltered Instruction Observation Protocol* (SIOP). The curriculum and instructional materials used in immersion programs are adapted for second language learners and incorporate language as well as content areas. Length of program depends on state and local school district policies, but it can range from one to four years.

Structured English immersion is appropriate for schools that have:

* ELLs from multiple language backgrounds
* no access to certified bilingual teachers
* access to qualified ESL teachers

* access to quality ESL instructional materials
* state policies that restrict the use of bilingual education

Newcomer Centers

These programs provide academic, language, cultural, and social support to recently immigrated students, usually in middle schools and high schools. They are designed to address the needs of ELLs that have had interrupted schooling or no schooling in their home countries. Because these ELLs have had limited or no schooling they are not able to cope academically in bilingual or ESL classrooms and so require more support than what these programs can offer. A key feature of most newcomer centers is an emotionally safe learning environment that supports quick second language learning, adaptation to U.S. culture as well as school culture, and development of a positive self-image. Newcomer centers often offer other supports for families in the form of training or by facilitating access to information related to social services and legal matters.

Newcomer centers are appropriate for schools that have:

* middle and high school ELLs with interrupted schooling or no schooling from their home countries, including refugees
* access to certified ESL teachers with specialized training in working with this population
* access to specialized instructional materials for older ELLs with limited academic and literacy knowledge
* ability to create small classes and one-on-one tutoring

SELECTING THE APPROPRIATE MODEL

Decisions about which programs and models are best for a particular school population require a multistep approach that follows a process of:

* collecting information
* determining needs
* knowing strengths and weaknesses
* identifying priorities

* designing new programs or modifying existing programs/ approaches

* creating an implementation plan

* establishing an ongoing evaluation system

Going through these steps is critical for determining not only what is most appropriate for ELLs but also what is realistic for a particular school to implement. For example, many rural schools don't have access to qualified bilingual teachers and therefore cannot offer bilingual programs. Other schools where students speak multiple languages are not able to offer full native-language support to ELLs. More often than not, the first and most critical decisions are whether to offer native-language or English-only instruction, for how long, and whether the goal should be bilingualism (through maintenance and dual-language programs) or monolingualism in English (through transitional bilingual programs). The quote below speaks to how important it is for schools to create a plan for addressing the language and academic needs of ELLs.

> English-language learners must be seen as the responsibility of all teachers, not as the exclusive concern of ESL teachers. Schoolwide language policies need to be developed in which the language problems present in each school are identified and the solutions to these problems are agreed upon ... the views and wishes of all stakeholders are taken into account (teachers, parents, community members, students) and an action plan is developed that addresses key issues and seeks to remove the causes of disagreement among practitioners. The intent is to have all members of the school community agree about the nature of the problem and the importance of addressing the problem as an entire school. (Valdés 2001, p. 149)

Schoolwide Needs Assessment

Educators often talk about the benefits of being reflective teachers: set goals, take action, monitor their actions, and make necessary adjustments to meet their goals (Pape, Zimmerman, and Pajares 2002). For the same reason, schools should also be reflective of their practices, goals, and beliefs. This can only be accomplished through comprehensive and ongoing schoolwide needs assessments. A solid planning process is based on how well a school can identify its strengths and weaknesses as well as priorities for improving student achievement and developing a strategic plan. Identifying these strengths, weaknesses, and priorities requires that schools examine academic experiences, expectations, and outcomes from all perspectives: students, parents, teachers, school leaders, and community members.

Understanding how the school works helps provide the type of information needed to identify sources of problems and create sustainable solutions. Teachers and school leaders should be mindful, though, that the focus of identifying problems be on school practices rather than on students and their families. Paying attention to what can be changed—such as school culture, teacher attitudes, programs, and instructional approaches—is more productive than focusing on things that are beyond the school's control—such as students' family circumstances, poverty, and family immigration status. Placing fault solely on students for their underachievement overlooks what schools and teachers could improve or change.

Such was the case of Green Creek Elementary, a K–8 school that struggled with chronic low student academic achievement and high levels of teacher dissatisfaction. School leaders and teachers at Green Creek were confronted daily with the many problems associated with poverty: unemployment, violence, delinquency, incarceration, substance abuse, single parents, teen pregnancy, poor health, and more. Teachers pointed fingers at the students and their families for their constant underachievement. Negative comments from frustrated teachers could often be heard in the school's halls and lunchroom: "These kids are never going to amount to anything because their parents just don't care," or "These kids never try, they just don't want to make a better life for themselves," and worse still, "They are here illegally and don't even care to learn English—they should go back to where they came from." Seldom were there any conversations about what the school was not doing or what the school could do better to address the persistent low performance of the students, including the many ELLs enrolled at Green Creek.

Recognizing that negative teacher attitudes and low expectations have bad academic consequences for students, the principal and several key teachers created a leadership team to improve the teaching and learning conditions of the school. The first decision was to do an in-depth needs assessment. They discovered that judgmental teacher attitudes and low morale were near the top of the list of issues needing attention. The leadership team realized that creating new programs or adapting existing programs would be pointless if teachers continued to have negative perceptions and expectations about students and their families. One of the first initiatives that came from the leadership team was to shift the nature of teachers' complaints and finger pointing by redirecting their energies to more proactive approaches and solution-based reflections. The leadership team adopted an "ethics of care" approach (Noddings 2002) that focused on mutual respect, understanding of diversity, encouragement, ownership, and affirmation. They accomplished this by having teachers participate in professional development on diversity, reading selected articles and chapters from researchers (like writings by Noddings and Nieto), engaging in discussions that now centered on solutions rather than problems, and by having more time for collaborating and planning together. From this, a new way of relating to students and their families emerged as most teachers began to shift their energies and attention from a "complain and blame others" approach to a positive problem-solving model. An interesting discovery for many teachers was that by changing how they viewed students and their families they were more successful in engaging them academically, which in turn gave teachers a greater sense of fulfillment and accomplishment.

Understanding where a school is and pinpointing areas of strengths as well as areas that need improvement is the first step in creating a cohesive and strategic schoolwide plan where all students, including ELLs, can succeed. As was the case for Green Creek, the first step is not necessarily to focus on programs but rather on how school staff, parents, and students relate to and understand one another. These improved relationships are the foundation for creating sound and interconnected programs. For ELLs, a school needs-assessment would also provide information on their general and specific needs. Figure 3-3 describes a set of elements that need to be considered for assessment under six critical categories: school, students, personnel, family, curriculum and instruction, and assessment.

Criteria for ELL Program Selection

Based on information collected from the schoolwide needs assessment, as well as records of existing resources, schools can make modifications to established programs or introduce new programs and initiatives. The criteria for selecting an appropriate program or modifying existing programs for ELLs should align to the school's vision and student goals, take into account student backgrounds and needs, consider availability of qualified staff, and follow state and district policies.

SCHOOL	Organizational structures, program compatibility, communication systems, shared decision making, leadership opportunities
STUDENTS	Language, academic, socio-emotional, health Placement procedures, inclusion, tutoring, one-on-one support
PERSONNEL	Specialized training and certification, professional development, support staff, planning and reflection time
FAMILY	Attention to language and cultural differences, communication, parent involvement, family work patterns, education or ESL needs
CURRICULUM AND INSTRUCTION	Learner-centered instructional approaches, appropriateness of materials, curricular alignment, culturally relevant and inclusive curriculum
ASSESSMENT	Assessments in the native language, multiple forms of assessment, authentic and performance-based evaluation

Figure 3-3 Considerations for Comprehensive School Needs Assessment

School Vision and Student Goals

As was mentioned in the previous chapter, the school's vision is fundamental because it is a statement of the goals and aspirations of a school related to teaching and learning. Schools that value opportunities for all students to learn a second language are well matched with a dual-language program, for example. A school's vision statement that clearly values bilingualism and diversity is more compatible with additive programs such as two-way or one-way immersion, maintenance, late-exit transitional bilingual, and developmental programs. Schools that have a vision that is focused on academic excellence in English are more compatible with structured English immersion or sheltered English programs.

Student Backgrounds and Needs

When there are sufficient ELLs in an elementary school with the same language background, the best option is to offer an additive bilingual model such as dual-language or maintenance programs. Research evidence favors bilingual programs, especially those that use bilingual strategies that teach reading in the native language, use English through content-based ESL and sheltered approaches, use culturally responsive curriculum, and use appropriate assessment measures (Genesee et al. 2006). Schools that value bilingualism but are not able to offer bilingual education because of lack of bilingual teachers, or because students come from multiple language backgrounds, can offer an ESL program aligned to a strong multicultural education curriculum that values students' cultural and language backgrounds.

Because high school ELLs have less time to catch up in English and keep up with academic subjects to graduate in four years, they often select ESL over bilingual programs. However, Walqui (2000) suggests that well-designed content bilingual programs that are aligned with content-based ESL programs result in positive benefits for ELLs in high schools. For secondary schools with ELLs from multiple language backgrounds, effective approaches include sheltered ESL content classes paired with language arts ESL.

Refugee ELLs who have had interrupted schooling present a different set of challenges. Many refugee children and adolescents live in refugee camps for extended periods of time and some may have even been born in one of these camps. Refugee students enrolled in U.S. schools often come from extreme traumatic situations that cause them to feel great anxiety and instability. This is made worse by the additional pressures of having to learn a new language, new customs, and a new culture while trying to advance through unfamiliar content subjects. Other ELLs may have had limited or no schooling in their countries of origin and therefore are not able to cope in ESL or bilingual programs designed for students who tend to be at or near grade level in their native language, especially in middle and secondary schools. For these students, newcomer centers may be the best option because they focus on accelerated English-language development paired with basic literacy instruction as well as introduction to school culture. These centers also offer family support in the form of ESL instruction for parents, help with navigating social services and healthcare, assistance with networking for employment, etc.

Qualified Personnel

One of the more important issues in selecting a language program for ELLs is access to certified and endorsed bilingual and/or ESL teachers. Teaching in a bilingual classroom requires a teaching certificate with an endorsement in bilingual education acquired through university coursework in bilingual education. Bilingual education teachers must also demonstrate proficiency in a language other than English by passing a state proficiency test in the target language, such as Spanish or Chinese. On the other hand, ESL teachers are not required to have proficiency in a language other than English, but they are required to have a teaching certificate with an endorsement in ESL also acquired through university coursework.

Recruitment and retention of qualified bilingual and ESL teachers are two critical aspects in the strategic planning of any school that has or is projected to have ELLs. Effective teacher recruitment and retention includes plenty of professional development opportunities related to ELL education. Additional benefits like extra salary or stipends for supplemental instructional materials can also help to attract and retain ESL and bilingual teachers. A study by the Texas A&M University Bilingual/ESL Teacher Retention and Recruitment Coalition (2004) reports that benefits and incentives for bilingual and ESL teachers serve to both recruit and retain them. For example, district superintendents reported that "we pay for teacher certification testing and preparation" and "we pay for certification fees and tuition/fees costs" (p. 14). A cautionary note on providing "extra perks" for bilingual and ESL teachers is that it can create resentment among general classroom teachers who may see this as unfair special treatment. A good way to respond to this is to make sure that general classroom teachers have a good understanding of the "extra" work and pressures that bilingual and ESL teachers have. The most effective way to do this is by increasing the opportunities for dialogue and planning between general classroom teachers and bilingual/ESL teachers.

Mentoring and other support systems are also critical components of teacher retention, especially for teachers working with special populations like ELLs that require more specialized and accelerated instruction. Most teachers experience burn-out at some point in their careers, but among bilingual and ESL teachers the pressures of accelerating students' English acquisition and doing well on English standardized tests creates increased stress and anxiety (see Figure 3-4). Figure 3-4 lists factors that can increase or decrease the stress and anxiety of bilingual/ESL teachers.

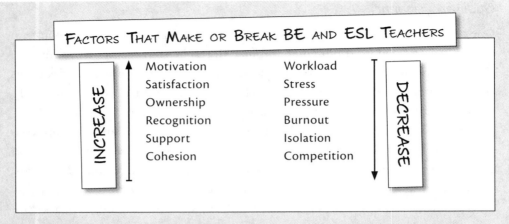

Figure 3-4 Factors That Make or Break Bilingual Education (BE) and ESL Teachers

A final suggestion for recruitment and retention is the "grow your own" programs that provide financial and/or time-release incentives for teacher assistants to become certified bilingual teachers or for general program teachers to become endorsed in ESL. For example, in 2006 Illinois enacted the Grow Your Own Teacher Education Act that states:

> The Grow Your Own Teacher preparation programs established under this Act shall comprise a major new statewide initiative, known as the Grow Your Own Teacher Education Initiative, to prepare highly skilled, committed teachers who will teach in hard-to-staff schools and hard-to-staff teaching positions and who will remain in these schools for substantial periods of time. The Grow Your Own Teacher Education Initiative shall effectively recruit and prepare parent and community leaders and paraeducators to become effective teachers statewide in hard-to-staff schools serving a substantial percentage of low-income students and hard-to-staff teaching positions in schools serving a substantial percentage of low-income students. Further, the Initiative shall increase the diversity of teachers, including diversity based on race and ethnicity. (Illinois General Assembly, 110 ILCS 48/1).

State and District Policies

According to federal law, public schools are required to provide specialized language instruction to ELLs through bilingual education, ESL, or both. Under NCLB's Title

III *Language Instruction for Limited-English-Proficient and Immigrant Students*, the purpose of the law is:

> (3) to develop high-quality language instruction educational programs designed to assist State educational agencies, local educational agencies, and schools in teaching limited English proficient children and serving immigrant children and youth; (9) to provide State educational agencies and local educational agencies with the flexibility to implement language instruction educational programs, based on scientifically based research on teaching limited English proficient children, that the agencies believe to be the most effective for teaching English. (Part A—English Language Acquisition, Language Enhancement, and Academic Achievement Act, SEC 3102, 3, 9)

Even though the law does not mention native-language instruction explicitly, there is an important statement under Part B related to the development of students' native-language and multicultural knowledge:

> ... help ensure that limited English proficient children master English and meet the same rigorous standards for academic achievement as all children are expected to meet, including meeting challenging State academic content and student academic achievement standards by: (2) developing language skills and multicultural understanding; (3) developing the English proficiency of limited English proficient children and, to the extent possible, the native language skills of such children. (Part B—Improving Language Instruction Educational Programs SEC 3202, 2, 3)

Federal law requires specialized language instruction for ELLs. The decision to offer native-language or English-only instruction is left up to each state. For example, California, Arizona, and Massachusetts have passed laws that greatly limit school districts' ability to offer bilingual education and instead require English-only instruction. In Texas, bilingual education is required for all ELLs, while states like New York, Illinois, New Mexico, and Nevada offer either bilingual education or ESL. Pennsylvania, for example, specifies the two types of language support programs in their policy:

> Every school district shall provide a program for each student whose dominant language is not English for the purpose of facilitating the

student's achievement of English proficiency and the academic
standards under code 4.12 (relating to academic standards). Programs
under this section shall include appropriate bilingual-bicultural or
English as a second language (ESL) instruction. (22 Pa. Code 4.26)

Implementation Plan

After conducting a comprehensive schoolwide needs assessment and selecting new
or modifying existing programs, a plan for implementation should be created.
Implementation plans typically include a description of the new program or of the
enhanced curriculum models, the targeted goals and objectives, timelines, needed
resources, and funding—staff, instructional materials, professional development,
strategies and action steps, and evaluation system (see Figure 3-5). Figure 3-5 illustrates these different steps needed for implementing a schoolwide plan.

About fifteen years ago, New Gates Elementary School began to experience a
steady flow of Spanish-speaking ELLs as more and more Latino families immigrated
directly into this suburban community, bypassing the usual ports of entry in the
nearby city. At the time, the school opted for an ESL pullout program because most
teachers and the principal believed that ELLs would be better served through this
type of English support service. Because the staff had little previous experience with
or knowledge of ELLs, the decision to offer ESL pullout was loosely based on their
success with the speech pullout program. Even though the needs of native-English
speakers who have speech problems are entirely different from the language needs
of ELLs, the staff was not aware of the differences between the second language
needs of ELLs and the speech pathology needs of native-English speakers. After a
while, the school began to get a sense about these differences and realized that there
were other options for ELLs besides an ESL pullout program. Because ELLs were
clearly not integrating well in the school and were not making adequate progress
academically in English, the principal and teachers decided to look into other types
of programs. They began by conducting a comprehensive needs assessment that not
only focused on ELLs but on all student needs. From the information collected
about what was working and what needed improvement, what resources they had
and what resources they would need, and what goals to focus on, the principal
and a group of teachers created a plan of action that included native-language
instruction for ELLs.

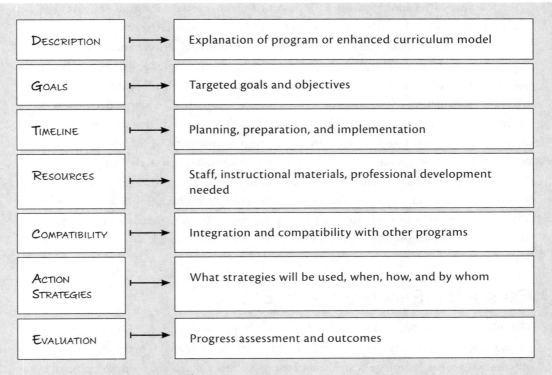

DESCRIPTION	⟶	Explanation of program or enhanced curriculum model
GOALS	⟶	Targeted goals and objectives
TIMELINE	⟶	Planning, preparation, and implementation
RESOURCES	⟶	Staff, instructional materials, professional development needed
COMPATIBILITY	⟶	Integration and compatibility with other programs
ACTION STRATEGIES	⟶	What strategies will be used, when, how, and by whom
EVALUATION	⟶	Progress assessment and outcomes

Figure 3-5 Implementation Plan

The first year, New Gates implemented a Spanish-English transitional bilingual education program in K–1 and continued offering ESL to students in grades 2–6. The second year, they were able to hire a second-grade bilingual teacher and the following year they added third grade. One of the challenges they faced was to increase the number of bilingual teachers. By creating a five-year strategic plan the school committed to replacing any teachers who retired, relocated, or left the teaching profession, with bilingual-certified teachers. The principal was careful to send the message to all teachers that their jobs were secure. A cause of concern when schools move from English-only to bilingual instruction, whether transitional bilingual or dual-language programs, is that nonbilingual teachers may feel that their jobs are at risk. This in turn can fuel mainstream teachers' negative feelings not only toward the bilingual program and teachers but also toward the ELLs themselves.

A few years after moving from ESL pullout to transitional bilingual education and experiencing a substantial increase in their ELL enrollment, the school decided to reevaluate their program and conduct another in-depth needs assessment. One of the needs that the school identified was to offer all students some type of world language learning opportunity, given that the district had identified foreign-language offerings in elementary schools as part of their strategic plan. The school decided to implement a dual-language program that would offer bilingual education services for ELLs and Spanish-as-a-second language program for native-English speakers. By selecting a 50-50 (partial immersion) model, the principal was able to design a dual-language program where bilingual teachers and monolingual English teachers team-taught and shared responsibility both for ELLs and native-English speakers. New Gates was able to evaluate their existing programs and successfully modify them to fit the changing demographics and needs of its students.

Preschool Programs and ELLs

The role of preschools in educating ELLs deserves special attention, given the long-lasting effects that early childhood education has on students' future academic outcomes. Because language is so closely tied to all aspects of a child's development in the early childhood years, ignoring their native-language acquisition processes greatly weakens teachers' ability to fully assess and promote young ELLs' language and literacy development. Outdated ideas about early bilingualism and misconceptions about the needs of young ELLs are common in preschool classrooms. For example, it is common for mainstream preschool teachers to believe that "young children are like sponges" and that "young children learn a second language quickly and easily," leading them to believe that there is no need for specialized language instruction for young ELLs. Beyond the need to provide appropriate language supports to young ELLs, educators must also create support systems that address factors related to poverty that impact their academic success later on. The lack of English language proficiency is not the only factor that affects ELLs' school outcomes. Factors such as parents having limited schooling themselves, working low-paying jobs that require them to have long work hours or multiple jobs, and having limited access to healthcare and other social services also contribute to the achievement gap for ELLs.

Early Childhood Education and Poverty

Children raised in poverty have more risks of negative life outcomes, like behavioral and socio-emotional difficulties, persistent poverty, and poor health. Studies have also linked poverty during early childhood and lower academic outcomes (Brooks-Gunn and Duncan 1997). Many low-income children between the ages of three and five are not enrolled in preschool. The belief that parents who don't enroll their children in preschool don't care about their education is far from true. The most common reasons parents give for not enrolling their children in preschool are concerns about safety in the area near preschools, not knowing that preschool is available, not being able to afford preschool, finding that preschools are at capacity and cannot take their children, and a belief that school begins in kindergarten (Williams 2007).

Consider for example the circumstances of Latinos, the largest ELL group. In 2007, of all Latino children under the age of three, 67 percent came from families with incomes 200 percent below the poverty line compared to 39 percent of white families with children of the same age (Latino Policy Forum 2009). Spanish is the dominant language of about three-fourths of preschool children in low-income Latino families. Fifty-six percent of Latino infants had a mother who was born outside the United States and of these, 19 percent of the parents reported only Spanish spoken in the home, while 35 percent reported mainly Spanish with some English spoken in the home (López, Barrueco, and Miles 2006). The likelihood for Spanish to be the primary language of the home was even greater for Latino families living in poverty, with 28 percent reporting only Spanish spoken in the home, while 15 percent saying that only English was used. Many young ELLs enter kindergarten considerably behind white children in early literacy skills. Research points to the link between high-quality preschool programs and higher academic achievement in elementary and high school resulting in economic and social benefits later in life. In addition, benefits to enrolling children in preschool programs include lower special education referral rates, higher rates of high school graduation, and increased college attendance.

Benefits of Early Bilingualism

Young children benefit cognitively from learning more than one language. For ELLs, transitioning from their first language to English before they have a strong foundation in their mother tongue can have long-lasting negative academic and linguistic effects. Preschool and kindergarten ELLs who are taught in English-only classrooms or transitioned to English instruction before they have solid oral language abilities in their own language often don't achieve high levels of English fluency and do not do as well as those who have opportunities to learn in two languages (Genesee, Paradis and Crago 2004). On standardized tests in English during the middle and high school years, young ELLs who had extended learning opportunities in their home language from ages three to eight consistently outperform those who attended English-only programs (Campos 1995).

Early childhood teachers should understand that acquiring more than one language does not delay the acquisition of English or interfere with academic achievement in English when both languages are supported. On the contrary, research on children who acquire English after their home language has been developed show that young children have the capacity to learn more than one language during the primary school years and that this bilingual ability offers long-term academic, cultural, and economic advantages (Hakuta, Butler, and Witt 2000). Neuroscientists and psycholinguists point to the positive effects of learning two languages during the infant-toddler years and also to the human brain's broad capacity to learn multiple languages. In addition, young children learning two languages have more neural activity in the parts of the brain associated with language processing. This increased brain activity can have long-term positive effects on cognitive abilities, such as those that require focusing on the details of a task and knowing how language is structured and used (Bialystok, Craik, and Ryan 2006).

Access to Linguistically and Culturally Responsive Preschool

The discussion earlier in this chapter about the importance of understanding ELLs' academic and language needs in the implementation of appropriate education practices is especially relevant for preschool-age ELLs. García, Jensen, and Scribner (2009) insist that in spite of well-documented effective policies and practices for young ELLs,

> evidence-based strategies are not implemented or are poorly implemented in many schools. The "implementation gap," therefore, is a mismatch between what works and what is commonly done in classrooms across the United States. It might also be referred to as a research-practice gap. In our view, at

least part of the reason this gap exists lies in the silos in which researchers, practitioners, and policymakers tend to work. (p. 5)

A starting point for early childhood educators is to recognize the research-based principles of educating preschool-age ELLs (García, Jensen, and Scribner 2009):

* Academic support for young children in their native language improves long-term English acquisition.

* Preschool-age ELLs who are immersed in English instead of participating in bilingual or ESL programs show decreases in reading and math achievement, higher high school dropout rates, and lower test scores.

* Neuroscientists and psycholinguists assert that oral language is the foundation for reading acquisition and that reading skills must be built on a strong oral language base.

Based on these principles, early childhood educators can provide the necessary language and academic foundations to better prepare ELLs to be successful in kindergarten and beyond. For ELLs, linguistic and culturally responsive preschool education must be an essential part of the overall improvement efforts of schools.

PROGRAM COORDINATION, COHESION, AND ALIGNMENT

Teachers and administrators should have a clear understanding about how programs fit together and in what ways they support or don't support one another. Because the education of ELLs is a process that happens over time and across grade levels and programs, attention should be given to how programs work with or against each other. Specialized programs such as ESL or bilingual education often work alone with little cross-program collaboration or sharing of information. Coordinating and aligning school programs along a set of common goals and objectives helps to ensure that they are compatible and complement each other. Schools that have well-aligned, coordinated, and cohesive programs have the most success with sustained student academic improvement. Ongoing articulation across programs also helps create a school culture that embraces the education of all students regardless of their subcategory—like ELL or special education—as the responsibility of the entire school staff.

Program Cohesion and Compatibility

Programs that share the same goals and follow similar approaches to teaching, curriculum, and assessment can complement one another because of a shared vision. This common vision is based on certain beliefs about learning, teaching, curriculum, and assessment. For example, teachers and principals who believe that learning is better when students are actively engaged in authentic and meaningful activities are likely to use instructional approaches and implement education programs that are learner-centered, integrated, interactive, and collaborative. This type of perspective on learning and teaching is known as *transactional* or *constructivist*. Teachers who follow a constructivist-transactional approach value and use students' background knowledge, encourage students to pose questions and reflect on their own assumptions, provide opportunities for real-life problem solving, and view learning as meaningful and purposeful. On the other hand, those who view learning as a process of rote memorization of facts supported by drill and practice tend to use direct-instruction approaches where prescribed knowledge and skills are transferred to students. This view is known as the *transmission* orientation to teaching (see Figure 3-6). Figure 3-6 lists the key differences between transmission- and transaction-based models of teaching and learning.

Tewei and Kavai are two schools that show how important program compatibility is: one school implements several cohesive interconnected programs while the other school implements several incompatible programs that seem contradictory to each other. At Kavai School, the principal and teachers are very motivated in providing their students with as many educational opportunities as possible. Because the school implements a dual-language program that follows a transactional-constructivist approach to learning, teachers use many learner-centered types of instructional approaches, such as cooperative learning and thematic strategies, as well as inquiry- and problem-based learning. In spite of the rich learning opportunities that the dual-language program offers, the principal felt pressured to adopt a highly scripted reading program because a significant number of students were not doing as well on the state standardized reading test.

Because the new reading program follows a strict timeline that requires a daily two-hour block dedicated to reading, teachers were forced to add an additional forty-five minutes of writing to their daily schedules. The result was that half the day ended up being dedicated to language arts, leaving very little time for content-area instruction. In addition, classroom teachers could no longer integrate the

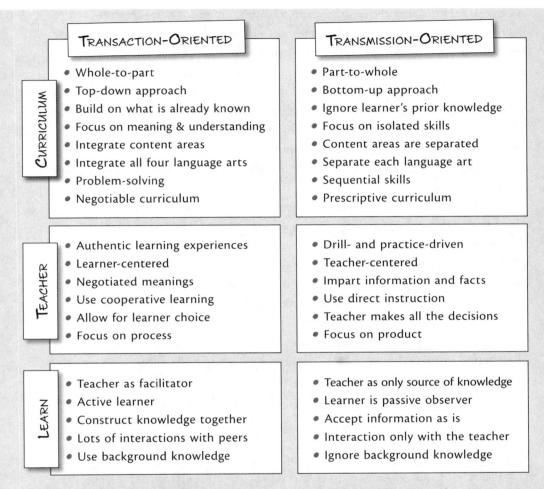

Figure 3-6 Transaction-Oriented vs. Transmission-Oriented Approaches (Soltero 2004)

curriculum or use thematic units during language arts because the new reading program followed a sequential set of lessons that used dry, decodable books with controlled text and focused on explicit, direct, and systematic skills instruction. Many teachers at Kavai felt torn and frustrated because they had to use two approaches that they thought of as polar opposite to each other: in the mornings they were expected to teach a scripted curriculum through direct instruction and rote learning using a transmission approach, while in the afternoons they were expected to teach through a hands-on learner-centered transactional/constructivist approach. Many other teachers felt that the highly scripted reading program not only narrowed the curriculum and affected what they could do with content-area instruction but also limited their ability to be flexible and creative, and to integrate the curriculum. Because both the reading program and the dual-language program were labor-intensive and "high-maintenance" programs, teachers felt that they were pulled in two opposing directions and had to choose which program to devote their energy and loyalty toward. The incompatibility of the two programs had many unintended consequences: the dual-language program began to lose its effectiveness, there was a decrease in morale among teachers, and several self-described "whole language" teachers left Kavai.

By contrast, the teachers and principal at Tewei School, which also has a significant number of students who are struggling academically, made programmatic decisions based not only on their shared vision and beliefs about teaching and learning but also on how well programs would align with and complement each other. Tewei is a multilingual school, with over twenty-seven languages represented in the student body. While the school has 38 percent ELLs, about 90 percent of the students come from homes where a language other than English is spoken by the parents. Teaching children from so many languages and cultural backgrounds is made more challenging in this school because the majority of the families live in poverty and many of the students' parents have low levels of education in their home countries. Tewei offers bilingual programs for the Spanish- and Gujarati-speaking ELLs, and ESL services for the rest of the ELLs in the school. Because of the multilingual and multicultural nature of the student population, and to promote multilingualism, they also offer all students world language classes in Chinese.

The school staff is well aware that teachers are most effective when they have knowledge about their students' backgrounds and that students learn best when they can relate to the curriculum. Because of this, the teachers and school leaders decided to rethink how they could shift the social studies curriculum from a narrow focus on the United States and Europe to a broader and more global focus that includes knowledge and perspective on other countries and cultures. Complementing their multilingual-multicultural vision, the school adopted a new social studies curriculum that follows a global and social justice perspective through authentic inquiry that promotes critical thinking rather than fact memorization. The new curriculum was well received by Tewei teachers because they felt it was more relevant to students' multiple backgrounds and because it gave students an opportunity to learn about each other's cultures and countries. More importantly, teachers felt that they were also learning alongside their students.

Vertical, Horizontal, and Cross-Program Articulation

Effective schools are those that adopt cohesive and well-coordinated programs with common approaches, philosophies, and goals. A key component is ongoing communication. These communication practices include vertical, horizontal, and cross-program coordination and articulation (see Figure 3-7). Figure 3-7 illustrates how vertical, horizontal, and cross-program coordination could work with different teachers at a school.

Ongoing communication between programs and across grade levels is especially important for integrating and engaging ELLs fully in school. Because many ELLs tend to be linguistically isolated at schools and at home, integrating them in all aspects of school and providing them access to English-speaking peers in supportive learning settings is essential to their academic success (Valdés 2001; Arias 2007). *Linguistic isolation*, a term introduced by the census in 1990 to identify households where all members fourteen years or older speak a language other than English and none speaks English "very well," is a serious problem that needs to be addressed both at the school level and through policy changes. For schools that have high

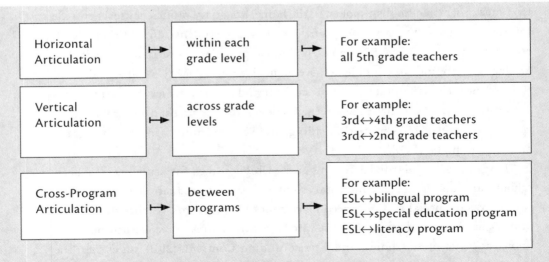

Figure 3-7 Vertical, Horizontal, and Cross-Program Articulation

concentrations of ELLs, the challenge is to create opportunities for ELLs not only to develop their academic native language but also to have educational interactions and experiences with native-English speakers. For schools that have few ELLs, the challenge is to provide supportive and meaningful learning experiences in mainstream classrooms with appropriate specialized support. To achieve this, teachers must engage in ongoing communication within and across grade levels and across programs to coordinate more effectively their efforts, objectives, and direction.

ASSESSMENT AND EVALUATION

Communication and coordination should be guided by how students are doing academically and by how well programs within a school are addressing their needs. Two key elements for effective program coordination are student assessment and program evaluation. Information gathered from well-planned and focused assessment and evaluation gives direction to and creates cohesion for programs serving all students, including ELLs.

Student Assessment: Standardized Tests

Title III of NCLB requires that students who might be identified as ELL be given a home language survey and then be given a language proficiency test if there is a language other than English spoken in the home. Language proficiency tests provide information about the language proficiency levels of students. In addition, NCLB requires that schools give ELLs a yearly English proficiency test that shows if they are meeting annual measurable achievement objectives (AMAOs). The goal is for ELLs to meet the same state academic content and student achievement standards as non-ELLs. ELLs who have been in the United States longer than a year must take yearly achievement tests in math, reading, and science from third to eighth grade and once in high school.

Large-scale standardized testing carries high stakes for students, teachers, schools, and districts. These high stakes include student graduation, grade promotion, access to special and Advanced Placement (AP) programs, teacher status and/ or merit salary, school sanctions or rewards, school closures or reconstitutions (also known as turnaround schools), and district funding. Contreras (2010) states that "the biggest losers in this 'high stakes' framework however are the students, as the myriad of achievement and exit exams are being utilized to withhold their school diplomas as well as make grade promotion decisions" (p. 194). Standards- and assessment-based reforms have been widely implemented in schools since the passage of NCLB, which requires that all students meet academic standards and that schools be held accountable for the progress of all their students.

Teachers as well as standardized test-makers recognize that for ELLs, large-scale standardized tests, especially when given in English, are a great source of concern. The misuse of these tests as well as the excessive testing of ELLs gives teachers and school districts inaccurate information about how ELLs are doing both academically and in their English development. August and Shanahan (2006) point to the limitations of existing English-language proficiency tests as poor predictors of ELLs' success on reading and content-area assessments in English over time. Teachers and researchers agree that scores on standardized tests in English of content knowledge are often not valid for ELLs. Genesee and Riches (2006) state that "a standardized test of mathematics or science administered in English to ELLs is just as much about the student's language proficiency as it is about his/her knowledge of mathematics or science" (p. 137). Schools and districts have other options for addressing concerns about the validity of standardized testing for ELLs. For example, evaluating ELLs in their native language can provide more accurate information about their progress in the content areas and reading, and this is especially true for ELLs who are enrolled in bilingual education programs. Another approach to testing ELLs is to provide accommodations such as giving students more time during testing or allowing students to respond in the native language. The most important consideration is that ELLs' academic progress not be based on a single test score and that schools include other assessments beyond standardized tests, such as authentic and performance-based assessment.

Student Assessment: Authentic and Performance-Based

According to Gottlieb (1999), "instructional assessment implies a partnership between instruction (the delivery system) and assessment (the information-gathering process). Performance-based instructional activities, tasks and projects form the basis for classroom assessment" (p. v). Katz (2001) suggests that for assessment to be most effective, educators should follow these steps in a cyclical way: 1) plan assessment, 2) collect and record information, 3) analyze and interpret information, and 4) report and make instructional and placement decisions based on this information and analysis (see Figure 3-8). This assessment cycle repeats as teachers and students progress through the learning standards and goals. For ELLs, well-thought-out assessment plans are especially important because language acquisition is an added element that needs to be considered. Figure 3-8 shows the different components of the assessment cycle.

Teacher-made, performance-based, and authentic assessment tools often provide a more complete picture of the abilities of ELLs in content subjects, literacy, and academic English. Authentic assessment is especially appropriate for ELLs because it involves students' actual learning processes and performances in specific academic and language tasks. Some of the most common authentic assessment tools for collecting information and documenting students' academic knowledge are portfolios, teacher observations, anecdotal records, checklists, rubrics, and self-assessment (see Figure 3-9). For ELLs who are at the beginner and intermediate levels of English proficiency it is especially important to have the opportunity to show rather than tell what they know and can do. Because beginner- and intermediate-level ELLs don't

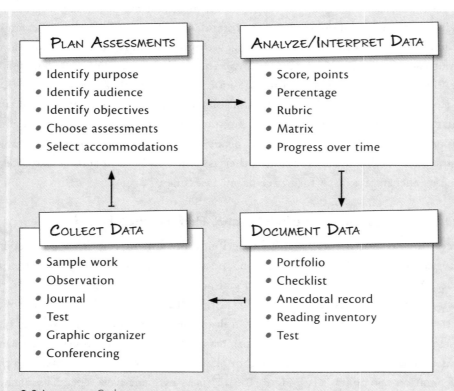

Figure 3-8 Assessment Cycle

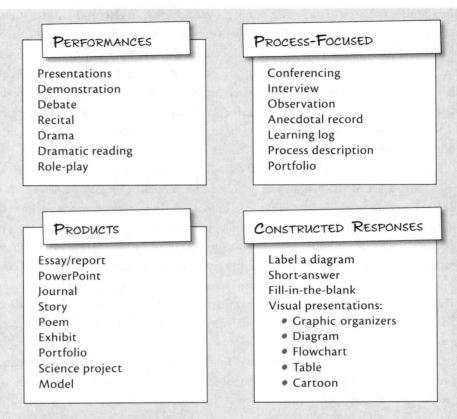

PERFORMANCES

Presentations
Demonstration
Debate
Recital
Drama
Dramatic reading
Role-play

PROCESS-FOCUSED

Conferencing
Interview
Observation
Anecdotal record
Learning log
Process description
Portfolio

PRODUCTS

Essay/report
PowerPoint
Journal
Story
Poem
Exhibit
Portfolio
Science project
Model

CONSTRUCTED RESPONSES

Label a diagram
Short-answer
Fill-in-the-blank
Visual presentations:
• Graphic organizers
• Diagram
• Flowchart
• Table
• Cartoon

Figure 3-9 Performance-Based Assessments

yet have enough vocabulary and language skills in English to express what they have learned, performance-based assessments such as the use of graphic organizers are especially valuable. Because these types of assessments don't require high levels of language proficiency or advanced skills in writing, ELLs can demonstrate their content knowledge and skills in ways that are not heavily dependent on academic language proficiency. For example, it is much easier for ELLs to show their knowledge of the water cycle by drawing a cyclical diagram than by writing an essay explaining it. Figure 3-9 lists a number of different types of performance-based assessments.

Program Evaluation

The academic achievement of ELLs cannot be measured in a vacuum. In other words, ELLs' academic progress and language development in English need to be evaluated in relation to the quality of programs and characteristics of schools in which students participate. For example, overcrowded, underfunded, and unsafe schools with weak leadership, high teacher turnover, many beginner teachers, teachers with provisionary certificates, and subtractive and remedial programs among other factors produce lower academic achievement among their students. On the other hand, schools that have visionary leadership, experienced and dedicated teachers, strong home-school partnerships, safe school environments, focused professional development, high expectations, and cohesive additive programs are more likely to produce higher academic results for students.

Steps for monitoring program and school effectiveness should include decisions on the purpose/s of the evaluation, who and what will be evaluated, who will be doing the evaluating, what tools will be used to collect information, and how the findings will be used. Establishing the purpose and objectives for conducting program or schoolwide evaluation usually includes determining program effectiveness, identifying areas that need improvement, recommending modifications, and setting new program goals. The critical program elements to be evaluated could include how well the program model is followed, what instructional approaches and materials are used, how effective the instructional delivery is, and how classroom management impacts learning.

In terms of who is responsible for doing the evaluation, the most valuable are those that are created by the entire school staff in collaboration with parents and in some case, the students themselves. A good approach is to have a team that represents teachers at different grade levels, school administrators, support staff such as librarians and nonclassroom teachers, parents, and students. Collecting the information needed for a comprehensive evaluation can be done through a number of ways: observations, surveys, portfolios, and checklists. In addition, data analysis of standardized and classroom-based assessment on students' academic progress and achievement should also be used.

Program evaluation usually involves measurable outcomes (such as test scores) and measurable processes (such as implementation elements). The evaluating of outcomes reveals the immediate effects of programs on the target audience and determines if the programs' objectives were met. Measurable processes enable a focus on how programs are implemented and allow an evaluation of the conditions under which programs function. Improving student academic achievement, enhancing teacher performance, expanding professional development, and increasing parent involvement are examples of outcomes and processes that should be part of program and school evaluation. A comprehensive evaluation would include all aspects of the program—or school—and an analysis of how the various elements influence their outcomes and processes. These evaluation targets not only include student test scores but also teacher and leadership effectiveness, curriculum and instruction, assessment practices, and family involvement (see Figure 3-10). Figure 3-10 lists examples of evaluation components. Once the necessary information has been collected and analyzed, the team can move to the final phase of identifying areas that need improvement and then develop strategic plans that include goals, tangible actions, timelines, persons responsible for those actions, and funding considerations.

STUDENTS	Academic knowledge and skills, improvement over time
TEACHERS	Knowledge, planning/preparation, goals, professional development, classroom management, communication skills, enthusiasm, respect
ADMINISTRATORS	Knowledge, leadership and problem-solving skills, communication, clear goals, shared decision making, innovation, clear planning
CURRICULUM	Aligned, integrated, rigorous, challenging, culturally relevant
INSTRUCTION	Organized and clear, creative, varied, engaging, active learning, differentiated, use of modifications
ASSESSMENT	Valid and reliable, multiple forms of assessment, formative and summative assessments
FAMILY INVOLVEMENT	Outreach, parent meetings and training, parent as advocates

Figure 3-10 Examples of Evaluation Components

Program evaluation at Toltec Middle School is a collaborative effort that involves teachers, parents, administration, community liaisons, and students. At Toltec, the Language and Culture Program is the central engine of the school to which all other programs are aligned. Because the vision and mission of the school are to maintain and develop bilingualism and multiculturalism, the rest of the programs coordinate their curriculum, instructional approaches, materials, and assessments to fit with the goals of the Language and Culture Program. Toltec is a school that is made up predominantly of Latino students, but recently Cantonese-speaking Chinese families have moved into the area. Because of this new influx of students, the school began a Chinese world language program a few years ago in which all students participate.

The leadership team coordinates the yearly evaluation of the other major programs in the school—such as the content-area programs, special education, world language, music and art programs—while also collecting data on smaller enrichment or supplemental programs such as the after-school and technology programs. Members of the leadership team include the principal, assistant principal, two resource coaches, a bilingual teacher, a special education teacher, a content-area teacher, the student council president, and the president of the Local School Council, who is a parent. Beyond the usual data collection of student standardized test scores, student retention rates, attendance, and truancy, the leadership team collects qualitative information from all stakeholders on issues such as student engagement, teacher and parent satisfaction with programs, level of leadership support, and family support and involvement. This information is gathered through meetings, interviews, surveys, and reports from the various teacher and school leader committees. In addition to program implementation and outcomes assessment, the leadership team also includes information from the two feeder primary schools as well as the neighborhood high school. Toltec's success at identifying areas of improvement through their program evaluation is made easier because of their focused curriculum and its schoolwide and interschool coordination and alignment.

Effective schoolwide curricular planning and program design should incorporate the needs of all students, including the academic, linguistic, and socio-emotional needs of ELLs. In order to identify the most effective and viable program models, schools need to increase the teacher and administrator knowledge base about ELLs, language program models, and basic requirements for their effective implementation. By conducting schoolwide needs assessments, schools are better able to select, modify, and/or create programs that are suited for their specific population of students. Once programs are in place, maintaining their effectiveness and sustainability requires coordination and alignment under a common shared school vision. Ongoing student assessment and program evaluation contributes to long-term effectiveness of programs. This chapter also gives special attention to the role that preschool education has on providing the necessary foundation to succeed in the primary grades and as an example of how critical it is for schools to align, coordinate, and integrate different programs in more seamless ways.

APPLICATIONS

1. Come up with four different ELL scenarios. For each scenario describe whether or not:

   * the school is rural versus suburban versus urban

   * the school is historically versus not historically populated by ELL school-age population

   * ELL group speaks the same language versus multiple languages

   * ELL group speaks a commonly spoken language versus a less-commonly spoken language

   * state policy allows native-language instruction versus policy that does not allow native-language instruction

   Based on the four different combinations of characteristics selected, decide what would be the best language education model for each ELL group.

2. Create a PowerPoint presentation for the board of education of a school district that explains each of the different program models for ELLs. Select one of the program models that would be best suited for a school that has (pick one):

   * a large number of ELLs from one language background (such as Spanish or Chinese)

   * ELLs from multiple language backgrounds

   * about half of ELLs from one language background and half non-ELLs

3. Select a second language program model and create a brochure that highlights the major elements of the program, such as vision, purpose, goals, characteristics, components, benefits, and special features.

4. Write a plan for cross-program alignment between the ELL program (bilingual or ESL) and the early childhood program, the special education program, the technology program, the literacy program, etc. Describe the coordination elements (assessment, language needs, cultural considerations, etc.), the ways that the coordination will take place (meetings, reports, professional development, book studies, etc.), and what the coordination will look like.

	Language Support	Cultural Considerations	Instructional Materials	Assessment
PreK Program				
Special Education Program				
Literacy Program				
Content Area Programs				
Library				
Technology				
Other				

SUGGESTIONS FOR FURTHER READING |||||||||||||||||||||||

Barone, Diane M., and Shelley Hong Xu. 2007. *Literacy Instruction for English Language Learners Pre-K–2*. New York: The Guilford Press.

Espinoza, Linda M. 2010. *Getting It Right for Young Children from Diverse Backgrounds: Applying Research to Improve Practice*. Boston: Pearson.

Gottlieb, Margot. 2006. *Assessing English Language Learners: Bridges from Language Proficiency to Academic Achievement*. Thousand Oaks, CA: Corwin Press.

Tabors, Patton. 2008. *One Child, Two Languages: A Guide for Early Childhood Educators of Children Learning English as a Second Language*. Baltimore: Brookes Publishing.

Chapter 4

Principles of Effective Teaching and Learning for ELLs

Current policy and practice do not align with what the scientific research shows about the value of the home language in promoting ELLs' school success. Nor as a nation are we taking advantage of ELLs as a source for developing the multilingual and multicultural resources of our society, which are so valuable in today's global economy.

(Hakuta, August, and O'Day 2009, p. 2)

According to Ballantyne, Sanderman, and Levy (2008)

> [m]easures of school performance indicate that ELLs are not
> performing as well as their EP [English proficient] peers. The
> National Assessment of Educational Progress (also known as "The
> Nation's Report Card") collects data on student performance at
> the fourth-grade and eighth-grade level. At the eighth-grade level,
> 76 percent of EP students scored at or above basic in reading; 74
> percent scored at or above basic in mathematics. ELLs' scores were
> considerably lower, with only 30 percent at or above basic in reading
> and only 31 percent at or above basic in mathematics. (p. 12)

Countering ELLs' academic underachievement requires that teachers and principals implement the types of instructional approaches and strategies that make the most of ELLs' learning potential. Instructional approaches and methods for ELLs are most effective when they are culturally responsive and linguistically appropriate. Culturally responsive instructional approaches include using students' cultural backgrounds, prior experiences, and learning styles to help them through the learning process (Gay 2000). Linguistically appropriate strategies take into account the developmental stages of second language acquisition, as well as the time and types of support needed to develop academic English. Effective instructional approaches also take into account ELLs' first language development—for example, whether or not ELLs are literate in the first language and/or have acquired academic language skills in their first language. For ELLs, becoming proficient in academic English is not the only aspect of their overall education needs. ELLs, like all students, must also develop content knowledge, high competency in literacy, and critical-thinking and problem-solving skills. Without a good understanding of ELLs' range and types of needs, teachers may develop low expectations toward ELLs and put in doubt their potential for success in school.

In this chapter I describe effective classroom instruction and learning practices that best help ELLs develop strong foundations in language, literacy, and content learning. I begin with a discussion on how teaching and learning practices, when combined with high expectations, result in the most positive education outcomes for ELLs. In the sections that follow, I introduce several types of classroom practices that support their language and literacy development, such as teaching for transfer and the use of scaffolding approaches. In the last two sections I describe culturally relevant and linguistically appropriate instructional approaches that help ELLs to access content-area knowledge and support their academic language acquisition. In the last section of the chapter I present a number of effective instructional practices that are based on active engagement, authentic learning, and learner-centered classrooms.

CONNECTING HIGH EXPECTATIONS AND ACADEMIC SUCCESS

Because ELLs interact daily with two languages and cultures, their experiences in and out of school greatly influence their learning. Understanding ELLs' individual, sociocultural, and language backgrounds allows teachers to form appropriate expectations that support their learning. There is widespread agreement that teachers should hold positive and high expectations for all students, including for ELLs. However, these high expectations have to be connected to appropriate learning-support systems, challenging and rigorous curriculum, and modifications based on ELLs' language proficiency levels. Teachers need to understand that ELLs' limited proficiency in English is not the same as limited intelligence or limited thinking ability. The same high standards expected for native-English speakers should also apply to ELLs. On the other hand, having high academic expectations for ELLs should not be unrealistic. For example, it is unreasonable to expect a middle school ELL at a beginner ESL level to be able to write paragraphs in English as well as a native-English speaker at the same grade level. Similarly, a high school refugee ELL with interrupted schooling should not be expected to perform in a biology class at grade level or as well as an ELL who is at grade level in her native language. Having high but appropriate expectations for ELLs requires that teachers have a clear understanding of their students' English language proficiency levels and their prior school experiences and academic knowledge. Freeman and Freeman (2007) advise that "[i]n order for educators to best serve ELLs, they must first know their students. They should have information about students' first languages, about their previous educational background, and to the extent possible, about their families and family histories" (p. 30).

The stories of two ELLs, Galina and Ofelia, show how important it is for teachers to have high but appropriate expectations based on students' backgrounds, experiences, and even individual aptitudes. On the surface, both Ofelia and Galina have similar circumstances related to age of arrival in the United States and English proficiency level—both were at a beginner ESL level when they entered school for the first time in the United States. A closer look, however, reveals that Galina and Ofelia came from very different situations that affected their learning and rate of English acquisition. Galina arrived in the United States from Bulgaria when she was twelve years old and was enrolled in sixth grade in a local public school close to her home. Although she scored at a beginner level in ESL, Galina had taken some English classes in school in Bulgaria and was familiar with conversational English. By the second semester Galina was advancing very rapidly in English and was doing very well in reading and the subject areas, especially in math and science. Ofelia on the other hand was struggling with learning English and was not doing well in the academic subjects. She arrived in the United States from El Salvador about the same time as Galina and enrolled in the same sixth-grade classroom. After the first semester Ofelia was moved to the fifth-grade classroom and was pulled out for an additional ESL class each day.

Mr. Walsh, the sixth-grade teacher, gave up on Ofelia almost immediately after she enrolled in his class, claiming that Ofelia came to school unprepared and "lacked motivation." The teacher often made comparisons between Galina and Ofelia and said that it was no surprise that Galina was doing much better because she was "highly motivated" and liked school. Mr. Walsh had no doubt that Galina was going to graduate from college and have a promising future. On the other hand, his low expectations of Ofelia were evident in his belief that she would probably end up working in a factory where "you don't really need to know English or how to read and write anyway."

The great difference in academic performance and English acquisition between Ofelia and Galina can be explained by considering their backgrounds, experiences, and circumstances. Ofelia's journey into the United States was long, difficult, and painful. She arrived in the United States with her mother and younger brother via Mexico with the services of a "coyote"—a human smuggler for hire. Ofelia's family fled El Salvador because of death threats from the violent Mara Salvatrucha gang after her father had been killed. Out of fear, Ofelia and her younger brother had stopped going to school after her father's murder and had also missed school while attempting the journey to the United States. It took her family more than seven months to reach the United States, with little money and few resources. The trauma of experiencing violence, persecution, and then escape, plus the two and half years of school that Ofelia missed, and the conditions of poverty in which she lived, shows a more complete picture of the personal struggles that ended up delaying her full learning potential. By contrast, Galina had lived a fairly comfortable life as an only child in Bulgaria, having been raised in a lower-middle-class family with both her parents employed in government jobs. Galina attended school without interruptions in Sofia, the capital of Bulgaria, where she was performing above grade level. Although Galina and her family arrived in the United States with undocumented status—the same as Ofelia's family—she was able to settle comfortably into a close-knit community of Bulgarians in the United States that provided social services support and helped them transition into English and the U.S. culture.

The backgrounds and experiences of these two ELLs, which on the surface seem to be so similar, are worlds apart. Galina and Ofelia not only need different support systems but also appropriate expectations related to their earlier education experiences. Ofelia's learning difficulties are not due to her lack of motivation. Her inadequate school preparation was not of her own choosing. Neither is Galina's academic success a result of her liking school and being more motivated than Ofelia. Indeed Ofelia was less prepared because of her interrupted schooling and traumatic experiences, while Galina "liked school" because she was already doing well and her teacher was constantly encouraging her. The connection between schools' high expectations and students' academic success is well documented and supported by research (Marzano 2003). Schools where teachers and administrators consistently hold high expectations for all their students tend to have higher student engagement and better academic outcomes. Because people tend to strive to accomplish what is expected of them, teachers have a great influence on how students internalize high or low expectations and often respond accordingly. For Galina, Mr. Walsh's high expectations reaffirmed that she was doing well and motivated her to keep working hard. For Ofelia, Mr. Walsh's low expectations only shut her down, intensified her apparent lack of motivation, and made her feel ashamed and guilty about her lack of "preparedness."

Holding high expectations for ELLs is necessary in helping them reach school success, especially for those who have experienced poverty, migratory trauma, and limited or interrupted schooling. Beyond academic types of support like tutoring and differentiated instruction, special attention should be given to students' emotional well-being and self-confidence. Teachers have great influence over how students view themselves: "For children who are used to thinking of themselves as stupid or not worth talking to or deserving rape and beatings, a good teacher can provide an astonishing revelation. A good teacher can give a child at least a chance to feel, 'She thinks I'm worth something; maybe I am'" (Kidder 1990, p. 3). Students generally internalize teachers' high expectations, resulting in increased self-confidence, higher motivation, and resiliency. On the other hand, teachers' low expectations result in students developing negative self-esteem, poor motivation, and apathy. It is important to note that having high expectations of students alone does not guarantee that they will do well academically. High expectations do not magically override students' individual abilities, the rate at which they learn, their particular educational background, or their socio-emotional state. Teachers can accommodate students' different needs while also holding high expectations for them.

In the school and within the classroom, teachers and school leaders can adopt coordinated and systematic ways to communicate high expectations such as the ones listed in Figure 4-1. A starting point is to create a climate of mutual respect by engaging students one-on-one and valuing their background knowledge. Personal interaction between teachers and students often results in higher student engagement because students perceive that the adults in the school care about them. Knowing each student's name, interests, concerns, family situation, and cultural background can help establish strong and caring relationships between educators and students, but also facilitates stronger relationships with their families and communities. Students also need to know that teachers have high expectations of them to succeed academically and will not be given what Ladson-Billings (2008) calls "permission to fail." Ladson-Billings recounts the struggles of Shannon, an African American first grader who struggled with writing and who was constantly given "permission to fail" by the teachers. In her own self-defense and to hide her inability to read, Shannon refused to write. While her white classmates were encouraged by the teachers to keep writing, young Shannon was given a pass by the teachers. Early on in this student's schooling the message to her was that teachers had little expectation for her to succeed in school. Shannon's teachers could have addressed her struggles by differentiated instruction and building her self-esteem through opportunities to experience success with writing. Encouraging Shannon to engage in challenging and engaging writing exercises with individual support would have motivated her to keep trying rather than to easily give up.

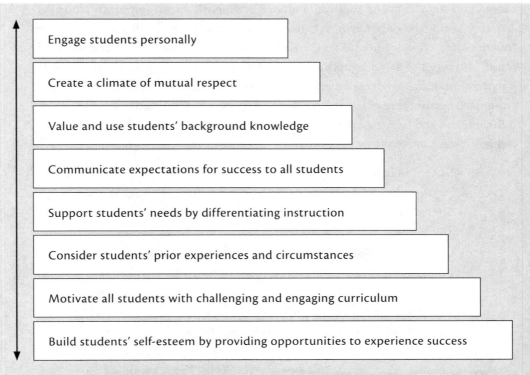

Engage students personally

Create a climate of mutual respect

Value and use students' background knowledge

Communicate expectations for success to all students

Support students' needs by differentiating instruction

Consider students' prior experiences and circumstances

Motivate all students with challenging and engaging curriculum

Build students' self-esteem by providing opportunities to experience success

Figure 4-1 Strategies for Increasing High Expectations

THE LANGUAGE-LITERACY CONNECTION

> Language-minority students who cannot read and write proficiently in English cannot participate fully in American schools, workplaces or society. They face limited job opportunities and earning power. Inadequate reading and writing proficiency in English relegates rapidly increasing language-minority populations to the sidelines, limiting the nation's potential for economic competitiveness, innovation, productivity growth, and quality of life. (August and Shanahan, 2006, p. 1)

Developing strong reading and writing skills is necessary for ELLs' overall academic success. Even though the language of instruction for ELLs' early reading development—whether the native language or English—is an important consideration, it is not the only factor that needs to be considered. Quality of instruction, orientation to literacy instruction, types of instructional approaches and materials used, and types of assessments can have either positive or negative effects on ELLs' language and literacy development. A recent U.S. Department of Education's report summarizes current research on how best to improve the education outcomes of ELLs (Tanenbaum and Anderson 2010) and points to the types of classroom practices and school conditions that best support ELLs' chances of academic success:

* ELLs' English language and literacy development can be promoted by initially learning to read in their first language (August and Shanahan 2010; Goldenberg 2008; Hakuta, August, and O'Day 2009).

* While instructional approaches that are most effective for native-English speakers are also most effective for ELLs, students not yet proficient in English need specific modifications and adaptations since they are simultaneously learning academic content and the language in which the content is taught (Hakuta, August, and O'Day 2009).

Language development is fundamental to learning. Because literacy is so interconnected to oral language and vocabulary, early literacy development should be, whenever possible, in the language that students know best, their native language. Extensive research on biliteracy shows that the ability to read and write well in two languages has been linked to long-term academic, sociocultural, and economic advantages. The National Literacy Panel (NLP) on Language Minority Children and Youth concluded that oral proficiency and literacy in ELLs' first language can help literacy development in English, and inclusion of first-language instruction in ELL programs can have long-term benefits (August and Shanahan 2010). This conclusion is supported by five recent meta-analyses comparing bilingual and English-only programs (Genesee et al. 2006; Krashen and McField 2005; Rolstad, Mahoney, and Glass 2005; Slavin and Cheung 2003; Collier and Thomas 2009). Goldenberg (2008) summarizes key findings of two major reviews of the research on educating ELLs completed in 2006 by the NLP and by the Center for Research on Education, Diversity, and Excellence (CREDE). These reviews provide a comprehensive analysis of the most effective approaches that support ELLs' success in school. The findings correspond to other research conclusions and can be summarized in three major points:

* Teaching students to read in their first language promotes higher levels of reading achievement *in English*.

* What we know about good instruction and curriculum in general holds true for English learners as well; but

* When instructing English learners in English, teachers must modify instruction to take into account students' language limitations.

Callahan (2006) found that programs that focus only on reading at the expense of English language development fall short in supporting ELLs' academic achievement. Several studies have pointed to the shortcomings of instruction that emphasize word recognition, spelling, and decoding skills alone, because ELLs do not develop comprehension or vocabulary necessary to succeed academically (Genesee et al. 2006). ELLs need to acquire extensive content-area and academic vocabulary as well as strategies for comprehending and analyzing difficult expository text and challenging narrative text. Snow (2002) notes that for teachers to understand the development of literacy in a second language they need to know about the complexities of the reading process, language and cognitive development, ELLs' individual differences, and the context in which ELLs develop reading.

Acquiring a second language happens in stages as ELLs progress through increasingly more proficient levels. Even though the time it takes to go through these stages varies and depends on each individual learner, language proficiency levels guide teachers to make more appropriate and effective instructional decisions. The WIDA (World-Class Instructional Design and Assessment) language proficiency levels and standards provide benchmarks as ELLs progress through their English language development. The WIDA standards, based on the TESOL (Teachers of English to Speakers of Other Languages) standards, are available at no cost online (www.wida.us/). WIDA's five proficiency levels are based on expected performance indicators that describe what ELLs can do in academic English in listening, speaking, reading, and writing (see Figure 4-2). According to the WIDA standards, the performance definitions for each proficiency level are based on three criteria related to students' increasing knowledge of:

* comprehension and use of the technical language of the content areas

* linguistic complexity of oral interaction or writing
* phonologic, syntactic, and semantic understanding of usage as they move through the second language acquisition continuum

Figure 4-2 shows these criteria and the language expectations for each level.

The WIDA standards, proficiency levels, and recommended instructional strategies provide teachers a helpful framework for creating focused, cohesive, and developmentally appropriate language programs for ELLs. A common challenge for teachers of ELLs is providing instruction for all the different levels of language proficiency within one classroom. Relying solely on ESL series and textbooks that are often designed for a grade level, rather than multiple language proficiency levels, makes

---

Performance definitions for the levels of English language proficiency

At the given level of English language proficiency, ELLs will process, understand, produce, or use:

5 Bridging	• the technical language of the content areas; • a variety of sentence lengths of varying linguistic complexity in extended oral or written discourse, including stories, essays, or reports; • oral or written language approaching comparability to that of English proficient peers when presented with grade level material
4 Expanding	• specific and some technical language of the content areas; • a variety of sentence lengths of varying linguistic complexity in oral discourse or multiple, related paragraphs; • oral or written language with minimal phonological, syntactic, or semantic errors that do not impede the overall meaning of the communication when presented with oral or written connected discourse with occasional visual and graphic support

Figure 4-2 Language Proficiency Levels Performance Definitions (WIDA Consortium, http://www.wida.us/)

it difficult for teachers to plan for differentiated instruction. The WIDA proficiency levels and standards help teachers organize instruction by language proficiency level so that students in the same classroom who are at the *Entering* level are not receiving the same instruction and have the same language objectives as students who are at the *Bridging* level. ELLs with varying language proficiency levels within the same self-contained classroom should have a combination of:

* homogeneous language-level grouping so that the instruction can be focused and designed for their language level

* heterogeneous language-level grouping so that higher and lower language proficiency level ELLs can help each other

3 Developing	• general and some specific language of the content areas; • expanded sentences in oral interaction or written paragraphs; • oral or written language with phonological, syntactic, or semantic errors that may impede the communication but retain much of its meaning when presented with oral or written, narrative or expository descriptions with occasional visual and graphic support
2 Beginning	• general language related to the content areas; • phrases or short sentences; • oral or written language with phonological, syntactic, or semantic errors that often impede the meaning of the communication when presented with one to multiple-step commands, directions, questions, or a series of statements with visual and graphic support
1 Entering	• pictorial or graphic representation of the language of the content areas; • words, phrases, or chunks of language when presented with one-step commands, directions, WH-questions, or statements with visual and graphic support

Figure 4-2 Continued

     * whole-group instruction that is designed to reach all students
       through multilevel lessons and strategies

Regardless of ELLs' language proficiency level, the key foundation for developing strong English and literacy skills is oral language development at all grades and for all ELL proficiency levels.

Oral Language Development and Vocabulary Building

Most educators recognize that oral language provides the fundamental base for literacy development. Researchers have pointed to the strong correlation between oral language proficiency—both in the first and second language—and literacy in the second language and academic development (Freeman and Freeman 2006). The ability to read and write—literacy—depends heavily on the ability to speak and understand a language orally. For ELLs, vocabulary is especially important in supporting both oral language and literacy development.

Oral Language Development

For native-English speakers who have developed the language since birth and who were surrounded by continuous language experiences before entering school, their oral language development happens over time and in supportive contexts. Even though there are differences in the oral language proficiencies of native-English-speaking children—compare for example the oral language skills of children from middle-class, educated backgrounds to those of children who come from poverty—they develop an intuitive knowledge of the language that children who have not grown up speaking English at home do not. Because of this, Goldenberg and Coleman (2010) suggest that "teachers have a greater challenge in managing, promoting, encouraging, and stimulating both oral and written language development simultaneously for ELLs" (p. 41).

    How can teachers support oral language development for ELLs? First, ELLs must have many opportunities not only to hear, but more importantly, to use academic language. Traditional transmission-oriented classrooms where the teacher is doing most of the talking are not helpful in developing strong speaking skills in any student, but especially in ELLs. Researchers point out that on average, teachers are talking to students—giving lessons, directions and commands—up to 75 percent of the time during an average school day (Zahed-Babelan and Kia 2010).

The amount of teacher-talk is even higher in classrooms that use direct instruction throughout the day and where students have few opportunities to talk to each other. On the other hand, classrooms that use cooperative-learning and learner-centered approaches provide more opportunities for students to engage in authentic oral discussions about academic content (see Figure 4-3).

Cooperative learning allows ELLs to practice language at their own level of English proficiency in meaningful and authentic ways. Because cooperative approaches are based on students interacting with each other, they

COOPERATIVE LEARNING
Numbered-Heads-Together Think-Pair-Share Jigsaw
Instructional Conversations Collaborative Talk

Figure 4-3 Strategies for Supporting Oral Language Development

provide ELLs with rich language and academic opportunities and access to both comprehensible input and output. Cooperative learning is a very effective instructional method for ELLs because students work collaboratively in small groups, engage in many meaningful experiences with language and content, and receive more individualized support from the teacher who acts as a facilitator. ELLs, who are at different levels of academic and second language proficiencies, can also help each other through cooperative learning by exchanging ideas and by processing information with each other. Strategies used in cooperative learning, like jigsaw, think-pair-share, and number-heads-together, are especially useful in promoting academic oral language. These strategies provide structured but authentic ways for students to use academic oral language through focused discussions about academic content. Although there are several other cooperative-learning grouping strategies, jigsaw, think-pair-share, and number-heads-together, are the most commonly used (Johnson, Johnson, and Holubec 1993; Kagan 1992).

In *Numbered-Heads-Together*, small groups of students solve a problem or answer a question together. The first step is for each student in the group to pick a number, one through four. The teacher then provides all the groups time to research and discuss possible solutions or answers. All members of the group make sure that everyone understands and can provide the answer or solution to the other groups. After students have solved the problem or answered the question together, the teacher calls a number from one to four at random and asks all the students with that number to report back to the class. For example, the teacher calls on all the students who have the number two to share the group's solution/answer with the rest of the class (see Figure 4-4). The students who report the correct answer or solution then win points for their team. In this cooperative-learning strategy, all students in the group are responsible for knowing the answer to the problem since the members of the group do not know what number the teacher will call. Numbered-heads-together provides ELLs a support structure for understanding a text through discussions with other peers.

In *Think-Pair-Share*, the teacher asks an open-ended question and gives students time to think about the question, first on their own and then with a partner. After each individual student has thought about the problem or question, they then pair with a partner and discuss their ideas about the question for several minutes. The teacher then invites students to share their responses to the question (see Figure 4-5). This collaborative strategy gives ELLs the opportunity to discuss their ideas and allows them to confirm or reformulate their responses together with another learner. Students are less inhibited in sharing their responses because they have already discussed their thoughts with a partner. Think-pair-share engages students first in thinking individually, then pairing with a partner for discussion and reflection,

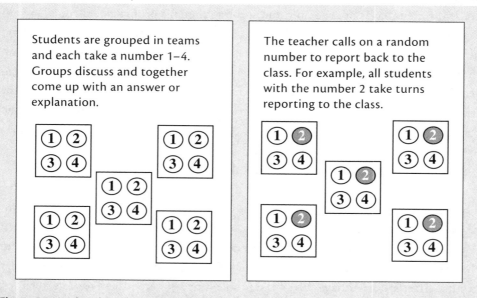

Figure 4-2 Numbered-Heads-Together

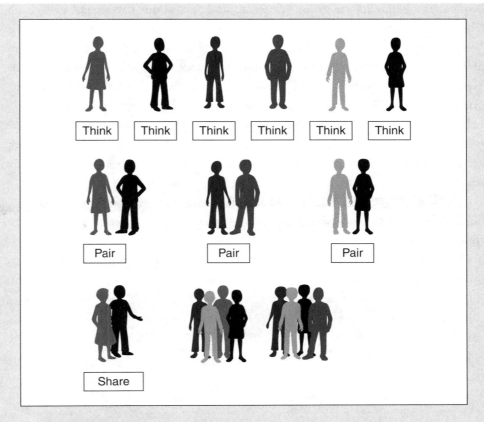

Figure 4-5 Think-Pair-Share

and finally sharing their findings or ideas with the whole class. This strategy helps ELLs improve their oral communication skills as they talk about their ideas with one another.

In *Jigsaw*, students are grouped in "base" teams of four where each member is given a number, one through four. Each number in the group is responsible for one section of the reading. For example, all students who have the number one are responsible for reading, understanding, and reporting back the first paragraph of the text to the base (original) group; all number two students are responsible for the second paragraph, number three students for the third paragraph, and number four students for the fourth paragraph. The class then regroups by numbers in "expert" groups to read and discuss their section of the text. For example, all the number one students are grouped to read and talk about the first paragraph and all the number two students are grouped to read and talk about the second paragraph. The rest of the numbers do the same. After the students in each numbered team become familiar or an "expert" about their understanding of the text, they regroup and return to their base groups to explain or report on their assigned section (see Figure 4-6). This strategy can be adapted for lower or higher levels of second language proficiencies. For example, instead of dividing the text by paragraphs, the reading can be assigned by sentences or by entire pages. Jigsaw engages every student in the group, helps to increase reading comprehension skills, and helps to develop students' oral language proficiencies. In jigsaw, all the students are responsible for their own understanding as well as that of their teammates.

Providing opportunities for ELLs to engage in meaningful language "output" is critical for their continuous development of academic oral language (Swain 1985). In addition to cooperative-learning approaches, instructional conversations—also known as collaborative talk—are very effective in helping ELLs develop oral language (Goldenberg 2008). Instructional conversations involve interactions between students

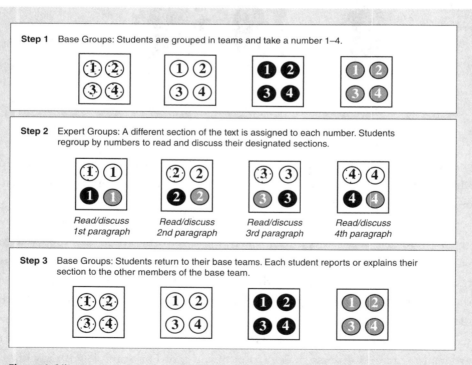

Figure 4-6 Jigsaw

and also between students and teacher talking to each other to make meaning, solve problems, and think critically together. The difference between instructional conversations and traditional instruction is in the teacher's assumption that students have something valuable to say beyond answering questions the teacher already knows (Tharp 1994). Because talk is a major tool for learning, young children learn by talking and also learn to talk by talking. Britton (1992) suggests that children "must practice language in the sense in which a doctor 'practices' medicine and a lawyer 'practices' law, and not in the sense in which a juggler 'practices' a new trick before he performs it" (p. 130). Collaborative talk offers authentic opportunities for problem-solving, making sense of new information, and linking new ideas and concepts to what students already know. Through talking, students can try out new ways of thinking, reshape their ideas in mid-sentence, respond instantly to others' comments, and collaborate in constructing meaning.

ELLs can build language through collaborative talk because not only are their backgrounds validated but they also can tap and expand on their prior experiences. This approach is especially effective for ELLs because content is familiar and of interest to them. They also become active learners by engaging in real communication about events in their lives, and they are more likely to take ownership of their language learning in the context of their own experiences. While ELLs may have opportunities outside the classroom to develop social oral language, the only place where they can build their oral academic language is in the context of the classroom. This is especially important for building academic and content vocabulary and word knowledge.

Vocabulary Building and Word Knowledge

Vocabulary plays an important role in both oral language and literacy development. Without knowing a sufficient number of words, it is not possible to understand what we read or hear. The more words students know the better they are able to understand oral language and comprehend texts. In addition, having a large and rich vocabulary improves students' abilities to speak and write in clearer and more sophisticated ways. Educators and researchers agree that vocabulary and word knowledge contribute to improved reading comprehension and better writing skills (Genesee et al. 2006). Where there is room for debate is on which are the best instructional approaches to building vocabulary and word knowledge. Current research has not identified the best method or program for improving students' vocabulary development and word knowledge. However, research does point to extensive independent reading as the most effective word-learning strategy (Snow 2002). Students who engage in wide reading and independent learning of words have much better results in vocabulary acquisition than those who receive only direct instruction in learning words. Adams and other researchers such as Krashen (1993) also suggest that students who read independently each day have higher vocabulary growth, improved writing skills, and higher reading comprehension than students who don't engage in independent reading.

Waring (2002) describes six aspects of vocabulary development that shed light on how best to teach and learn words. These include the number of times a word must be encountered to learn it, the rate at which we forget words, the impact of vocabulary on reading comprehension, how words are related to each other, stages of word learning, and the difference between written and spoken words (see Figure 4-7).

Teaching vs. Learning

Most teachers would agree that teaching words to students does not mean that they will learn them. This is especially true if vocabulary is taught in isolation and with few opportunities to hear, see, and use the words in context and through multiple exposures. Even though direct instruction in vocabulary can be of value, using this approach alone has limitations. Adams (1990) reports on the growth of vocabulary for a typical native-English-speaking student to be above 3000 words per year, which translates into more than eight words per day or forty new words per week. If this is the case, then direct instruction in vocabulary alone could not possibly accomplish this.

Forgetting and Remembering Words

Knowing that students must encounter a new word five to sixteen times to learn it can help teachers create enough opportunities for them to read, write, hear, and speak these new words in context. The number of encounters necessary for a new word to be stored in long-term memory varies, depending on how specialized or abstract the word is. The word *habitat* may require fewer encounters to learn because it is more concrete and used more often than words like *coniferous* and *deciduous*, for example. Some words are easier to learn than others. Words are easier to learn when they are connected to other familiar words, to words in the native language,

Teaching a word does not mean it will be learned.	It takes 5–16 encounters to learn an average word and for it to go into long-term memory.
It is easier to forget a word than remember it.	Of 10 new words, it is normal to forget most of them within a few days. Only 1–2 are retained in medium- or long-term memory.
The meaning of an unknown word cannot be guessed from context if the surrounding text is too difficult.	Readers need to know 98% or more of the other words in the text to guess the meaning of an unfamiliar word.
There are two major stages in word learning.	1. Matching the word's spelling and pronunciation with its meaning 2. Understanding deeper aspects of the word.
Words function with other words, not in isolation.	Language is made up of sets of words that go together to make individual meanings.
Written words and spoken words are different.	Written language is more formal, precise, and sophisticated than spoken language. Spoken language is more communicative due to cues like gestures, tone, and context.

Figure 4-7 About Vocabulary Teaching and Learning (adapted from Waring 2002)

or to what is already known. For example, Spanish shares many similar words with English, such as *furioso/furious* and *increible/incredible*.

It is more natural to forget new words than to remember them. Of a list of ten new words that students learn in a typical week, most are forgotten, and only one or two of these words are remembered after a few months. A common but ineffective classroom practice is to give students a list of ten unrelated words at the beginning of the week and test students at the end of the week on their ability to spell and use each word in a sentence. If teachers were to test students again on the weekly list of words a few months later, it is likely that students would remember very few of the words. More effective strategies include selecting words that are related to each other and to a content lesson, having students select their own words, previewing the text, and using prereading vocabulary strategies such as word banks and graphic organizers. Memorizing lists of words that are unrelated and not tied to any context is not an effective way to learn new words and expand students' vocabulary.

Guessing the Meaning from Context

Using context clues for reading comprehension and for making sense of unknown words is a good strategy but one that has limitations too. Students are not able to guess the meaning of a new word from context alone if the text is too difficult. The reader needs to know 98 percent or more of the words in a passage to be at an independent reading level. According to Waring (2002), for students to be at the instructional reading level, they must know 93–97 percent. Coming across 7 percent or more unknown words in a text puts readers at the frustration level (see Figure 4-8). Consider the very convoluted and exaggerated example below. The target word here is *gallimaufry*. As this example shows, the meaning of the word cannot be guessed by surrounding words or the context of the text, especially if students don't have sufficient background knowledge.

> The gallimaufry of opinions augmented as a polyglot society languorously emerged from a state of invisibility. Perfunctory nomenclatures and pedantic proclamations only exacerbated the ontological debate and reduced it to a pedestrian draconian outburst.

Gallimaufry is a very obscure word for "hodgepodge," which interestingly is another word that would be difficult for ELLs to grasp. In the example below (Dugger 2007), we know all the words but are not likely to understand the meaning because the words are being used in ways that don't make sense to most of us.

> The difficulty of your set could be increased
> if you do a jam followed
> by a peach.

Given their prior knowledge, gymnasts would not have a problem understanding this sentence. In this case, *set* means a gymnastic routine, *jam* refers to a gymnast

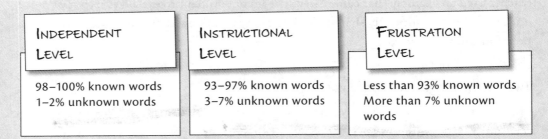

INDEPENDENT LEVEL	INSTRUCTIONAL LEVEL	FRUSTRATION LEVEL
98–100% known words 1–2% unknown words	93–97% known words 3–7% unknown words	Less than 93% known words More than 7% unknown words

Figure 4-8 Word Knowledge and Reading Comprehension

that stays sitting on the high bar, and *peach* refers to a gymnast moving from a high to a low bar. Students need to understand that words change meaning depending on how they are used and on the context. Prior knowledge allows students to use the appropriate meaning for the text. For ELLs this is especially challenging because they don't yet have sufficient content, language, or cultural background knowledge to interpret text.

In Omar's Level 1 ESL high school class, an amusing exchange between ELLs illustrates the shared cultural knowledge students need to be able to interpret words correctly. Omar is a Somali refugee enrolled in the tenth grade in a very linguistically diverse urban high school. In his Level 1 ESL class there are twenty-six students from sixteen countries who speak nine different languages, including Somali, Gujarat, Spanish, Polish, Urdu, Pashto, Yoruba, Amharic, and French Creole. He and his classmates were engaged in a small-group guided conversation about the differences and similarities between their home countries and the United States. At one point in the conversation Anita, a student from Puerto Rico, shared with her group that the police had put a "boot" on her father's car the night before. Omar was very puzzled by this and expressed, in his emergent English, how that must be a very big boot to put on a car, and anyway why would anyone want to put a boot on a car? This made absolutely no sense to him because he was thinking of a boot that is used for walking rather than a contraption put on the wheel of a car by police so that is not driveable until a fine is paid. The teacher took this teachable moment to talk with the class about word meanings and culturally shared knowledge in interpreting those meanings. For homework, she asked students to find two more examples of words that have both a concrete meaning and a culturally shared meaning, including examples from their native languages. In doing this exercise, the teacher used an example that came directly from one student to extend everybody's understanding of culturally shared word meanings and how those compare to the literal meanings of words.

Two Major Stages in Word Learning

The process of learning new words has two main stages. The first stage is to match the word's spelling and pronunciation with its meaning—for example, knowing the spelling, pronunciation, and meaning of the word *highly*. The second stage is to understand the deeper aspects of the word, such as what words it goes and does not go with ("highly important" is okay, but "highly happy" is not); restrictions on how the word is used ("the building is highly tall" is not acceptable); whether it is formal or informal (*highly* tends to be formal); whether it is spoken or written (*highly* tends to be used more in writing than in conversation); its similarity to other words (*high*, *highlands*, *highlight*); whether it is frequent or not (*highly* is infrequent); and its shades of meaning. Teaching and learning words typically stop at the first stage. This usually involves memorizing the word's spelling/pronunciation and looking up the meaning in a dictionary. Going beyond the first stage and having students really become immersed in learning vocabulary at a deeper level will help them improve in speaking, understanding, reading, and writing.

Words Function with Other Words

The meanings of many words change when combined with other words. Because words do not function alone but in combination with other words, teaching words in isolation does not help ELLs to know how they relate to one another. For the native-English speaker, words that often go together "sound right" to them because they have heard and used these word combinations often. In addition, native-English speakers do not get stuck trying to attach individual meaning to each word. Think for a moment how a beginner ELL would imagine these common English phrases: "I see what you mean" or "pretty sure." Both examples would probably be very confusing; the ELL would wonder how one can "see" meaning or how being sure about something can be "pretty." These word combinations, also known as collocations, have specific meanings when the words are combined, meanings that are different from each word when they are used separately. "Pretty sure" means "very sure," but an ELL would never find the word *pretty* in the thesaurus as a synonym for *very*.

Words: Difference Between Speech and Writing

It is important to note that written language is very different from spoken language. When we try to use spoken language in writing, such as in text messages or emails, there are often unintended interpretations of what we were trying to say and the message may come off as inappropriate or offensive. In the reverse, when we try to use written language when speaking, what we say may come off as strange or pretentious. In general, written language is more formal, precise, and sophisticated than spoken language. Spoken language on the other hand can be more communicative than written language because nonlinguistic cues like gestures, tone, and context help to clarify meaning immediately. We use different words for speaking and listening than for reading and writing. For example, even though the words *thus* and *vehicle* are familiar words to adult English speakers, we don't normally use them when we are having a conversation. We would not sit around the dinner table with our family and say something like this: "My vehicle broke down, thus I will take it to the mechanic tomorrow." The word *thus* is usually found in books or novels and used in formal speaking. The only place where ELLs would most likely come across it would be in school and in books.

Vocabulary-Building Routines

Teachers can create routines for building vocabulary and word knowledge by providing scaffolds for ELLs before, during, and after a lesson or reading a text. The following steps can help teachers organize instruction in meaningful and authentic ways:

1. Teacher and/or students select important and connected words (by theme, topic, book).

2. Teacher presents new words by introducing the lesson, topic, or book:

   ☑ *Activate prior knowledge:* use predicting, inferencing, discussions, KWL.

   ☑ *Build background knowledge:* use anticipatory guides, picture-walks, previews.

   ☑ *Create an interest in words:* use word histories, crossword puzzles, jokes and riddles, word sorts, word walls, word banks, word games.

3. Teacher provides multiple opportunities for students to see, hear, and use new words in context and use strategies on their own:

☑ *Read books, Internet, periodicals:* use word searches, word sorts, word banks, highlighting.

☑ *Write stories, poems, summaries, reports, plays:* use peer-editing, outlines, brainstorming, graphic organizers.

☑ *Speak in presentations, discussions, debates:* use instructional conversations, collaborative talk, role-playing, storytelling.

☑ *Listen to dramatizations, read-alouds, presentations, discussions:* listen to discussions, presentation, storytelling, interactive lessons.

Because teachers do not have enough time to teach everything about a word, students need to become independent word learners. In addition to providing ELLs with lots of opportunities for independent reading, other effective approaches to building vocabulary, increasing word knowledge, and promoting independent learning of words include teaching students how to use word-learning strategies (Graves 2006). Two strategies that students can use are *word analysis* and *context analysis*. Through word analysis students can make sense of vocabulary by examining word parts—compound words, prefixes, suffixes, roots—and focus on chunks of meaning. For example, the word *redesign* can be chunked into *re-* (meaning "again") and *design* (meaning "to create"). Through context analysis students can learn to look for clues in the text such as in the examples in Figure 4-9, which shows different ways that context provides clues to meaning. Teachers can help students by giving them practice to look out for these clues in the text.

Teaching for Transfer

Monolingual instructional strategies predominate in the teaching of bilingual students (in both monolingual and bilingual programs). As a result, there has been minimal exploration of the potential of bilingual instructional strategies. Teaching for transfer (L1-L2-L1) is largely ignored in the education of bilingual students despite massive evidence that students themselves constantly draw on their prior knowledge which is encoded in their L1. (Cummins 2008)

Explicit definitions	_She was averting her eyes_, which means to avoid looking at him.
Opposite	A cow is a _herbivore_, not a carnivore.
Synonym	Her _dwelling was dark_ ... her house had few windows.
Function indicator	The _auger_ drilled into the wall to get the cat out.
Example	He is _shrewd_. Remember when he intercepted her mail?
Comparison	I would rather be _wealthy_ than poor.
Classification	_Vertebrates_ are mammals that include horses and whales.

Figure 4-9 Context Analysis

An important aspect of second language acquisition that affects instruction and learning is the relationship and interdependence between the first and second language. According to Cummins' (1979) _Interdependence Hypothesis_, the development of academic language proficiency in one language helps to develop a common underlying proficiency that can be used in acquiring a second language. Knowledge of the first language can be transferred effectively during the process of second language acquisition. In other words, the linguistic knowledge and skills that learners have in their first language can be very useful in the development of abilities in their second language. For effective interdependence, the native language needs to be well developed before positive transfer can take place. Understanding this cross-linguistic transfer helps teachers and students to better understand how first language knowledge helps language acquisition and literacy development in the second language. Cross-linguistic transfer happens when ELLs use and access their linguistic resources in their first language to assist in developing the second language (Cárdenas-Hagan, Carlson, and Pollard-Durodola 2007).

Types of Transfer

Many aspects of language and literacy are universal and transfer from the first to the second language. These language and literacy elements are called universal because they exist in all or most languages. Once students learn one of these universal skills in their first language, it does not have to be relearned in the second language but rather the concept is transferred and applied to the new language. For example, the basic elements of story structure are universal across languages. Regardless of whether a story is in Russian, Hmong, or French, it will have a beginning, middle, and end, as well as characters, plot, setting, problem, and solution. Once young children learn these universal aspects of story structure they do not have to be relearned in English. Other examples of universal elements of literacy include reading strategies like inferencing, predicting, summarizing, and questioning. Readers from all language backgrounds use these strategies to make meaning from print, as they are fundamental to the process of reading. Cross-linguistic transfer also depends on similarities and differences between the first and second languages. For example, differences in writing systems—alphabetic in Spanish or logographic in Chinese—or directionality—horizontal left to right in Spanish, horizontal right to left in Arabic, or vertical top to bottom in traditional Chinese—affect the level of transfer between languages.

Some aspects of language and literacy do not transfer, either because they don't exist in one or both languages or because they are culturally based. For example, idiomatic expressions are especially difficult for ELLs, not only because the words do not follow the literal meaning but also because they refer to culturally shared knowledge. For example, consider this exchange between Duni, a Swahili-speaking ELL from Kenya, and her teacher:

Duni:	"My family is family with Mr. Obama."
Teacher:	"Oh, get out!"
Duni:	"Teacher, I go out?"

Duni's puzzled reaction is common because she does not understand the idiomatic expression as meaning "that is amazing," but rather interprets it literally as "leave the room." Cross-linguistic transfer between the first and second language can be positive, negative, or have zero transfer.

Positive Transfer

The closer two languages are—like having similar writing systems, phonology, grammar, and shared word origins—the more positive the transfer (August and Shanahan 2010). For example, Spanish and English share the same writing system, follow similar grammar rules, and have many Latin and Greek root words in common. These similarities make possible the use of the first language to assist in developing the second language. Spanish and English share many cognates that include both high-frequency words like *color/color* and more academic abstract words like *circulation/circulación*. Phonological awareness also has positive transfer, especially between many English and Spanish consonants. Two languages that are more distant and dissimilar, such as Korean and English, still have universal aspects of language and literacy that result in positive transfer, such as text structure and literacy strategies (Krashen 2003).

Negative Transfer

Negative transfer happens when a linguistic or literacy element is present in one language but not the other. For example, the sound for *th* in English does not exist in Spanish and the letter *h* is silent in Spanish but not always in English. Spanish-speaking ELLs may rely on the closest sound in their language and may pronounce *that* as "dat" or *hospital* as "ospital." A Chinese speaker learning English may leave out articles like *the* and *a* because they are not used in Chinese and may say "I have book from library." A German speaker may say "vat" for *what* because the *w* sound does not exist in German. Understanding some basic language characteristics of ELLs' first language, especially grammar and phonology, can give teachers valuable information about why students make particular errors. This understanding can in turn help teachers to organize instruction and minilessons more effectively.

Zero Transfer

When the rules or aspects of one language make no difference to the other language there is neither positive transfer nor interference. In Spanish, most nouns have gender attached to them but in English most nouns are gender-neutral. *La mesa* in Spanish has a female designation but in English it is simply *the table*, and it is neither female nor male. For Spanish speakers learning English this does not cause a problem because they do not need to attend to word endings or to using the correct gender article. In the reverse situation where an English speaker is learning Spanish, this may cause many headaches to Spanish language learners because they have to apply a rule that does not exist in English—selecting the appropriate gender for nouns.

Strategies for Teaching for Transfer

Knowing what transfers and what does not transfer from one language to another, as well as what has no impact on the second language, is important for both teachers and students to understand. Too often, teachers work under the assumption that allowing ELLs to use the native language is bad practice because they either view the first language as a "crutch" that students never let go of or as unnecessary to the development of English. For Eduardo, being told by his fourth-grade teacher that he needed to think in English and not in Spanish had many negative consequences that he only realized later as an adult. Eduardo, now a sophomore in college, remembers his first year in a suburban U.S. school as a difficult and unhappy time. Before arriving in the United States, he had been an A student in Mexico and was excited about school and learning. What he remembers most from that first year was how hard it was to follow the teacher's request not to use Spanish in school and to think only in English. Eduardo now says, "I remember thinking—in Spanish—how on earth I was going to force myself to think in English if I didn't know English yet. Because I was always told to respect teachers, I tried very hard to do what she asked. In the end, I spent all my fourth-grade year sitting there alone, not participating, and bored. And I had to repeat fourth grade! Have you ever tried thinking in a language that you don't know well?"

Even though it was probably not what the teacher intended, in asking Eduardo to stop using Spanish and think only in English, she had essentially asked him to stop thinking. Because Eduardo did not yet have enough command of English he was not able to process information, think through a problem or question, or make sense of new concepts, including his acquisition of the English language—all things he could have done in his more dominant language, Spanish. The teacher in this case did not understand how Eduardo's Spanish language could have supported his

English acquisition, especially because his first language was well developed and he was literate in it. Had the teacher been aware of cross-linguistic transfer she could have used strategies that would have helped Eduardo transfer many of his already-acquired Spanish skills to his emergent English.

The same way in which metacognition involves thinking about our thinking, metalinguistics involves thinking about our language. Metalinguistics is defined as the ability to reflect on the use of language. Balanced bilinguals—those that have developed strong first and second language proficiencies—have an advanced awareness of language processing because they interact with the world through two languages. This gives bilinguals higher cognitive and language awareness as well as better analysis and control of language processing.

This awareness and ability to interpret and manipulate two languages develops as ELLs become increasingly more proficient in English but also continue to develop the native language. Teachers who use metalinguistic strategies support ELLs' cross-language transfer and help them to develop deeper language awareness. The best way for students to develop awareness about the similarities and differences between the first and second language and to internalize cross-language transfer is for the teacher to provide explicit instruction and modeling of these strategies. Contrastive analysis and the cognate strategy are two effective ways to engage ELLs in thinking about the similarities and differences between their first and second languages. These strategies are also helpful for ELLs as they use metalinguistic knowledge to help in their second language development.

Contrastive Analysis

Using contrastive analysis as a teaching and learning tool can be very effective for ELLs. Contrastive analysis involves comparing the similarities and differences between the first and second language in a conscious and purposeful way. For example, a teacher of Spanish-speaking ELLs may do minilessons on the comparisons of word order between Spanish and English, especially as they relate to noun and adjective. The teacher presents a few examples in Spanish and English, such as "the hungry dog was looking for food" and "el perro hambriento estaba buscando comida." Teacher and students discuss the similarities and differences between the examples and then focus on word order of the adjective and noun. The teacher can then create games and activities where students apply this knowledge. The teacher could also set up a "Compare and Contrast Language" center with different games and activities for students to analyze similarities and differences between the two languages.

Finally, the teacher can organize word and language research projects. For example, students can search for idiomatic expressions that exist in the two languages and analyze differences and similarities in language use and meaning. See the English and Spanish idiomatic expression examples in Figure 4-10. Idiomatic expressions are especially difficult for ELLs because they have figurative meanings that cannot be understood in literal ways. ELLs must have explicit instruction with meaningful activities to develop understanding about idiomatic expressions. Teachers can guide students to look for idioms in text and do activities that compare literal versus figurative meanings. Figure 4-11 shows two examples of students' analysis and understanding of idiomatic expressions. The first photo shows a fourth-grade student's artistic representation of the difference between the literal and figurative meaning of the idiomatic expression "Tío Luis' face hardened like a rock" that he found in *Esperanza Rising* written by Pam Muñoz Ryan. The second photo is a written explanation of idioms by a third-grade ELL after the class had spent several weeks studying idioms.

Spanish:	Más loco que una cabra.
Literal Translation:	*Crazier than a goat.*
English:	As mad as a hatter.

Spanish:	Como quitarle un pelo a un gato.
Literal Translation:	*Like plucking a hair from a cat.*
English:	Like a drop in the bucket.

Spanish:	Camarón que se duerme, se lo lleva la corriente.
Literal Translation:	*The shrimp that falls asleep, the current carries away.*
English:	You snooze, you lose.

Figure 4-10 Comparing and Contrasting Idiomatic Expressions

Figure 4-11 Figurative vs. Literal Language Activities

Cognate Strategy

A cognate is a word that has similar meaning, spelling, and pronunciation in two or more languages and comes from a common origin. The cognate strategy works well with languages that have Greek and Latin influences, especially Spanish, Portuguese, French, Romanian, and Italian, as well as English, German, Greek, and Dutch. For example the English word *color* has cognates in several languages: *color* (Spanish), *couleur* (French), *colore* (Italian), *cor* (Portuguese), *culoare* (Romanian), and *kleur* (Dutch). Spanish and English share many high- and low-frequency cognate words. Low-frequency cognates tend to be more academic and content-related vocabulary (see Figure 4-12). These low-frequency cognates are especially important to support academic language in both English and the native language. Teachers should be aware that although cognates are common between Spanish and English, Spanish-speaking ELLs may not necessarily know the word and concept in the native language. For example, a second-grade ELL learning about perimeters in English may not have yet learned the concept or know the word *perímetro* in Spanish. For the cognate strategy to be effective, ELLs need to already know the concept and word before it can be used in language transfer.

Words that are similar in spelling and pronunciation but not in meaning are called false cognates—or false friends. There are two types of false cognates: nonrelated (total) and related (partial) false cognates (see Figure 4-13). Nonrelated false

HIGH-FREQUENCY COGNATES		LOW-FREQUENCY COGNATES	
animal	animal	constellation	constelación
family	familia	exclaim	exclamar
class	clase	respiratory	respiratorio
group	grupo	assassinate	acecinar
list	lista	inculcate	inculcar

Figure 4-12 Cognates in Spanish and English

TOTAL FALSE COGNATES		PARTIAL FALSE COGNATES	
exit	éxito [success]	molest	molestar [bother]
quit	quitar [take off]	sequester	secuestrar [kidnap]
choke	chocar [crash]	policy	póliza [insurance policy]
delight	delito [crime]	arena	arena [sand]

Figure 4-13 False Cognates

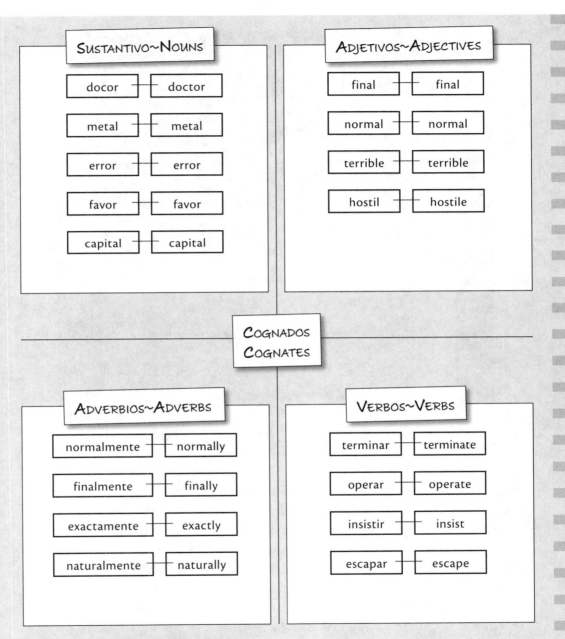

Figure 4-14 Spanish-English Cognate Word Wall

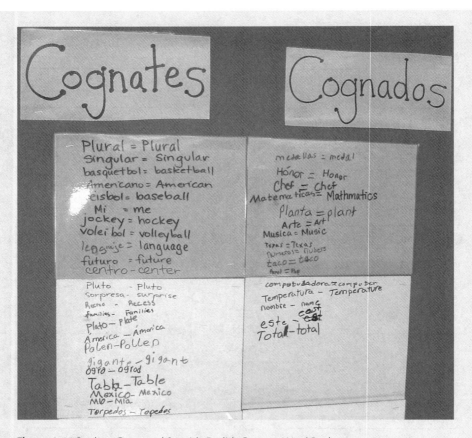

Figure 4-15 Student-Generated Spanish-English Cognate Word Bank

cognates are those that have no root word in common, such as the Spanish word *éxito* (means "success") and *exit* in English. These two words don't share a linguistic origin and are completely unrelated. On the other hand, related false cognates are those that do share a common origin but have different meanings in each language. For example, the English word *molest* and the Spanish word *molestar* have a common origin—in Latin *molestare* means 'to trouble or annoy' and *molestus* means 'troublesome'. Even though these two words share a common Latin root, the two words have taken on different meanings: in English the word specifically refers to physical and/or sexual abuse but in Spanish it retains the broader meaning of annoying or being annoyed. It is very common for a Spanish-speaking child to say that so-and-so *me está molestando*, which means that so-and-so is bothering me.

Figure 4-16 Spanish-English Cognate Word Hunt

The cognate strategy needs to be explicitly taught to ELLs. Teachers should not assume that students are either consciously aware of cognates or know how to use them to help in the acquisition of English. For ELLs to internalize this strategy and use it on their own, they can participate in a number of engaging activities and games like finding cognates or false cognates on the Internet, in newspapers, books, and textbooks as well as in their own writing. Other activities related to cognate strategy include cognate word wall (see Figure 4-14), cognate word bank (see Figure 4-15), cognate word hunt (see Figure 4-16), cognate word sort, and underlining and highlighting cognates. In addition, students can play false versus true cognate games like Memory. The Memory false cognate game has a set of false and true cognate pairs (eight to ten word pairs in English and Spanish, for example) where each word is written on index cards or other thick paper. The cards are mixed up and placed face down on a table or rug. Students take turns turning over each word until there is a match of a false cognate.

LITERATURE-BASED INSTRUCTION

As has been mentioned earlier in this chapter, reading is the most effective strategy for building vocabulary. Providing ELLs many opportunities to read, and to read many different types of text, is also the best way to support their English acquisition, literacy development, and content knowledge. Through authentic books and texts, ELLs not only strengthen their reading and language skills, but also increase their knowledge of new concepts and the world.

Authentic Literature

Teaching and learning to read and write are best accomplished through authentic literature, not through basal reading programs alone. Although there are many types of reading basals—from highly scripted and skills-focused to literature-based holistic programs—most tend to rely on decodable readers that use controlled text, especially in the early grades. Controlled text is made up of many high-frequency and one-syllable vocabulary, as well as selected words with the sounds and letters that students have already learned. The language in decodable texts (for example, "The dog is in the mud. The day is very hot. The mud is cool and fun. The dog likes the mud.") tends to be simplified, artificial, and dull.

Rather than relying on decodable texts and basal readers, teachers should use an abundance of authentic children and adolescent literature that also includes authentic nonfiction materials like newspapers and magazines, as well as reference, historical, and biographical books. High-quality adolescent and children's literature not only promotes a love of reading but also exposes students to rich language and vocabulary. In addition, authentic multicultural literature is an ideal medium for integrating culture into the language arts and content curriculum, and is easily integrated to social studies.

Literature-Based Strategies

A balanced literacy approach is based on authentic and rich literature. In a balanced literacy approach students' reading, writing, speaking, and listening develop in the context of rich language and literacy experiences while also receiving explicit instruction needed for fluency and comprehension. While the focus is always on meaning, balanced literacy instruction engages students in modeled, shared, guided, and independent reading and writing. A balanced literacy model uses a number of instructional strategies including read-alouds, shared reading and writing, guided reading, literature circles, and readers' theater, among other approaches and strategies.

Read-Alouds

In read-alouds, the teacher reads a book, poem, or other print aloud to the whole class or a group of students. Before the read-aloud the teacher engages students in prediction and inferencing. After the read-aloud students respond to questions about the text and also confirm their prediction. Hearing a proficient reader provides ELLs a model both for reading and the English language. Because read-alouds also give ELLs the opportunity to hear words and language structures they may not be ready to read on their own, they can be used effectively with middle and high school students. Read-alouds can be done in ELLs' native language or in the context of ESL lessons.

Shared Reading

During shared reading, the teacher typically reads a predictable or pattern language book or text—one that follows a predictable pattern and is repetitive. Figure 4-17

Predictable Texts	Example and Description (adapted from Education Oasis 2009)
Chain or Circular	*If You Give a Mouse a Cookie* by Laura Numeroff *Why Mosquitoes Buzz in People's Ears* by Verna Aardema The ending leads back to the beginning.
Cumulative	*The Napping House* by Audrey & Don Wood *The Sandwich That Max Made* by Marcia Vaughan Each time a new event occurs, all previous events are repeated.
Familiar Sequence	*The Very Hungry Caterpillar* by Eric Carle *Cookie's Week* by Cindy Ward Organized by theme (days of week, numbers)
Patterned	*The Three Bears* by Robert Southey *Are you there, Bear?* by Ron Maris Scenes are repeated with some variation.
Question & Answer	*Brown Bear, Brown Bear* by Bill Martin Jr. *I Went Walking* by Sue Williams The same or similar questions are repeated throughout the story.
Repetition of Phrase	*Goodnight Moon* by Margaret Wise Brown *The Important Book* by Margaret Wise Brown Word order in a phrase or sentence is repeated.
Rhyme	*Is Your Mama a Llama?* by Deborah Guarino *Abiyoyo* by Pete Seeger Rhyming words or patterns are used throughout the story.
Songbooks	*Baby Beluga* by Raffi *Over in the Meadow* by Ezra Jack Keats Familiar songs with predictable elements or repetitive phrases

Figure 4-17 Types of Predictable and Pattern Language Books

offers examples of pattern language and predictable texts such as *chain* or *circular stories* in which the end of the story leads back to the beginning, and *cumulative stories* in which each time something new happens all earlier events are repeated. Other pattern language structures include: *familiar sequence*, which are stories organized by a theme that repeats, such as days of the week or numbers; *patterned stories* and *repetition of phrase*, where a sequence or phrase is repeated; *question and answer*, in which the same or similar question is repeated and answered throughout the story; and *rhyme* and *song books*, where rhyming words or patterns are used throughout the story or have predictable elements or repetitive phrases.

Shared reading is an interactive experience where students join—or *chime in—* during the reading of a big book or other enlarged text. In shared reading, a book or text is read multiple times over several days. During each reading the teacher and students attend to certain literacy skills, such as punctuation, letters, sounds, and words. Nonpattern language nonfiction books can also be used for shared reading. For ELLs shared reading is especially effective because it can be used in the native language to support literacy development in their mother tongue or it can be used in the context of ESL instruction. ELLs go beyond listening by chiming in as they anticipate rhymes and the pattern or repetitive language of the text. Shared reading is a multilevel approach to language and literacy that can reach all students regardless of their English proficiency. In addition, shared reading uses minilessons to teach skills in a meaningful context.

Shared Writing

In this interactive writing experience students join in the teacher-led writing of a collaborative written text. The teacher and students together compose a story, report, or poem while also attending to literacy skills, while the teacher acts as the scribe and writes the majority of the text on large paper. Also known as interactive writing, it can be done with the whole class or in a small group where both teacher and students contribute to the piece. Shared writing is usually done after a shared experience, like reading a pattern language book in shared reading, returning from a field trip, or a hands-on lesson or experiment. For example, after reading a pattern language or predictable book, the teacher and students write a similar pattern story with some variations. For example, after reading a patterned book like *Goodnight Moon* by Margaret Wise Brown, a shared writing follow-up might be to compose an interactive writing text that uses "goodnight school" or "goodnight zoo." The pattern is repeated, but in these versions the objects are different from the original story, for example, animals or school-related things. Shared writing can engage students in a variety of writing forms, genres, and purposes as well as providing an authentic means to teach writing and reading skills. For ELLs, shared writing is especially effective because the teacher models writing mechanics and processes while students participate in writing the text with the teacher.

Guided Reading

In guided reading, students read leveled books in small groups guided by the teacher, who does minilessons according to the needs of the students. The teacher provides support as students learn to use different reading strategies such as inferencing, predicting, summarizing, and questioning. The teacher helps students to use context, visual, and structure cues presented in the stories to create meaning. For ELLs guided reading can be done in the students' native language or ESL instruction. If done in English, the teacher should make appropriate modifications for second language learners and select both language and literacy objectives that are matched to ELLs' English proficiency levels.

Literature Circles

In literature circles, small groups of students select a book based on their shared interest in a particular genre (such as adventure or mystery) or topic (such as sports or family). Each student reads the book independently, and it is also read aloud when the group meets to discuss certain parts of the story. The discussions are guided by students' response to what they have read. Students also have specific roles connected to assignments about the book that they share with the other members of the literature circle group. For example, the *connector* is responsible for making connections between something in the book and the outside world or their own lives, while the *word detective* is responsible for selecting an unfamiliar word and finding its meaning and origin. Other roles include discussion director, literary luminary, checker, character captain, and artful adventurer. In *Esperanza Rising*, written by Pam Muñoz Ryan, about a young wealthy girl from Mexico who through a family tragedy ends up as a farm worker in California, the roles and discussions in a literature circle would look like this:

Connector: Makes comparison to a situation like Esperanza's when someone in the group has had to do something they don't like or are not used to doing, like Esperanza has to do by working in the camp. The goal of the connector is to make connections between new information and something that is already known by the group.

Word Detective: Selects the words untethered from the book, and provides a definition and a sentence accompanied by a drawing to illustrate the meaning of the word. The purpose of the word detective is to clarify word meaning and pronunciation.

Discussion Director: Leads a discussion on the sequence of events that led Esperanza to the fields of California. The discussion director can formulate a list of questions to lead the discussion. The role of the discussion director is to increase comprehension.

Literary Luminary: Selects several paragraphs in the book that describe the U.S. Great Depression and guides the group into a discussion about how the author uses language to illustrate this period. The principal goal of the literary luminary is to point out the literary structures used by the author, such as figurative language, thought-provoking examples, or impact of the dialogue between characters.

Checker: Makes sure that all members of the group participated and completed the tasks connected to their assigned roles.

Character Captain: Describes and compares Tío Luis and Esperanza's father's personalities and the relationship they have with each other. The role of the character captain is to describe the personalities of the main and secondary characters in the book and their relationships with other characters.

Artful Adventurer: Draws a map of Esperanza's journey from Mexico to the United States. The role of the artful adventurer is to visually represent an important piece of the story.

For ELLs, literature circles help them to interact with more proficient readers and engage them in reading a text that is of interest to them. Because the roles in literature circles also allow for different levels of participation, ELLs can select roles that don't require as much knowledge of English, such as the artful adventurer.

Readers' Theater

In readers' theater, students read from a script by telling a story in the form of a play. Students read with intonation and gestures appropriate to their characters and the dialogue. Readers' theater provides ELLs authentic opportunities to read, speak, and act out roles that they read or write themselves. This multilevel activity accommodates ELLs from all proficiency levels because more proficient ELLs can take roles that require more knowledge of English while beginner ELLs can take roles that have fewer language demands.

Literature-based balanced literacy instruction offers the most engaging and authentic approach for developing language proficiency, literacy, academic content, and cross-cultural knowledge. Using authentic literature and meaning-based approaches, such as the ones described above, provides a strong foundation for integrating the curriculum. A balanced literacy approach that incorporates multicultural literature can also provide the base for inclusion of culturally relevant and culturally responsive curriculum for ELLs.

CULTURALLY RELEVANT CURRICULUM

Schools and classrooms that serve ELLs are by default multicultural and diverse. ELLs come from a variety of backgrounds, languages, cultures, and experiences. Even in schools where the majority of ELLs are from the same language and ethnic background, such as Latino Spanish speakers, there are many cultural variations. Spanish-speaking ELLs are often perceived to be all the same. Although families originating from Latin America share many aspects of the culture and language, not all follow the same customs, play the same music, follow the same religion, or prefer the same food. Even within the same ethnic or national origin group many follow very different cultural practices. Take the United States for example. Saying that all Americans are Protestant, eat hot dogs on a regular basis, listen to country music, and speak with the same accent would be inaccurate. In the same way, saying that all Latinos are Catholic, eat tacos on a regular basis, listen to mariachis, speak Spanish with the same accent, and use the same words would also not be accurate.

Spanish-speaking Latinos come from more than twenty countries and territories. They speak a variety of Spanish dialects with different accents and often use different vocabulary, much in the same way that U.S. English differs from Australian or British English. Latinos are very ethnically diverse: white, indigenous, black, and mixed. They are also diverse in many cultural aspects. Take for example music or food. It would be difficult to find a lot of Argentine tango in El Salvador, Mexican mariachi music in Bolivia, or Dominican merengue in Uruguay. Tamales and guacamole would not be common in Chile, and *alfajores* (a caramel cookie sandwich popular in Argentina) would not be common in Puerto Rico.

Schools where diversity is celebrated and where ELLs' language and cultural backgrounds are seen as resources tend to have better academic results (Nieto 2010). Combining high standards with high-quality instruction should integrate ELLs' real-life sociocultural experiences in the school curriculum. Developing partnerships with the families and communities of ELLs can increase the effectiveness of instructional programs, develop intercultural sensitivity and competence among teachers and students, and create stronger commitment and advocacy. Culturally responsive and linguistically appropriate instructional approaches should adapt the curriculum to be more culturally relevant to ELLs' life experiences, use ELLs' cultural prior knowledge as a bridge to learn new content, align curricular planning to state-mandated standards and multicultural education, and select instructional materials that are culturally relevant, rigorous, and appropriate to ELLs' language proficiencies.

School and classroom libraries should include a variety of resources on the history, literature, music, folklore, and art of different ethnic and cultural groups.

These would include books, magazines, films, music, software, posters, and artifacts. Ethnic and cultural diversity should be reflected in assemblies, hallways, cafeteria menus, and extracurricular programs. In addition, teachers should make sure that instructional materials do not have racial, ethnic, or gender stereotypes. For example, materials and books that show Mexicans always wearing *sombreros*, Japanese wearing *kimonos*, or women wearing aprons are not authentic representations of these groups. The same goes for studies of indigenous Americans, like Mayans or Cherokees who are often portrayed as living centuries ago and not in contemporary America. Multicultural curricular materials that are based on stereotypes could be used as a teaching tool only if the teacher engages students in analyzing and reflecting on what aspects are stereotyped and why.

A culturally responsive curriculum goes beyond celebrations of holidays or exploring what is "exotic." Teachers should avoid the "tour and detour" approaches to multicultural education. The "detour" approach is when teachers drop what the class was studying for one day to focus on a holiday or event, and then return to their original topic of study. For example, a class that has been studying the planetary system for a few weeks stops for just one day on *Cinco de Mayo* to do a day of celebrating Mexican-related topics. These one-day detours are often filled with arts and crafts and a few surface-culture activities. The next day, the class returns to studying about planets. The "tour" approach is not much better and happens when students take a virtual or real tour, much like a tourist, of a cultural or ethnic group. An example would be taking a field trip to Chinatown while studying Chinese New Year. Students study the superficial characteristics of a culture such as traditional dance, food, and celebrations without exploring the deeper aspects of the culture, which would include contemporary issues and current events, historical perspectives, belief systems, and norms. These are weak forms of multicultural education because they provide simplified representations of cultures while continuing to maintain or even create new stereotypes.

For ELLs, developing positive self-identities and pride in their heritage helps them to persevere, be resilient, and increase their motivation to do well in school. ELLs may often not feel entirely accepted by society or may not fully feel a part of their new environment. ELLs who have developed positive self-image and who value their heritage language and culture can develop healthy bicultural identities. These bicultural identities in turn help ELLs better navigate two sociocultural systems and two languages. A multicultural curriculum can help ELLs understand

and appreciate their personal backgrounds and family heritages. Family studies in school can contribute to increased self-understanding and a positive personal sense of heritage. When parents and relatives are invited to school to share their "funds of knowledge," stories, and experiences, both ELLs and native-English students come to understand that ethnic groups and diversity are a meaningful part of our collective heritage. The notion of funds of knowledge is defined as "historically accumulated and culturally developed bodies of knowledge and skills essential for household or individual functioning and well-being" (Moll et al. 2001, p. 133).

For Alex, a third-grade self-contained ESL teacher, the use of his students' and their families' cultural funds of knowledge provided the most authentic, engaging, and rigorous integration of academic subjects with multicultural topics. An integrated project that increased Alex's knowledge about the linguistic and cultural backgrounds of his predominantly Chinese ELLs relied on Moll's "funds of knowledge." Alex often used the talents and expertise of his students' families to supplement his classroom instruction. There was a well-established parent and family participation in this school, which helped Alex and other teachers in getting information about families' funds of knowledge and their willingness to share these in the classrooms.

Alex invited the father of one of his students who managed a local Chinese restaurant to speak about all that was involved in running a restaurant. He asked the father to not only talk about Chinese cooking styles and ingredients but also about things like marketing, accounting, legal permits, creating menus, hiring staff, supplies, and so on. The father agreed to visit the class as a guest speaker over a period of three days in which he brought and talked about different types of typical Chinese cooking utensils and ingredients, and spoke about a variety of traditional dishes from different parts of China, connecting these discussions to Chinese geography, history, culture, and language. He also showed and discussed U.S. influence on Chinese dishes. The final day he spoke to the students about managing a restaurant. The discussion with the father resulted in cooperative-learning groups creating a plan to open an ethnic food restaurant that entailed research via the Internet and the library (reading and social studies), writing plans, advertising, and persuasive pieces (writing), presenting their work to their peers (listening and speaking), calculating costs (math), and much more.

Multicultural education is not limited to teaching students about their own cultures. In a preschool in Chinatown where all the three- and four-year-olds are

Cantonese-speaking ELLs, they studied a unit on Guatemala. Their teacher, Clara, had recently returned from a vacation in Central America and was also engaged to a Guatemalan American. For several weeks the young Chinese children studied aspects of Guatemalan culture, geography, languages, and history, and they made comparisons between Chinese and Guatemalan traditions, foods, musical instruments, dress, and other characteristics of the two countries (see Figure 4-18). Even though the children were young, they were very engaged and interested, especially because the teacher made regular connections and comparisons to what they already knew. In addition, the children showed much interest in the unit on Guatemala because Clara had brought many hands-on artifacts, photographs from her trip, and even her fiancé—who met the children as a guest speaker on several occasions.

The integration of the study of ethnic and cultural content into the curriculum is especially important for ELLs, not only for their own development of a positive self-concept but also to promote broader understanding and harmony among diverse groups. Multicultural education should include the study of present culture, historical experiences, geography, social and political current events, contributions,

Figure 4-18 Chinese PreK Children Learning About Guatemala

and many other aspects of diverse groups. It should not be narrow and limited to special occasions only or to "heroes and holidays." Multicultural content can be a perfect vehicle for teaching and learning language and literacy, developing higher-order and critical thinking, and integrating content knowledge.

APPLICATIONS

1. Create a plan for promoting high teacher expectations toward ELLs. Explain how high expectations would be reflected in the school's vision and mission statements, included in teachers' professional development, measured and evaluated by administrators, and integrated into the curriculum and instructional practices. Describe what role ELLs' language, culture, education backgrounds, immigration experiences, etc. would play in creating the school's high expectations plan. Explain how teachers might develop appropriate methods for ELLs according to their language proficiency levels without lowering their expectations.

2. Describe how you would have handled Ofelia's situation differently than Mr. Walsh. What would have been more appropriate academic and linguistic expectations for Ofelia, considering her experiences and background? What support systems would have been appropriate for Ofelia related to her academic, linguistic, cultural, and socio-emotional needs? What types of learning activities would have increased Ofelia's motivation?

3. Step 1: Review the WIDA English Language Proficiency (ELP) Standards 2007 Edition:

   * Grade level cluster PreK–5
     www.wida.us/standards/PreK-5%20Standards%20web.pdf

   * Grade level cluster 6–12
     www.wida.us/standards/6-12%20Standards%20web.pdf

   Step 2: Select a grade level and then select one of the ELP standards:

   * Standard 1—Social and Instructional Language

   * Standard 2—The Language of Language Arts

   * Standard 3—The Language of Mathematics

* Standard 4—The Language of Science

* Standard 5—The Language of Social Studies

Step 3: Select two of the language domains (Listening, Speaking, Reading, or Writing).

Step 4: Create a unit with activities for your grade level, select standards, and two language domains that are appropriate for each of the five proficiency levels: Entering, Beginning, Developing, Expanding, and Bridging. For example, create a science unit on the solar system, focusing on reading and speaking for a fourth-grade class that has ELLs from all five proficiency levels. Make sure that the activities and English language expectations are appropriate for each proficiency level.

4. Consider each of the phrases below, reflect on your own, and then discuss with a small group. Draw a picture that illustrates the meaning of each phrase and discuss with your group. Arrange the phrases in order of value, from the least valuable to most valuable. From your reflections and discussions identify the implications for integrating multicultural elements into the curriculum.

   * *I tolerate you.*

   * *I am aware of you.*

   * *I understand you.*

   * *I respect you.*

   * *I appreciate you.*

   * *I accept you.*

SUGGESTIONS FOR FURTHER READING |||||||||||||||||||||||||

Au, Wayne. 2009. *Rethinking Multicultural Education*. Milwaukee: Rethinking Schools.

Cloud, Nancy, Fred Genesee, and Elsie Hamayan. 2009. *Literacy Instruction for English Language Learners: A Teacher's Guide to Research-Based Practices*. Portsmouth, NH: Heinemann.

Goldenberg, Claude, and Rhoda Coleman. 2010. *Promoting Academic Achievement among English Learners: A Guide to the Research*. New York: Corwin.

Lee, Enid, Deborah Menkart, and Margo Okazawa-Rey. 2007. *Beyond Heroes and Holidays: A Practical Guide to K–12 Anti-Racist, Multicultural Education and Staff Development*. Washington, DC: Network of Educators on the Americas.

Walqui, Aida. 2000. *Access and Engagement: Program Design and Instructional Approaches for Immigrant Students in Secondary Schools*. Washington, DC: Center for Applied Linguistics.

Chapter 5

Leadership, Advocacy, and Engagement

Some ELLs do not speak a word of English and are not literate in their native language. Others have some conversational English, but are not yet fluent, and in their native language they are not only literate, but have mastered a great deal of academic content. There will probably never be a formula for educating ELLs, just as there is no formula for educating students who already know English. What we can do is provide guidelines based on our strongest research about effective practices for teaching ELLs.

(Goldenberg 2008, p. 8)

As the quote above states, there is no formula for educating ELLs and no "one-size-fits-all" solution to the complex academic challenges of students who are not yet proficient in English. We do, however, have a significant amount of research that consistently points to the types of conditions and elements that can help advance the education of ELLs, and should be used when making decisions about the best ways to promote and improve the academic achievement of ELLs. Findings from these research studies give teachers and school leaders the type of information needed for making sound decisions. For example, this research is invaluable in helping teachers, administrators, and policymakers to identify the best classroom practices and instructional materials, choose the most appropriate assessment tools, design highly effective program models, and build sustainable family and community partnerships.

It is important to note that selecting best education practices for ELLs should be based on research that specifically focuses on ELLs and not on native-English speakers alone. It is not unusual for districts and schools to use research findings that are based on studies of English-speaking students for making decisions about ELLs. Research studies that focus on native-English-speaking students do not include issues like bilingualism or the influence of the native language on the second language, for example. Native-English-speaking students intuitively know the basic elements of the English language while ELLs do not have this automatic understanding. Research findings that don't reflect this are not appropriate for guiding decisions about ELLs.

A common thread in current research emphasizes the need to make the education of ELLs a schoolwide effort. ELLs and their teachers can no longer be isolated and disconnected from the rest of the school. Implementing effective schoolwide practices to improve the education of ELLs requires full commitment, participation, and advocacy from all stakeholders: teachers, students, support staff, families, and school leaders. Developing a sense of schoolwide ownership is essential for providing ELLs the best learning opportunities. Fundamental to creating this sense of collective responsibility for the education of all students, including ELLs, are the roles of school leaders, families, and communities.

Claiming Opportunities: A Handbook for Improving Education for English Language Learners Through Comprehensive School Reform (2003)—a comprehensive guide on ELLs and school reform—proposes a set of nine principles based on current research on ELLs (see Applications section at the end of this chapter). The Handbook offers concrete recommendations to help schools be more responsive to the academic needs of ELLs. The first and fourth principles are especially relevant to the discussions in this chapter about school leadership and family participation. The first principle speaks to the idea of a schoolwide approach to ELL education and the role of school leadership: "School leaders, administrators, and educators recognize that educating ELLs is the responsibility of the entire school staff." The authors argue that promoting the academic success of ELLs requires that the "school leadership's support of the education of ELLs is seen in the explicit inclusion of ELLs in a school's vision, goals, and reform strategies" (p. 37). Regarding the value of establishing strong relationships between school, home, and community, the Handbook's fourth principle affirms that for ELLs to experience success in school there need to be "strong and seamless links connecting home, school, and community" (p. 41). Among the many recommendations that the Handbook presents about home and community participation is this basic premise: "Educators recognize the importance of family participation in education and, through family and community activities, reinforce connections among students' home, school, and the broader community in which the school operates" (p. 41).

A wide range of topics related to ELLs has been covered in the previous chapters: second language acquisition and literacy development; schoolwide reform elements such as school climate and professional development; curricular planning and program design; culturally responsive and transactional instructional approaches; and school evaluation and student assessment practices. In this chapter, I discuss the three remaining aspects of schoolwide improvement for ELLs: school leadership, advocacy, and family/community partnerships. I begin by highlighting the vital role that school leaders play in the education of ELLs. In the following section, I offer specific suggestions on how to create effective and collaborative leadership structures and how to implement the most flexible and responsive leadership strategies that best address the needs of all students, including ELLs. I also discuss the importance of advocacy and provide specific ideas for classroom, school, district, and national advocacy. In the final section I focus on family and community participation and offer concrete ideas on ways to build strong family-involvement models and ongoing community partnerships.

EFFECTIVE AND VISIONARY LEADERSHIP

School leadership is one of the most important characteristics of successful schools. Because good school leaders are those who have wide professional knowledge and deep understanding about their schools' population and needs, they know how to select and use the best strategies, practices, resources, and tools that are most appropriate for their students, families, and staff. Research points to school leaders as having significant influence on teachers, instruction, and learning outcomes for students. A recent study by Delfino, Johnson, and Pérez (2009) illustrates this critical role of school leaders, especially for ELLs. The researchers studied four rural schools with a high percentage of ELLs who consistently performed well academically. The study identified a number of school features that promoted their ELLs' academic success. These are the same elements as those discussed in the previous chapters, including a school culture of high expectations, a focus on conceptual understanding, a rigorous and challenging curriculum, and a positive school climate. Another critical characteristic of these schools that had positive education outcomes for ELLs was "focused, dedicated, and caring leadership" (p. 68). The authors found that "[p]rincipals at each of the schools have focused on goals that resonate with their faculties and communities. Teachers and parents express enthusiasm for the goals and directions that the principals articulated—perhaps in part because principals help them see the connections between these goals and student success" (p. 68).

Research on school improvement over the past twenty years has shown that school leadership is the single most important factor for instructional improvement (Reyes 2006). Reyes summarizes findings from several research studies that focus on what school principals do to support learning and increase achievement of ELLs. The findings identify a number of leadership practices of effective programs for ELLs. Principals in the study commonly engaged in the following strategies and activities, most of which have been discussed throughout this book:

* Integrate the ELL program into the school vision/mission, staffing, professional development, parental participation approaches, instructional goals and programs, and assessment.

* Support and empower ELL teachers to actively participate in the school organizational and governance activities.

* Discuss ELL program goals, implementation, progress, and assessment with ELL teachers.

* Provide ELL professional development for non-ELL teachers and staff.

* Value the use of two languages and people who use different languages, including parents.

* Increase their knowledge of ELLs and second language acquisition.

* Provide appropriate and accurate information about second language development to parents.

Higher levels of program effectiveness for ELLs have been linked to strong school leadership guided by principals' commitment to and knowledge of ELL education. The main task of a principal is to create the best conditions for teaching and learning. This requires not only a focus on classroom instruction but a broader effort at creating a schoolwide collaborative and supportive teaching and learning climate that extends across the school building and beyond. Principals and other school leaders can draw on existing education leadership principles to create frameworks for success for ELLs as discussed below.

Education Leadership Frameworks

The Institute for Educational Leadership's Task Force on the Principalship (2000) offers one such framework that school leaders can use to integrate the needs of ELLs and their families, identifying three key roles. The specific practices listed under each leadership focus—Visionary, Instructional, Community—are interdependent and support one another (see Figure 5-1). The educational needs of ELLs can easily be connected to these leadership practices typically used for the general student population. For example, in Instructional Leadership, strengthening teaching and learning could include elements like modifications for ELLs and native-language instruction. Professional development could incorporate second language acquisition and ESL instructional strategies, while data-driven decision making and accountability would integrate appropriate assessment tools for second language learners. For Visionary Leadership, demonstrating "commitment, innovation, energy, values and belief that all children will learn at high levels" could make an explicit statement that "all children" also includes ELLs. In Community Leadership, the relations and shared leadership with staff, families, and community could include the needs of ELLs, their teachers, and their families. Because of ELLs' economic conditions, emerging English proficiency, immigrant status, and other factors that are beyond their control, the advocacy piece in Community Leadership is especially important for principals to follow.

The *Standards for School Leaders* developed by the Interstate School Leaders Licensure Consortium (ISLLC) also offers a similar framework that can be adapted to

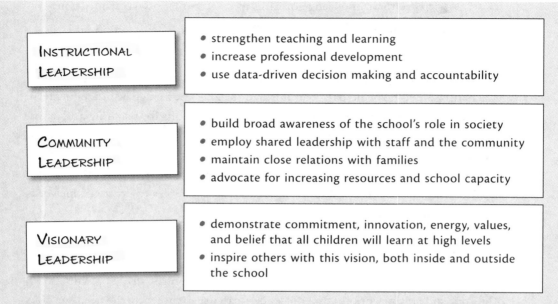

| INSTRUCTIONAL LEADERSHIP | • strengthen teaching and learning
• increase professional development
• use data-driven decision making and accountability |

| COMMUNITY LEADERSHIP | • build broad awareness of the school's role in society
• employ shared leadership with staff and the community
• maintain close relations with families
• advocate for increasing resources and school capacity |

| VISIONARY LEADERSHIP | • demonstrate commitment, innovation, energy, values, and belief that all children will learn at high levels
• inspire others with this vision, both inside and outside the school |

Figure 5-1 Key Roles of Effective Principals

include ELLs. The six standards are used nationwide by state boards of education, institutions of higher education, and school districts. The standards define the knowledge and dispositions that principals and other school administrators need to have to be effective leaders (see Figure 5-2). Based on current leadership research, the standards reflect the core aspects of effective schoolwide practices discussed earlier. These include creating a shared vision, a positive school culture, a safe and effective learning environment, structures for family and community involvement, and advocacy for ELLs. Even though the Standards for School Leaders don't directly speak to diverse language learners, each can easily be linked to the education needs of ELLs.

Smiley and Salsberry (2007) do just this by explicitly connecting the ISLLC standards to ELL-related indicators. They developed a self-assessment survey based on the ISLLC standards that includes specific connections to ELLs to help principals evaluate their own knowledge of ELLs. For example, references to ELLs are included in Standard 1 regarding principals having a "clear understanding of the elements that are necessary for an effective program for ELLs with a focused vision ..." and also having "thorough understandings of the research findings and pedagogical principles underlying programs for ELLs" (p. 21). In Standard 2, language is added

A school administrator is an educational leader who promotes the success of all students by:

1. facilitating the development, articulation, implementation, and stewardship of a vision of learning that is shared and supported by the school community
2. advocating, nurturing, and sustaining a school culture and instructional program conducive to student learning and professional growth
3. ensuring management of the organization, operations, and resources for a safe, efficient, and effective learning environment
4. collaborating with families and community members, and mobilizing community resources
4. acting with integrity, fairness, and in an ethical manner
6. understanding, responding to, and influencing the larger political, social, economic, legal, and cultural context

Figure 5-2 ISLLC Standards for School Leaders (1996)

about principals advocating for the "inclusion of ELLs," ensuring "sustained attention to these students by explicitly keeping language and culture in the reform agenda ..." and placing "high priority on professional development for all school staff with training that is designed to serve ELLs more effectively" (p. 22). One of the indicators in Standard 3 states that principals should "hire bilingual staff who have cultural backgrounds similar to those of the students" (p. 23).

The ISLLC Standards for School Leaders and the Institute for Educational Leadership's Task Force on the Principalship framework discussed above are examples of how school leaders can address issues specific to ELLs within broader practices. Principals of schools with ELLs, whether they are a small or large percentage of the student body, have the professional, moral, and ethical responsibility to respond to their needs and to create the best opportunities for their academic success. To do this in the most effective way, principals and other school leaders must make conscious and deliberate efforts to increase their own knowledge and understandings of ELL education.

The type of school-leader self-assessment described above was successfully implemented by the principal of a rural elementary school that had recently experienced an influx of ELLs. Patricia, a twelve-year veteran principal, had always engaged in some kind of informal reflection and self-assessment about her leadership skills and accomplishments, especially in preparation for her yearly central office evaluation. As her school began to enroll more language- and ethnic-diverse students and her staff had to increasingly communicate with non-English-speaking parents, Patricia realized that she needed to integrate the specific needs of this new population into her own yearly goals. She integrated specific areas related to ELLs within the mandated district's principal standards and assessment. One of the standards in the principal assessment rubric was to "communicate effectively with all stakeholders," including parents. As Patricia completed the self-assessment piece on communication, she quickly realized that this was an area that needed much improvement as it related to ELL families. Patricia had prided herself on creating excellent communication structures at her school through newsletters, phone trees, and recently, through an interactive school website. After completing the self-assessment, which had now incorporated ELLs, she realized that she had not made the appropriate accommodations to communicate effectively with culturally diverse families who did not speak English. Because the ELL population at her school came from different religions, languages, and cultural backgrounds, Patricia realized she had to offer both written and verbal information in the language represented in her school. She also realized that to be an effective communicator with her ELL families, she would need to become more knowledgeable about their cultural practices and norms.

Developing a Knowledge Base

> The principal must not only be a change agent, but must also be an instructional leader. The literature has consistently identified the strong instructional leadership of the principal as playing a critical role in providing instruction that responds to the needs of ELLs and making their achievement a priority. (Smiley and Salsberry 2007, p. 18)

Effective school leaders not only support and promote the success of all students by collaborating with their families and the community, but also by responding to their diverse interests and needs. To do this, school leaders need to increase their understandings of the students, families, and communities they serve. Researchers and educators in the field agree on the general type of core knowledge needed to provide the most effective learning conditions for ELLs. These include language and literacy development, sociocultural dimensions, instructional approaches, and assessment (see Figure 5-3).

LANGUAGE & LITERACY DEVELOPMENT

- how a second language is acquired
- stages of second language acquisition
- the differences between academic and conversational language
- length of time it takes to acquire academic second language
- factors that influence the rate of second language acquisition
- the relationship between the first language and second language
- bilingualism and its benefits
- how literacy skills transfer from the first to the second language
- ELL background knowledge and reading comprehension

SOCIOCULTURAL DIMENSIONS

- ELLs' cultural and social norms
- the differences among ELLs
- the immigrant experience and its effects on ELLs' learning
- acculturation vs. assimilation
- the connection between language and culture
- differences between home culture and school/society culture

INSTRUCTIONAL APPROACHES

- active learning through hands-on and authentic activities
- integrated curriculum
- language learning through content
- modifications and scaffolding strategies
- adapting instruction to different language proficiency levels
- connecting instruction to ELLs' home culture and community
- adapting instruction for challenging and rigorous curriculum

ASSESSMENT

- assessment appropriate for second language learners
- classroom assessments that test content, not language proficiency
- testing accommodations

Figure 5-3 What Teachers and School Leaders Should Know About ELLs

To be responsive to ELLs, school leaders must have additional skills that go beyond what traditional leadership preparation programs offer. It then falls to the principal and other school leaders to increase their knowledge base about ELLs on their own or in collaboration with their staff. School administrators who have neither classroom experience with ELLs nor formal university coursework in ESL and/or bilingual education have several options to increase their knowledge (see Figure 5-4). Enrolling in university courses on ESL and/or bilingual education would offer the most complete and comprehensive understanding about ELLs. School administrators often return to universities interested in pursuing doctoral degrees. Elective courses in such programs can be in the areas of ESL and/or bilingual education. In addition, school leaders pursuing a doctorate may choose to do their dissertation studies on ELL-related subjects.

Principals can also focus their professional development on topics related to ELLs and participate with their staff in these trainings, which could include second

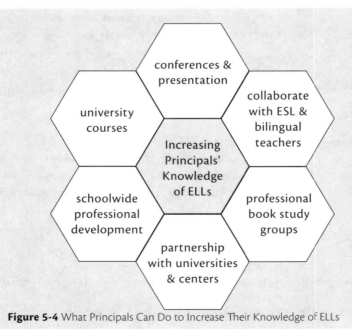

Figure 5-4 What Principals Can Do to Increase Their Knowledge of ELLs

language acquisition, ESL instructional approaches, or second language assessment strategies, for example. Professional book study groups where principals and teachers read and discuss books relevant to ELL topics is also an effective way to develop knowledge in a collaborative way. Included at the end of each chapter in this book are a number of recommended books on ELL-related topics that can be used for book study groups of this kind. In addition, principals and other school leaders can attend conferences and presentations on ELLs as well as establish action-research partnerships with universities or education centers. A more informal but very effective way to increase principals' knowledge about ELLs is for them to work closely with bilingual and ESL teachers. Principals and other school leaders can gain great insights from teachers by listening to their concerns and needs, observing in their classrooms, meeting with them often, and including their voices and concerns in all school decision-making processes.

In one urban middle school, the principal and assistant principal take turns attending teachers' weekly department meetings, acquiring firsthand information on teachers' concerns and needs. The school has both self-contained bilingual content-area teachers, who meet with their respective English-language peers, as well as two pullout ESL teachers, who also attend the department meetings. The principal also created an ELL advisory council made up of bilingual, ESL, and mainstream teachers who provide him with updates and information on ELLs' progress as well as concerns related to instructional materials, professional development needs, assessment practices, and communication with families.

Leadership Practices

Principals have considerable influence in shaping school culture and setting school-wide expectations for students, teachers, and families. Beyond managerial and administrative tasks, the principal has the responsibility for nurturing shared beliefs and a sense of community among all members of the school, including students and their families. ELLs and their teachers often find themselves at the margins of school, both literally and figuratively (Gándara and Hopkins 2010). School leaders have the ability, authority, and responsibility to reverse practices that often leave ELLs on the sidelines.

The case of Lil, the new principal at a suburban middle school, shows how a principal can promote change and shift perceptions about ELLs even in a school that is unaware of and sometimes resistant to ELL needs. Lil was able to accomplish this with the help of several staff, most importantly the ESL teacher, Henri.

The school had been experiencing a fast demographic change, from mostly white middle-class students to a more linguistically, ethnically, and economically diverse population. Within a ten-year period the area near the school had experienced a 30 percent increase in the immigrant population, from a few immigrant families to a significant community of recent arrivals, mostly from Latin America. The previous principal had responded to the school's increasing immigrant population with little effort and limited resources to address the needs of ELLs and their families. The only service available was a part-time ESL instructor, Rachel, who taught ELLs two-to-three periods of ESL a week while the rest of the time they were mainstreamed in other classes with no extra support. Because the school had so many ELLs, Rachel often had groups of thirty-five or more students in each period, and often had multiple language proficiency levels within one group. Adding to these challenges was the fact that she did not have her own classroom and had to teach in the cafeteria before and after lunch. Because the cafeteria also served as the school auditorium, any performance or event resulted in the cancellation of her ESL classes. Not surprisingly and given the nearly impossible working conditions, Rachel was the third part-time ESL teacher in five years at this school. She did not last long either, and left the school midyear.

Henri had not started as an ESL teacher. Fresh out of university, Henri taught English/language arts at this school for the first five years. He experienced firsthand the changes in the community and school. He noticed the increasing number of ELLs in his classroom who were having academic difficulties and struggling to learn English. His own struggles trying to help his ELLs catch up in English reading and writing compelled him to get his ESL endorsement. After Henri earned his endorsement and Rachel left, he set out to become the full-time ESL teacher at the school. He wanted to make a difference for all the ELLs at his school by creating what he called a "real" ESL program. Henri convinced the then principal to make the ESL position full time and allow him to take the ESL teacher position. The principal was resistant at first, but eventually could not deny the need for a full-time ESL position, with so many ELLs in need of services. The principal warned Henri that he would not be able to have his own classroom and would need to continue to use the cafeteria. Henri did so for several years until Lil became the new principal. She recognized how, in so many ways, both Henri and his ELLs were relegated to the status of second-class citizens in the school. Lil called them "the forgotten."

Lil made it her priority to change the way the school staff saw ELLs. Working closely with Henri and a few other interested teachers and staff, Lil created a strategic plan to address the needs of ELLs at the school. Her first positive changes were to find a permanent classroom for Henri and to make him a member of her leadership team. These two moves by the principal not only elevated the "status" of ELLs and their ESL teacher but also signaled a new approach to teaching and responding to the needs of ELLs and their families. Lil also included ELLs in the School Improvement Plan (SIP) under the *Improvements for Teaching and Learning* priority by focusing part of the yearly professional development on ELL instruction as well as allocating funds for teachers to attend an ELL-related conference. In addition, she integrated issues related to non-English-speaking parents in the *Parent Participation* section of the SIP by providing them with written and oral information in Spanish as well as offering parent trainings in Spanish. Slowly, Lil changed teachers' and other staff's perceptions about ELLs. She not only created a climate of shared responsibility for the education of all students, including ELLs, but also managed to have the teachers view this as a worthwhile challenge rather than an additional burden.

Lil's ability to make teachers and other school staff view the shared education of ELLs as an enriching experience rather than "one more thing we have to do" is an especially important accomplishment. Changing from a narrow isolated approach for addressing the needs of ELLs to a schoolwide effort cannot be effectively done from a top-down mandate by school leaders. If a principal does not have buy-in from the school staff, not only might teachers become resistant to viewing ELLs as their responsibility, they may also develop resentment toward these students and their families. Principals and other school leaders are more effective when they use collaborative and shared decision-making approaches. The most effective ways of building a common purpose as well as a sense of ownership is by creating professional learning communities and building collaboration among teachers to improve curriculum, instruction, and assessment practices. Because teacher leaders, counselors, and assistant principals share responsibility as well for many functions and activities across the school, they should incorporate the needs of ELLs and their families throughout the decision-making process.

In this school, the principal's efforts translated into concrete improvements for ELLs and their ESL teacher. Both Lil and Henri's strategic planning and advocacy played an important role in gaining support from the rest of the school staff. Educators' lack of knowledge, unawareness, and even prejudice are all factors that keep ELLs segregated in schools, with less access to school resources, and few options available to them to change their own conditions. Principal and teacher advocacy is essential in helping advance ELLs' education opportunities and academic outcomes.

ADVOCACY FOR THE EDUCATION OF ELLS

ELLs are one of the groups most at risk for academic failure. Many in the field would argue that in fact ELLs might be the most vulnerable of any student group. Other at-risk populations, such as racial- and ethnic-minority students, white students living in extreme poverty, and non-ELL students with disabilities, are often perceived as being more "American" and having more rights than the children of immigrants and immigrant children. Even though other ethnic groups like Native Americans and African Americans also experience a great deal of prejudice and discrimination, they don't have to deal with adverse circumstances related to immigration. In addition, ELLs have to cope with considerable linguistic, sociocultural, and legal challenges that other disadvantaged groups do not experience. For example, many ELLs face the frightening prospect of being deported or having their parents deported. Out of fear of deportation or imprisonment, parents of ELLs sometimes keep their children away from school. Living under the cloud of being from an undocumented family, even when the children themselves are U.S.-born citizens, takes a heavy psychological toll on students and often interferes with their learning.

According to López and López (2010), "the children of undocumented migrants in the United States are trapped in the intersection of two systems in crisis: the public education system and the immigration law system. These young people, who have come to the U.S. 'through no fault of their own,' are caught in the crossfire of the harsh law, policy and rhetoric that currently pervade these two systems" (p. 1). Immigration status and language barriers present significant challenges for most ELLs and their families, often restricting their potential for success and future opportunities. The fierce anti-immigration attitude reappearing across the United States cannot be ignored when discussing approaches to improve the education of ELLs. The fact is, many ELLs live daily with deep fears associated with society's language and ethnic prejudices. Anti-immigrant schemes, often targeting Latinos and particularly Mexicans, resurface often and in many different forms. California and Arizona offer examples, described in the next section, of the types of restrictive and harmful policies that have long-lasting negative effects on ELLs' education. In the following section I focus on one particular case in Arizona—the banning of teachers with accents from teaching ELLs—to illustrate how educators can advocate against these types of misguided mandates.

State- and National-Level Advocacy

Over the past several decades California has passed a number of legislative policies aimed at limiting the educational opportunities for immigrant children. Proposition 187, interestingly named "Save Our State" and passed in 1994, eliminated all government-funded social services to undocumented immigrants, including access to public education for their children. Although the federal court in California struck this provision down in 1997 citing *Plyler* v. *Doe*—a United States Supreme Court ruling that guarantees undocumented children the right to a free public education—the stage was set for a climate of fear, distrust, and anxiety for ELLs and their families. Not long after, in 1998, Californians passed proposition 227, titled "English for the Children," ending most bilingual education programs and mandating one-year structured English immersion for ELLs instead.

Arizona followed suit in 2000 with a similar law prohibiting bilingual education for ELLs. More recently, in 2010, Arizona banned ethnic studies and passed legislation criminalizing the undocumented. Another misdirected Arizona policy is the recent mandate to remove teachers with accents from ELL classrooms. Several national education organizations, made up mostly of teachers as well as academics and researchers, have come forward to advocate in defense of ELLs and against these discriminatory policies. The official public statements by the Teachers of English to Speakers of Other Languages association (TESOL), the National Council of Teachers of English (NCTE), and the Linguistics Department of the University of Arizona provide examples of the types of advocacy efforts used to defend ELLs and their teachers, and to protest unfair policies.

TESOL released a public joint statement with its affiliate AZ-TESOL condemning the Arizona Department of Education mandate to remove teachers with accents from classrooms that have ELLs. Arizona officials defended their policy by citing NCLB's requirement that teachers of ELLs must be "fluent in English and any other language used for instruction, including having written and oral communications skills." It is important to point out that neither NCLB nor the U.S. Department of Education say anything about teachers' accents. In this case, noneducators are misinterpreting "fluent" as being unaccented. While requiring that teachers of ELLs be "fluent in English" is entirely appropriate, requiring ELL teachers to be "unaccented" is simply not possible. Whether people's accents come from the mother tongue or from different regions of the United States, all linguists agree that everyone has an accent. Determining which teacher accent is suitable for teaching ELLs and which is not is both impractical and dangerous. Officials from the Arizona Department of Education incorrectly claim that ELLs must have teachers who speak the language without an accent in order to learn English well. TESOL's *Joint Statement on the Teacher English Fluency Initiative in Arizona* (2010) counters that

> [f]or decades the field of English language teaching has suffered from the myth that one only needs to be a native English speaker in order to teach the English language. The myth further [implies] that native English speakers make better English as a second language (ESL) or English as a foreign language (EFL) teachers than nonnative English speakers because native English speakers are perceived to speak "unaccented" English and understand and use idiomatic expressions fluently. ... With the recent state legislation targeting undocumented immigrants in Arizona (SB 1070) and other legislation banning ethnic studies in Arizona (HB 2281), TESOL and AZ-TESOL are deeply troubled by what appears to be an environment of fear and xenophobia being fostered by lawmakers in the state without consideration of the consequences upon student learning and achievement. (See Appendix A for complete statement.)

NCTE, a professional association of teachers of English, literacy, and language arts, also issued a statement denouncing Arizona's policy on banning teachers with accents from instructing ELLs:

> This edict is dangerously misguided. Confirmed by research and by policy positions adopted by the National Council of Teachers of English, what matters most in teaching non-native English language learners is not elocution or adherence to a single dialect or speech pattern. What matters most is understanding

students and the dynamics of language learning. Teachers who have deep roots in the culture and linguistic experiences of their students are well equipped for success in teaching English, regardless of their spoken dialect or accent.... . The urgent need for more highly-adept teachers to meet the demand makes the Arizona ban so invidious: teachers who may best understand the cultural and family dynamics of their ELL students, who are living the gradual developmental process that characterizes second language acquisition, are barred from the classrooms where they are needed most. (See Appendix B for complete statement.)

Another official statement from the Linguistics Department of the University of Arizona sent to Arizona's Governor and Superintendent in 2010 outlines scientifically backed facts about language and accents:

1. "Heavily accented" speech is not the same as "unintelligible" or "ungrammatical" speech.

2. Speakers with strong foreign accents may nevertheless have mastered grammar and idioms of English as well as native speakers.

3. Teachers whose first language is Spanish may be able to teach English to Spanish-speaking students better than teachers who don't speak Spanish.

4. Exposure to many different speech styles, dialects, and accents helps (and does not harm) the acquisition of a language.

5. It is helpful for all students (ELLs as well as native speakers) to be exposed to foreign-accented speech as a part of their education.

6. There are many different "accents" within English that can affect intelligibility, but the policy targets foreign accents and not dialects of English.

7. Communicating to students that foreign-accented speech is "bad" or "harmful" is counterproductive to learning, and affirms preexisting patterns of linguistic bias and harmful "linguistic profiling."

8. There is no such thing as "unaccented" speech, and so policies aimed at eliminating accented speech from the classroom are paradoxical.

Strongly worded official public statements from credible and established teacher organizations and other groups are essential in opposing uninformed and unfounded state and district policies. More importantly, publicly denouncing these discriminatory practices not only helps to advance ELLs' education opportunities but also helps to educate the public. Negative public sentiments against bilingual education, as well as toward ELLs and their families, are often based on false assumptions and lack of understanding. Disseminating information about ELLs must target both the education profession and also the general public. To do this most effectively, communication about ELLs aimed at noneducators must be in everyday accessible language that presents concise and clear information.

One organization that is especially helpful in advocating for ELLs is the Institute on Language and Education Policy (see Appendix C for a list of advocacy web links). ILEP is a nonprofit organization committed to promoting research-based policies and advocacy for ELLs and heritage language learners. The Institute's website states: "In an era of misguided 'accountability' measures, high-stakes testing, cutbacks in school funding, and English-only activism, strong advocacy for children is essential. Scientific knowledge about what works—not ideology or political expedience—must guide public policy." ILEP is an excellent resource for up-to-date information, events, news, and opportunities for advocacy.

Other professional organizations such as the National Association for Bilingual Education (NABE) have also recognized the need for active and ongoing advocacy for ELLs. NABE has identified a set of core advocacy areas aimed at promoting educational excellence and equity for ELLs.

* Advocacy for federal and state legislation to address the unique needs of ELLs.

* Advocacy for adequate funding, well-trained teachers, appropriate assessments, and other resources for ELL programs.

* Advocacy for equal educational opportunity, including strong civil-rights policies and aggressive enforcement of the *Lau* v. *Nichols* decision.

* Advocacy against political attacks on language-minority communities, such as the English Only movement and anti-bilingual-education initiatives.

Classroom, School, and District Advocacy

The main purpose of ELL advocacy is to help reach full education equity and inclusion for ELLs and their families. The examples above show how ELL educators can mobilize and advocate at the national and state levels. Advocacy to improve the working conditions of teachers and increase the academic outcomes of ELLs also must happen in classrooms, schools, and districts.

Advocacy at the District Level

The Council of the Great City Schools (2009) recently conducted a study in four large urban school districts analyzing the conditions, context, and instructional practices that explain why ELLs progress academically in some districts but not in others. According to their report, each district that showed improvement in the education of ELLs had "a particularly effective, vocal advocate for improvement of ELL instruction and services who helped shape and advance the reform agenda" (p. 18). This advocate was often the district's ELL director, but in some cases it was the chief academic officer, superintendent, or a board member. In one of the districts there was overwhelming agreement among teachers, principals, and district staff that "the driving forces behind the changes in the district's ELL strategy were the superintendent and ELL director, who developed a clear vision for ELL reform and aggressively advanced this vision" (p. 18). The report also identified several characteristics and priorities shared by the leadership in each district, as outlined in Figure 5-5.

An important finding in the study was how the empowerment of the office of ELL programs and its director had a positive effect on district and school improvement efforts. The role and importance of the ELL office was enhanced by including them in "the highest levels of decision making, such as the superintendent's cabinet, and [giving them] the authority to establish district-wide ELL practices and to work with other central office departments and schools to oversee progress" (p. 22). ELL directors who were most involved in the higher-level decision-making process were more successful at getting district resources—both funding and staff—to support instructional improvement for ELLs. These types of districtwide efforts are often spearheaded by people who understand and recognize the special needs of ELLs and who are also skilled advocates.

- Had expertise and a commitment to quality ELL instruction
- Formed strategic partnerships and successfully rallied support behind reform agendas
- Took proactive steps to break down the compartmentalized organization of the central office and build a culture of collaboration
- Worked closely with directors of content-area and grade-level departments and encouraged similar collaboration at the school level
- Connected with people outside the district office, having a regular presence at school sites and community meetings
- Set high standards for ELL achievement and provided the tools and oversight schools needed to meet these high standards
- Recognized the importance of research and data, mandating and supporting the use of student data to improve instruction and services for ELLs

Figure 5-5 District Leadership Characteristics for Improving ELL Achievement

Teacher-Led Advocacy

At the school level, teachers of ELLs are in the best position to advocate for their students by providing information and educating school leaders and non-ELL teachers about ELLs and their families. The stories of the three ESL teachers—Sharon, Rachel, and Henri—described above and in Chapter 2, show the types of difficulties they can experience in schools. While Rachel was overcome by so many challenges that she quit midyear, Sharon and Henri used their knowledge and training to advocate for themselves and their students.

Teachers of ELLs need to ensure that there is a fair distribution of resources and that ELLs are included in the allocation of funds for materials, professional development, and other activities (de Oliveira and Athanases 2007). In addition, there should be equitable distribution of human resource services and parental support for ELLs. Teachers of ELLs cannot assume that school leaders will automatically know what they and their students need. Teachers' communications to school leaders about their needs should always come with clear explanations and justifications. Lower class size for ELLs is a good example of a request that needs convincing explanations. Most if not all teachers prefer to have smaller rather than larger class size. Why then would a district or a principal decide to have small class sizes for

ELLs and not for classrooms with native-English speakers? A convincing argument would explain the pressures that ELLs and their teachers face in accelerating their English acquisition to do well in state and district tests. For teachers to help ELLs "catch up to a moving target" they need to have accelerated and focused instruction that can be better accomplished in classrooms with fewer students. The "moving targets" are native-English-speakers who make gains every year in reading, writing, and vocabulary in a language they already know. According to Cummins (2009), for ELLs to catch up to native-English-speaking students and reach grade-level competency within six years, ELLs must "make 15 months' gain in every 10 month school year. By contrast, the typical native-speaking student is expected to make 10 months' gain in a 10 month year" (p. 24). Understanding this challenge might help convince administrators to consider the benefits of smaller class size for ELLs in which teachers can provide more individualized and small-group instruction.

Family and Community Advocacy

Parents and families can be powerful and effective advocates as well. However, families of ELLs may be less likely to become involved in their own advocacy efforts when they lack sufficient knowledge, are afraid, or don't view themselves as having any influence or role in improving the education of their children. Navigating the school system and the power structures of state and district education politics is not easy, and much less so for ELL parents. Many are not fluent in English, may have had interrupted schooling themselves, may be undocumented, and may not be familiar with how the school system works in the United States. Just as teachers and school leaders need to increase their knowledge about ELL education issues, parents and families must also become well informed about the very issues that affect their children's education. Teachers and school leaders can help to educate families about school programs and curriculum, inform them of their rights, and raise their political awareness. Educators can support families, and even older ELLs, to become engaged in the improvement efforts of their schools and programs.

Advocacy partnerships between school, families, and community can have very positive results in policy changes and improved responses to students' needs. An example of this type of successful parent and community advocacy is the nineteen-day hunger strike in 2001 by seventeen community members, mostly mothers of high school students, in a large urban school district. They demanded the construction of a new high school because the only secondary school in their community was overcrowded, had a dismal record of academic performance, had very high dropout rates, and suffered from frequent violence. District officials had promised to build a new high school in their predominantly Latino and African American south-side neighborhood but postponed the project indefinitely claiming lack of funds, even though they had continued with construction of two north-side high school preps. After many failed attempts at getting the school board to respond, success came through the efforts of these parents and community advocates. Even after the board agreed to build the new high school, parents and community members continued to be involved in all aspects of the planning of the school, from physical aspects to the focus of the curriculum. Responses from several parent surveys conducted by the community and parent leaders were used to design the school programs and curriculum. Several parent surveys indicated their desire for a safe, small, and academically rigorous school where bilingualism and biculturalism are valued; where fine arts are integrated into the curriculum; where students are prepared to compete in math, science, and technology; and where students develop a deep sense of social justice and equity. Their advocacy and engagement efforts resulted in four small schools within the high school that integrated the community and families' wishes: the World Language High School, the Multicultural Arts High School, the Math, Science, and Technology High School, and the School for Social Justice.

Parent Beliefs and Perceptions

As the example above shows, the parents and community members who were involved in creating their new high school had a very positive self-image and strong ties to their home language and culture, as evidenced by their desire for the school to value bilingualism and biculturalism. This is not always the case. Language-minority students and their families sometimes internalize the stigma linked to their origins, making them reject their language and culture. Research studies that examine parents' attitudes and opinions about native-language instruction point to a general lack of understanding by immigrant parents about the work-ings of bilingual education. In their study of parent attitudes toward bilingual education, Shin and Kim (1996) found that most Korean-immigrant parents sup-port the general principles of bilingual education. However, when the parents were asked specifically if the use of Korean in the classroom helped their children to be at the same level as their peers academically while they developed English, only 32 percent of the parents agreed. Conflicting views about bilingual education are common among immigrant groups in the United States. Opposition to bilingual education is strongest when an extreme view—the program only has native-language instruction—of bilingual education is presented, but when parents are asked about using both languages or about bilingual education in general, responses are more positive (Krashen 1996). Shin and Gibbons (1998) found that Latino parents tend to support the general principles of bilingual education. In their study, the majority of Latino parents felt that reading, writing, and basic subjects should be taught in both English and Spanish.

A number of factors shape parents' perceptions about bilingual education. ELL parents' positive attitudes toward native-language instruction are often based on their desire to maintain and pass on the native language and culture to their children. Parents of ELLs who see bilingualism as an asset also recognize that their children are more likely to have better job opportunities if they have well-developed literacy in two languages. Immigrant families may also have hopes of an eventual return to their native country and may be concerned that their children will not be able to fit in if they no longer speak their home language.

Some ELL parents, on the other hand, favor quick assimilation to English-speaking U.S. culture and adopt negative attitudes toward programs with native-language instruction. The most common motivation for immigrant families to reject bilingual education is fear that their children will suffer from discrimination and prejudice because they will not learn English quickly or well enough. ELL parents also recognize that to succeed in an English-dominant society, English proficiency is critical for better education and job opportunities—but they don't always understand that it is not necessary to lose the native language in order to learn English. As illustrated by Mirka's mother in Chapter 1, ELL parents sometimes believe that bilingualism is a liability. They assume that bilingual education delays English language development and stigmatizes children who participate in these programs. The assumption that bilingual education programs are inferior to English-only programs is also a common reason for ELL parents to reject native-language instruction for their children. As was mentioned earlier, educators play a very important role in helping families become well informed about education issues so that they can make the best decisions about their children's schooling. Parents should always have the right to decide whether they want their children enrolled in native-language or English-only instruction, but they should not make these decisions based on pressures, misinformation, or an incomplete understanding of bilingual education.

For ELL parents and families to be effective in their own advocacy efforts they must be well informed about how different education programs work. Engaging in advocacy is one of the many ways that parents, families, and the community can be involved and participate in their children's education. Developing strong and trusting relationships between families and schools is critical for this to happen. In the last section of this chapter I speak to the important roles that family participation and community engagement play in the improvement of ELLs' academic outcomes and school experiences.

PARENT, FAMILY, AND COMMUNITY PARTICIPATION

Educators recognize that involvement of parents and families in the education of their children leads to increased academic achievement, better school attendance, and lower dropout rates. Research points to a strong relationship between parental involvement and increased student achievement regardless of income level or ethnicity. In a recent meta-analysis of forty-one research studies on parental involvement in urban schools, Jeynes (2005) found that efforts by schools to increase parent support of their children's education produce positive results for all students. The studies also show that parent-involvement programs can help reduce the achievement gap for struggling students, especially in urban areas. Jeynes concludes that "parent involvement programs that were effective for urban students [are] particularly encouraging because studies have indicated how low SES, urban parents are generally less educationally supportive than most other parents" (p. 261).

Jeynes' analysis also focused on identifying the specific aspects of parent involvement that most help minority student achievement and the kinds of parent participation that are most important. He found that the strongest features of parent involvement were the subtler aspects of family support, such as high parent expectations of their children and creating a supportive home environment. He found that traditional aspects of parent involvement, such as attending school functions and checking homework, were not as significant as the subtler types of family support. Jeynes suggests that this meta-analysis "questions current beliefs about parental support mechanisms considered exemplary (e.g. checking homework, attending school functions)" (p. 263). Schools tend to give preference to certain types of mostly white middle-class interactions between families and schools that are perceived as the ideal types of parent involvement. Parent participation that relies on middle-class social and cultural capital, which low-income minority families are likely not to have, excludes them from successfully engaging in their children's school and education (Bakker and Denessen 2007). The common standard for parent involvement is based on "visible and active" participation in school activities such as attending parent workshops, volunteering in the classroom, helping children do their homework, and attending parent meetings. The less traditional and less observable types of parent involvement are often not recognized by schools as valuable alternatives to family participation or important support systems for students (see Figure 5-6).

TRADITIONAL PARENT INVOLVEMENT

- Volunteer in the classroom
- Attend assemblies and school events
- Attend parent-teacher conferences
- Organize fundraisers
- Join the PTO
- Participate in field trips
- Help children with homework
- Attend parent workshops
- Respond to written notices
- Communicate with teachers during school hours

NONTRADITIONAL FAMILY INVOLVEMENT

- Show they value education
- Be attentive to their children's well-being
- Send their children to school regularly
- Give encouragement and support at home
- Respond to school notices through their children
- Work additional jobs to provide for school supplies and uniforms
- Teach children self-discipline and perseverance

Figure 5-6 Traditional and Nontraditional Parent Involvement

Models for Meaningful ELL Family Participation

Most teachers and school leaders place high value on parent and family participation because they recognize the connection between parent involvement and increased student achievement. A framework developed by Epstein (2001) presents six types of family involvement that can be used as a guide for creating strong and sustainable school and family partnership programs (see Figure 5-7). *Parenting* involves support systems provided by the school that help families improve their parenting skills. This type of family involvement also helps families transform their home environments to offer the most favorable conditions for child development and learning. This also enables families to share their backgrounds, culture, and needs with teachers and school leaders so that they can provide culturally and socially appropriate support.

Communicating is based on establishing two-way communication systems from home to school and from school to home. In this type of involvement, families and school staff share information, communicate needs, and provide opportunities for collaborative problem solving. Communication is essential for creating mutual understanding and respect between families and school staff. *Volunteering* is a type of

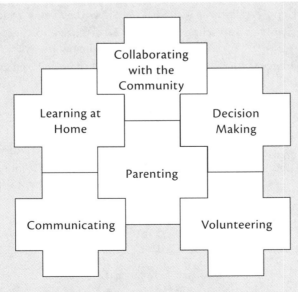

Figure 5-7 Epstein's (2001) Framework for Six Types of Involvement

involvement more commonly found in the early elementary grades but one that can be expanded up to secondary school. Creating effective volunteering programs that support the school and students involves careful planning and training. Optimizing the time and talents of parents and other family members in schools requires organization and coordination. The *Learning at Home* type of involvement helps families create supportive learning conditions at home. Schools can provide information to parents and other caregivers on how to engage in home activities that promote learning. Families helping students with homework is one but not the only way to create a learning-at-home environment. Families that have limited schooling may not be able to help their children with homework but can certainly offer other kinds of support like encouragement, guidance, and praise. *Decision Making* involves families in the school decision-making process and helps them develop leadership and advocacy skills. This is a very important type of engagement, especially for ELL families, because it can create opportunities for self-empowerment and a real sense of ownership in their children's education.

The final type of family involvement is *Collaborating with the Community*, where schools can help to establish partnerships with community centers and agencies to share resources and services between families, students, school, and community.

Because of the significant achievement gap between ELLs and English-proficient students, it is especially urgent to identify practices that can help increase ELL family participation. In schools with a high percentage of low-income and ethnic-minority students, school leaders and teachers are often at a loss about how to increase and improve parents' participation in their children's education and in the school. Teachers frequently point out that the students who struggle the most academically tend to come from families where there is little participation in their children's education. Many teachers come to the mistaken conclusion that these parents and families are not committed or concerned about their children's education. Rather than a lack of commitment to education, low parent involvement is more often the result of a number of other factors that schools need to help them overcome.

> [P]arents of ELLs face daunting barriers as they try to become informed or involved in their child's school. These barriers, which include the inability to understand English, unfamiliarity with the school system, and differences in cultural norms and cultural capital, can limit parents' communication and school participation. (Arias and Morillo-Campbell 2008, p. 1)

For parents of ELLs, there is a long list of obstacles that may interfere with their school participation. They may not understand the language or culture of school, may be struggling to make a new life in a unfamiliar culture, may come from countries where they are not expected or allowed to participate in schools, may be under financial stress and therefore have heavy workloads, may have little formal education, may be fearful and not fully trust schools, or may lack resources and knowledge of how to navigate the education system. The challenge for teachers and school leaders is to understand the types of circumstances that lead parents and families to stay away from school and then to work at creating innovative ways to involve ELL parents and families and help them overcome these barriers.

Schools with high numbers of ELLs and minority students sometimes fail to create effective systems for meaningful and ongoing parent and family involvement. Schools either don't make much of an effort to involve ELL families or they apply traditional expectations and approaches for parent involvement that don't take into account linguistic, social, and cultural differences. Recognizing how these factors affect the amount and the kinds of parent participation can help explain the real reasons for low parental participation. Understanding why parents and families are not involved in their children's education is the first step in identifying best strategies and approaches for creating meaningful and long-lasting partnership between families and schools.

Alvaro, a veteran first-grade bilingual teacher, recounts his frustration with lack of parental involvement during his first few years in the classroom. His negative perceptions about the low levels of parent participation were often fueled by the other first-grade teachers. Bothered by the persistent lack of parent participation, and in an effort to dispel some of his peers' negative perceptions, Alvaro began to reflect on how he could increase parent involvement in his classroom. He soon realized that the first step was to understand what impeded parents from participating in school. He created a survey asking parents about their work hours, means of transportation, age of siblings, whether they were taking care of elderly relatives, familiarity with the system, time in the United States and city, and other residency, family, and employment issues that might interfere with their participation in school. He also wanted to know what parent involvement was like in the areas where many of his ELL families originated. Because Alvaro realized that all these personal questions might be seen as intrusive by the parents, he approached the school's Parent and Teachers Association (PTA) and Parent Bilingual Advisory Committee (PBAC) to get a better sense about these issues. From the feedback and recommendations he received, Alvaro created a checklist that asked parents to provide information on such issues as their preferences for times and days to volunteer in his classroom, their desire to carpool and organize childcare with other parents, and the types of training they would like in order to be more competent in their parent-involvement activities. Alvaro found that gaining better understandings about families' situations and needs was the first step in creating better parent-involvement conditions. His yearly routine of getting to know his students' families and asking for specific preferences on ways to participate in their children's education spread to the other primary classrooms.

School programs that aim to increase ELL parent involvement must consider differences in culture, income, education, and language. A recent policy brief by Arias and Morillo-Campbell (2008), "Promoting ELL Parental Involvement: Challenges in Contested Times," analyzes factors related to the implementation of effective family involvement with ELLs. The authors examine the types of barriers to ELL family engagement with schools as well as characteristics of traditional and nontraditional parent-involvement models. They argue that for schools to be successful at improving parent involvement they must look beyond traditional models that are based on white middle-class families. According to Arias and Morillo-Campbell, nontraditional models of ELL parental involvement give the best results when "variation in language proficiency is acknowledged, communication is facilitated and maintained, and communities are recognized and integrated within the school culture" (p. 1).

Creating a Welcoming School Environment

The most important aspect of effective family-involvement efforts is a welcoming and nonthreatening school environment. A school can have a very well thought-out and comprehensive parent-involvement program that is ineffective simply because the overall school climate is unwelcoming and not responsive to the needs of ELL families. Creating an inviting, caring, and receptive school environment is especially useful in helping ELL parents and families overcome their apprehensions about being involved in their children's school. Sometimes, though, what we consider to be a welcoming school environment might not be perceived as friendly or open for parents unfamiliar with U.S. school culture. For example, parents may not understand why in some schools there might be a security or police officer at the front door or why they have to sign their names every time they come to the school if the school staff already knows them. Other, subtler messages, such as culturally based communication differences, can be interpreted as unwelcoming by families. For example, in many countries when parents visit their child's school they are expected to wait until an office staff member approaches them. In U.S. schools, the office staff may well ignore parents waiting to be helped or may be annoyed that the parents don't communicate why they are there or what they need.

A good way to understand what may or may not be welcoming is to walk into a school and see it through the lens of an ELL parent. This simple exercise can be quite revealing by bringing things to our attention that we normally take for granted. In putting ourselves in the shoes of ELL parents, we might be able to understand how they feel, for example, when they find the school's front door locked or when they have to go through a metal detector to get into their child's school.

Mrs. Nguyen, a recent immigrant from Vietnam, recalls her early experiences in her children's new school in the United States. She and her family moved to a large urban school district in the United States from a rural Vietnamese village where her oldest child attended a small multigrade school. Both Mr. and Mrs. Nguyen had little experience with schooling in Vietnam because both had only completed primary education. Recognizing their own lack of opportunities because of their limited schooling, they were very committed to having their children do well in school in the United States, with high hopes that all three would eventually attend college. Even though Mrs. Nguyen was very enthusiastic about helping her children do well in school, she found it difficult to connect and communicate with the teachers and principal. She felt intimidated by the school staff and didn't perceive them as being very welcoming or open. Mrs. Nguyen, who years later joined the school's PBAC and became a very involved parent, remembers feeling scared and nervous whenever she was at the school and trying to avoid it as much as possible. She remembers feeling intimidated by the office assistant, who was always very busy and showed little patience. She also felt unwelcomed because the front door of the school was locked, and she was scared by the security guards.

However, Mrs. Nguyen felt it was her embarrassment at her lack of English proficiency that kept her from participating in her children's school.

She remembers feeling especially inadequate about not being able to read or understand the written notices that her children brought home from school. Over time, Mrs. Nguyen began to understand the school culture and overcame her fears about going to her children's school. She later shared these negative experiences with teachers and staff to help the school become more welcoming and nonthreatening for ELL parents.

The purpose of understanding what might be unwelcoming to parents is not only to adjust how and what we do but also to clarify to parents those issues about U.S. school culture and norms that might be unfamiliar or uncomfortable to them. Ongoing and open communication is essential for creating a welcoming climate for ELLs and their families. Interactions between ELL parents and schools should be through two-way communication, where parents have regular opportunities to express their needs and concerns and to share their ideas. Improving ELL family participation and engagement can be done through multiple methods, including bilingual newsletters, community liaisons, home visits, regular phone calls, and after-school-hours meetings and trainings (see Figure 5-8).

Community Outreach

Because childrearing and learning development are often a joint effort between parents, families, schools, and communities, Epstein and Sheldon (2006) believe that "school, family, and community partnerships" is more appropriate than the narrower term "parent involvement." Epstein's (2001) theory of "overlapping spheres of influence" suggests that home, school, and community interact with one another in influencing children's education and development. In addition, the term "parent involvement" may unintentionally exclude students who are cared for or raised by extended family members, grandparents, or other adults. Shifting to a family-community approach to involvement offers a broader and more meaningful engagement by all stakeholders.

Community Centers and Agencies

Partnerships between schools and community-based organizations, local government agencies, and neighborhood businesses not only help to support ELLs' education but also can improve the quality of life for communities and families. Community-based centers and government agencies offer assistance on issues that directly or indirectly affect children's learning, such as health, safety, nutrition, legal services, and educational support. Schools that have close relationships with community and local government agencies can tap into the types of services they are often not able to provide themselves. These services include after-school tutoring, ESL classes and continuing education for adults, immigration assistance and citizenship classes,

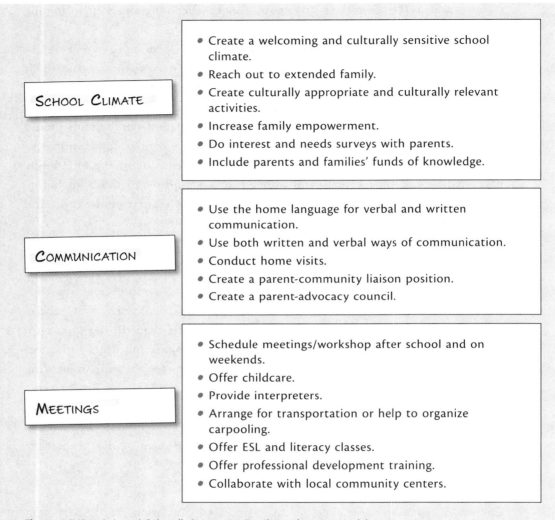

SCHOOL CLIMATE

- Create a welcoming and culturally sensitive school climate.
- Reach out to extended family.
- Create culturally appropriate and culturally relevant activities.
- Increase family empowerment.
- Do interest and needs surveys with parents.
- Include parents and families' funds of knowledge.

COMMUNICATION

- Use the home language for verbal and written communication.
- Use both written and verbal ways of communication.
- Conduct home visits.
- Create a parent-community liaison position.
- Create a parent-advocacy council.

MEETINGS

- Schedule meetings/workshop after school and on weekends.
- Offer childcare.
- Provide interpreters.
- Arrange for transportation or help to organize carpooling.
- Offer ESL and literacy classes.
- Offer professional development training.
- Collaborate with local community centers.

Figure 5-8 Linguistic and Culturally Responsive Family Involvement Model

medical and social services, and clothing/food bank aid. Community youth centers also provide the types of after-school activities that help ELLs become better adjusted to their new language and culture in a less academic and more fun environment than in schools. ELLs can participate in social and sports activities that help build their self-esteem, teach them about cooperation and leadership, encourage positive personal and social growth, and increase their cross-cultural understandings. For ELLs who live in high crime areas, community youth centers also provide a welcome relief from a dangerous environment.

For adults, community centers provide helpful information, resources, and training. They often serve as liaisons between the community and government agencies like the public library, department of transportation, health department, police department, and legal aid. Some community-based organizations also assist communities in setting up effective school-family advocacy partnerships to promote positive change in schools and districts. A school-family-community partnership approach offers the best opportunities for participation and engagement and also involves everyone in more meaningful ways. Creating better coordination between schools, families, and communities allows parents to have a more active role in school improvement efforts. School-family-community partnerships can be a powerful force that results in positive change for students' quality of education. At the district and state levels, such partnerships can be very effective in persuading officials and administrators to address problems that result in overcrowded, underfunded, and unsafe schools.

Establishing ongoing partnerships requires open communication, a shared vision, and building of trust between families, community, and schools. There are many ways to go about creating strong and long-lasting partnerships. For example, adult classes and trainings offered by community centers can be hosted at the school so that families can more easily access these services during school hours. Such is the case in the partnership between an urban elementary school and a neighborhood social service agency that offers adult ESL classes at the school. Schools and community centers can also coordinate efforts to create sustainable volunteer programs.

Community agencies that have a senior center, for example, can tap into their rich language and cultural backgrounds and train these seniors to work as volunteers in schools and classrooms. A Chinatown agency does just this by having their senior center participants volunteer in their preschool program. The seniors help children during center time, read to them, tutor them in math and writing Chinese, and share traditional songs and poetry from China. Another idea to create sustainable structures for effective collaboration is by forming a school-family-community council made up of school leaders, teachers, parents, students, and community members. A school-family-community council can serve as the place to

discuss issues, solve issues and problems, consider new ideas, and help create ways
to implement new systems and approaches for improvement.

School-Business Partnerships

In addition to joining forces with local community centers and government agencies, schools can set up partnerships with local businesses to help improve the
academic and social well-being of students. Partnerships between local business
and schools tend to be in the form of contributions from the businesses to the
schools, such as donations of funds, goods, or services to support instructional
programs and activities. Businesses can provide curriculum materials, volunteers
and mentors, products and services, and can organize special events, fundraising,
or other activities. More recently, schools and local businesses have moved to a more
collaborative model that includes a socially responsible approach that results in
mutually beneficial outcomes for students, community, and businesses. School and
business leaders recognize the benefits in supporting community-building and collaborative efforts that improve the quality of life for the whole community. More
in-depth school-business partnerships may offer college scholarships, work-study
programs, school-to-career partnerships, field trips to workplaces, internships, and
job shadowing.

A well-known private high school in a poor Latino neighborhood of Chicago has
successfully implemented a work-study model for almost fifteen years. All students
work once a week in entry-level jobs in downtown firms. The program offers them
valuable work experience and also helps them partially fund their education at this
college-preparatory school. The school has partnered with over sixty businesses
and agencies, including healthcare centers, law firms, banks, community colleges,
consulting agencies, and engineering companies.

A word of caution in establishing a school-business partnership: educators need
to make sure the companies they collaborate with share values and goals similar
to those of the school. Businesses that aim to use the school for commercial and
publicity gains by advertising on school grounds, selling products and services, and
marketing to students and their families would compromise the spirit of the partnership. In response to concerns about the increasing presence of "commercialism"
in schools, the National Association of Secondary School Principals (NASSP) pro-

vides a number of recommendations for educators looking for appropriate business partners. Some of these recommendations include:

* *Choosing companies that promote academics and learning:* Businesses that promote a field of study or skill and support student achievement are likely to be well received and less controversial.

* *Assessing the school's needs:* Conduct a cost/benefit analysis to determine whether to accept corporate support.

* *Determining the corporate motives:* Consider the expectations that businesses may have of the school. These can range from companies' "marginal" commercial benefits and philanthropic efforts to more aggressive direct marketing to students and families.

* *Avoid making decisions in a vacuum:* Get input from parents, teachers, administrators, and student leaders.

* *Considering the political climate:* Be aware of companies' connections to controversial issues or practices that may carry negative consequences for the school.

* *Doing the research and knowing the facts:* Seek insight from consumer groups that have focused on business education partnerships, including Consumers' Union, the Society of Consumer Affairs Professionals, and the International Organization of Consumers' Unions.

Epstein and Sheldon's (2006) view, that engaging families in their children's education through school-family-community partnerships is a highly effective way to promote students' success, is especially relevant to ELLs. Implementing the types of practices described above to help improve and increase family and community engagement requires commitment and well-planned coordination among all stakeholders. At the heart of successful and sustainable family-involvement programs and community partnerships is a shared commitment to improve the education opportunities and academic achievement of all students, including ELLs.

APPLICATIONS ||||||||||||||||||||||||||||||||||||||||||||||||||||||||||||||||||||||||||||||||||||||||||||||||

1. In *Claiming Opportunities: A Handbook for Improving Education for English Language Learners Through Comprehensive School Reform* (2003), the authors present nine research-based principles (listed below) for building an "ELL-responsive environment." For each of the principles think of two or three additional recommendations that could be implemented at your school site. Included under each of the principles is one example of a concrete recommendation to better guide you in thinking of additional suggestions.

Principle 1: School leaders, administrators, and educators recognize that educating ELLs is the responsibility of the entire school staff.

Recommendation—All staff have access to appropriate professional development in educating ELLs.

Principle 2: Educators recognize the heterogeneity of the student population that is collectively labeled as "ELL" and are able to vary their responses to the needs of different learners.

Recommendation—Consider ELLs' age when designing instruction, especially for older beginner-level proficient students.

Principle 3: The school climate and general practice reinforce the principle that students' languages and cultures are resources for further learning.

Recommendation—View ELLs' backgrounds and experiences as valuable assets that can be used to bridge instruction.

Principle 4: There are strong and seamless links connecting home, school, and community.

Recommendation—The school staff includes adults from students' heritage communities and speakers of their languages.

Principle 5: ELLs have equitable access to all school resources and programs.

Recommendation—ELLs have access to all enrichment and extracurricular activities.

Principle 6: Teachers have high expectations for ELLs.

Recommendation—Make appropriate modifications according to ELLs' language proficiency levels while maintaining a challenging and rigorous curriculum.

Principle 7: Teachers are properly prepared and willing to teach ELLs.

Recommendation—Teachers foster meaningful relationships with students.

Principle 8: Language and literacy are infused throughout the educational process, including curriculum and instruction.

Recommendation—ELL students have many opportunities to hear comprehensible language and to read comprehensible texts.

Principle 9: Assessment is authentic, credible to learners and instructors, and takes into account first and second language literacy development.

Recommendation—Teachers include native-language competence in assessment of an ELL's overall academic accomplishment.

2. Create an advocacy project with students to engage them in improving the conditions in their classroom, school, or community and connect it to academic content such as literacy, math, or social sciences. Select an issue that is relevant to students and their families (for example, dealing with overcrowded classrooms, an underfunded school library, neighborhood graffiti). Describe how the advocacy message will be delivered (for example, through performance, video, concert, art exhibition, poster, book, or PowerPoint presentation) and the type of follow-up activities to enact change in the classroom, school, or community.

3. Think of the most prominent challenges and problems in your school, or a school that you have observed recently, and create a plan of action for advocacy aimed at district administrators, government agencies, city/town officials, and policymakers. First, describe the issue and explain why it is important. Second, describe the types of advocacy activities that will be used (letters and presentations to decision makers, petitions, proposals for improvement, testifying in front of boards or legislation, collecting signatures, voter mobilization, physical protests, using the media, etc.). Third, create a follow-up plan of action. Refer to suggestions from this chapter to formulate the activities and follow-up plan.

4. Create a proposal for a family-engagement and community-outreach program to present to the leadership team at your school or to the board of a school district. Integrate the elements mentioned in this chapter and add at least two other ideas each for family, community, and local business partnerships.

SUGGESTIONS FOR FURTHER READING ||||||||||||||||||||||||||||||||

Delgado Gaitan, Concha. 2004. *Involving Latino Families in Schools: Raising Students' Achievement Through Home-School Partnerships*. Thousand Oaks, CA: Corwin.

Hamayan, Else, and Rebecca Freeman. 2006. *English Language Learners at School: A Guide for Administrators*. Philadelphia: Carlson.

Olivos, Edward. 2006. *The Power of Parents: A Critical Perspective of Bicultural Parent Involvement in Public Schools*. New York: Peter Lang Publishing.

Smiley, Patricia, and Trudy Salsberry. 2007. *Effective Schooling for English Language Learners: What Elementary Principals Should Know and Do*. Larchmont, NY: Eye on Education.

CONCLUSIONS: CHALLENGES AND OPPORTUNITIES TO ACHIEVE A PROMISING FUTURE FOR ELLS

The extent to which teachers and school leaders recognize and assume a shared schoolwide responsibility for educating ELLs directly contributes to their academic success or failure. Schools that affirm and promote ELLs' language and cultural backgrounds, take into account their social and economic circumstances, adopt a collective approach to their education, and promote the participation of their families and communities are in the best position to advance improvements in their education. Districts and schools across the United States face increasing challenges in providing ELLs culturally and linguistically responsive quality education that will help close the achievement gap between them and their English-speaking peers.

The rapid growth in the numbers of ELLs in PreK–12 schools, especially in rural and suburban areas not traditionally populated by immigrants, together with NCLB's accountability mandates to improve ELLs' academic outcomes, have compelled many districts and schools to rethink how ELLs are educated. Consistent underachievement among ELLs over the past decades shows that what we have been doing is not adequate in providing the best education opportunities for ELLs. Obstacles to providing the most favorable conditions for ELLs to be successful in schools begin with issues related to the education workforce. The shortage of trained bilingual and ESL teachers, inadequate teacher and school-leader preparation programs that lack ELL-related coursework, and insufficient ELL professional development opportunities are all factors that must be addressed and remedied to improve ELLs' education. Especially troubling is the limited number of school leaders with ELL training or knowledge of the relevant issues. Teacher and administrator certification programs at universities must respond by increasing and improving preparation of all educators to address the needs of ELLs. State boards of education must also review and reformulate their ELL policies so they are more closely aligned to current research findings and recommendations.

Bilingual education also needs to be reconsidered and reframed. On the surface the argument seems to be only about a choice of language of instruction, but a closer look shows that it is a political hot-button subject. Suárez-Orozco and Suárez-Orozco (2001) point out that language is "a marker of identity and an instrument of power" (p. 135). Opposition to bilingual education in the United States often comes from several sources: misinformation about second language acquisition; the perceived failure of native-language instruction programs; the belief that national unity and the English language are threatened; immigrants' perceived failure and/or resistance to learning English; and an assumed higher cost to educating ELLs. The most persistent beliefs are that native-language instruction prevents or slows down the development of the second language, and that immersion in the second language is the fastest way to develop it. Extensive research in second language acquisition and in education does not support the idea that native-language instruction is bad for second language development. There is strong evidence that a foundation in the primary language has positive effects on the development of the second language (Genesee et al. 2006).

One key premise repeated throughout this book is how important it is for all teachers and school leaders to become knowledgeable about the theories, research, and practices related to second language learners. Teachers and school leaders are more likely to make effective decisions about the education of ELLs if they have a clear understanding of the basic concepts of second language acquisition and language-minority education. Commonly held but mistaken beliefs about second language acquisition, bilingualism, and ELLs often result in inadequate and mis-guided policies that interfere with and delay ELLs' academic progress.

Another critical aspect is the idea of developing inclusive schoolwide frameworks that support the academic achievement of ELLs. This approach places responsibility for ELLs' education success on all aspects of the school organization rather than on bilingual and ESL programs and teachers alone. Such a collective and collab-orative approach includes creating a positive and safe school climate for ELLs and their families, providing opportunities for professional development that integrates ELL-related topics, school leaders actively engaging in advocacy and support efforts, building systems to improve school organization and programmatic elements, and promoting family-community involvement. Schools that can successfully coordinate and align programs are in the best position to support the educational attainment of *all* students, including ELLs. Such coordination ensures that there is compatibility and alignment between curricular programs, instructional and assessment practices, instructional materials, school policies, and family-community initiatives.

Schools with ELLs should also offer a culturally and linguistically responsive curriculum that takes into account the sociocultural and political conditions under which most ELLs and their families live. Culturally responsive and linguistically appropriate instructional approaches and materials can accelerate ELLs' language acquisition and academic progress. Instructional practices that use active engagement, learner-centered strategies, and authentic learning activities as opposed to remedial and direct instruction are the most effective approaches to engaging ELLs in meaningful learning. Other important elements of effective instruction include using ELLs' prior knowledge, increasing their motivation and maintaining interest, and helping them to become independent learners.

Family involvement and community outreach that enhance an affirmative and collaborative school climate are very valuable in helping to improve ELLs' learning and to give them a more positive school experience. With appropriate support from schools, families can become important "partners in learning" and provide their children added support systems for success in school. Community outreach efforts can offer expanded support systems for families and children through partnerships with local organizations, businesses, and universities. These collaborations can provide many types of assistance and support to the school and families. School-family-community partnerships can also provide an excellent forum for engaging in advocacy efforts to change conditions and policies that interfere with ELLs' academic progress. Undertaking advocacy efforts can be done both small- and large-scale, with community and educators joining forces to demand fair treatment and equitable distribution of resources.

This book presents the many aspects that need to be considered in creating sustainable and effective improvements for ELL education. The recommendations for schoolwide reform presented here are based on extensive research that points to the best practices and approaches for enhancing ELLs' learning experiences and advancing their academic achievement. Even though there has been increasing national attention to ELLs as well as some noteworthy advances in their education, there is still much that needs to be done to improve their school experiences, support their learning, and promote their academic achievement.

Appendix A

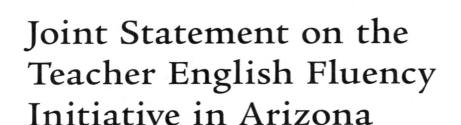

Joint Statement on the Teacher English Fluency Initiative in Arizona

According to recent media reports, the Arizona Department of Education has mandated that teachers whose spoken English it deems to be heavily accented or ungrammatical must be removed from classes for students still learning English. It is reported that the intent of this initiative is to ensure that students with limited English have teachers who speak the language flawlessly.

For decades the field of English language teaching has suffered from the myth that one only needs to be a native English speaker in order to teach the English language. The myth further implicates that native English speakers make better English as a second language (ESL) or English as a foreign language (EFL) teachers than nonnative English speakers because native English speakers are perceived to speak "unaccented" English and understand and use idiomatic expressions fluently. The distinction between native and nonnative speakers of English presents an oversimplified, either/or classification system that is not only misleading, but also ignores the formal education, linguistic expertise, teaching experience, and professional preparation of educators in the field of English language teaching.

TESOL has long opposed discrimination against nonnative English speakers in the field of English language teaching. All English language educators should be proficient in English regardless of their native languages, but English language proficiency should be viewed as only one criterion in evaluating a teacher's qualifications. English language proficiency, teaching experience, and professionalism should be assessed along a continuum of professional preparation; pedagogical skills, teaching experience, and professional preparation should be given as much weight as language proficiency.

TESOL and its Arizona affiliate AZ-TESOL have great concerns about this teacher English fluency evaluation initiative and its impact upon English language learners. Nonnative English-speaking educators should not be singled out because of their native language, nor evaluated based on arbitrary standards of language fluency. All educators should be evaluated in a transparent manner along the same criteria based on clearly articulated and valid standards. The *TESOL-NCATE Standards for P–12 Teacher Preparation Programs*, which provide standards and rubrics designed to help teacher education programs identify evidence of teacher performance, can be useful resources for institutions.

With the recent state legislation targeting undocumented immigrants in Arizona (SB 1070) and other legislation banning ethnic studies in Arizona (HB 2281), TESOL and AZ-TESOL are deeply troubled by what appears to be an environment of fear and xenophobia being fostered by lawmakers in the state without consideration of the consequences upon student learning and achievement. This impacts all educators and students, including U.S. citizens and legal permanent residents who speak a language other than English. The right of undocumented students to a K–12 public education has long been protected under U.S. law. TESOL and Arizona TESOL strongly urge lawmakers and education officials in Arizona to ensure that the education of all Arizona schoolchildren is not harmed by these developments, and that the right of all educators to be treated fairly and equally is protected.

www.tesol.org/s_tesol/bin.asp?CID=80&DID=13248&DOC=FILE.PDF

Joint Statement on the Teacher English Fluency Initiative in Arizona May 2010. www.tesol.org/s_tesol/bin.asp?CID=80&DID=13248&DOC=FILE.PDF.

Appendix B

Statement of NCTE Against Arizona Department of Education Ruling on Teacher Speech

NCTE Speaks Out on Arizona Department of Education Ruling on Teacher Speech

Evaluate Teachers on Their Competence, Not on Their Accents

June 7, 2010

The effects of a new Arizona Department of Education policy are reverberating in the literacy education community. According to numerous reports, the Department has told school districts that teachers whose spoken English it deems to be heavily accented or ungrammatical must be removed from classes for students still learning English.

This edict is dangerously misguided. Confirmed by research and by policy positions adopted by the National Council of Teachers of English, what matters most in teaching non-native English language learners is not elocution or adherence to a single dialect or speech pattern. What matters most is understanding students and the dynamics of language learning.

Teachers who have deep roots in the culture and linguistic experiences of their students are well equipped for success in teaching English, regardless of their spoken dialect or accent. A recent NCTE position paper on "The Role of English Teachers in Educating English Language Learners (ELLs)" emphasizes the importance of empathy, connections to ELL students' families and culture, and innovative teaching methods:

> Knowledge of the students is key to good teaching. Because teachers relate to students both as learners and as children or adolescents, teachers must establish how they will address two types of relationships, what they need to know about their students, and how they will acquire this knowledge. The teacher-learner relationship implies involvement between teachers and students around subject matter and language and literacy proficiency in both languages. Adult-child relationships are more personal and should include the family. Focusing on both types of relationships bridges the gap between school and the world outside it, a gap that is especially important for many bilingual students whose world differs greatly from school.

The NCTE position paper further asserts that all teachers of ELL students in all content-area subjects must provide effective instruction for students developing academic proficiency in English by:

- Recognizing that second language acquisition is a gradual developmental process and is built on students' knowledge and skill in their native language;
- Providing authentic opportunities to use language in a nonthreatening environment;
- Teaching key vocabulary connected with the topic of the lesson;
- Teaching academic oral language in the context of various content areas;

- Teaching text- and sentence-level grammar in context to help students understand the structure and style of the English language;

- Teaching the specific features of language students need to communicate in social as well as academic contexts.

Teaching English language learners well is difficult. The urgent need for more highly-adept teachers to meet the demand makes the Arizona ban so invidious: teachers who may best understand the cultural and family dynamics of their ELL students, who are living the gradual developmental process that characterizes second language acquisition, are barred from the classrooms where they are needed most.

We would have a different problem had the Arizona guideline directed reassignment of teachers of ELL students

* who are unsuccessful at teaching academic oral content in math, science, social studies, or the arts;

* who fail to teach key vocabulary or grammar in the context of helping students understand English for school or other purposes;

* who are unable to provide authentic challenges for applying language to solve problems in the lives of students or their families.

There would still be fewer ELL teachers in Arizona classrooms, but those missing wouldn't be identified by their accents. We would be focusing on the real problem: competence.

If the Arizona Department of Education wants to upgrade the quality of instruction for English language learners, it could heed the need for professional knowledge among all teachers about how to serve ELL students. Based on research, NCTE's policy states that:

> The majority of ELLs are in mainstream classrooms taught by teachers with little or no formal professional development in teaching ELL students (Barron & Menken, 2002; Kindler, 2002). Many teachers are not adequately prepared to work with a linguistically diverse student population (American Federation of Teachers, 2004; Fillmore & Snow, 2002; Gándara, Rumberger, Maxwell-Jolly, & Callahan, 2003; Menken & Antunez, 2001; Nieto, 2003).

NCTE encourages English teachers to collaborate and work closely with ESL and bilingual teaching professionals who can offer classroom support, instructional advice, and general insights into second language acquisition. School administrators should support and encourage teachers to attend workshops and professional conferences on bilingual learners, particularly in the areas of reading and writing.

It's time to put sound educational principles ahead of misguided cultural assumptions. We have real work to do unlocking the miraculous potential of a generation of ELL students. Let's use what educators know about language learning to make decisions about fostering the literacy skills of all students.

The National Council of Teachers of English, with 50,000 individual and institutional members worldwide, is dedicated to improving the teaching and learning of English and the language arts at all levels of education. For more information, please visit http://www.ncte.org.

www.ncte.org/library/NCTEFiles/Involved/Action/NCTEpositiononAZELL rules.pdf

Statement of NCTE Against Arizona Department of Education Ruling on Teacher Speech. June 2010. www.ncte.org/library/NCTEFiles/Involved/Action/ NCTEpositiononAZELLrules.pdf.

Appendix C

Organizations and Centers: Advocacy and Information

Professional Organizations	
ILEP	Institute on Language and Education Policy www.elladvocates.org
NABE	National Association for Bilingual Education www.nabe.org/advocacy.html
ASCD	Association for Supervision and Curriculum Development www.ascd.org/
DLENM	Dual Language Education of New Mexico www.dlenm.org/
NAME	National Association for Multicultural Education http://nameorg.org/

Centers	
CAL	Center for Applied Linguistics www.cal.org/
CREDE	Center for Research on Education, Diversity & Excellence http://crede.berkeley.edu/
IRC	Illinois Resource Center www.thecenterweb.org/irc/
NCELA	National Clearinghouse for English Language Acquisition www.ncela.gwu.edu/
NHLRC	National Heritage Language Resource Center http://nhlrc.ucla.edu/
	The Pew Hispanic Center http://pewhispanic.org/

REFERENCES

Ada, Alma F. 1995. "Creative Education for Bilingual Teachers." In *Policy and Practice in Bilingual Education: Extending the Foundations*, ed. Ofelia García and Colin Baker, 237–43. Philadelphia: Multilingual Matters Ltd.

Adams, Marilyn. 1990. Beginning to Read: Thinking and Learning about Print. Cambridge, MA: MIT Press.

American Federation of Teachers, AFL-CIO. 2006. "Where We Stand: English Language Learners." www.aft.org/pdfs/teachers/wwsell1106.pdf.

Arias, Beatriz M., and Milagros Morillo-Campbell. 2008. "Promoting ELL Parental Involvement: Challenges in Contested Times." East Lansing, MI: The Great Lakes Center for Education Research & Practice.

Arias, Beatriz M. 2007. "School Desegregation, Linguistic Segregation and Access to English for Latino Students." *Journal of Educational Controversy*. www.wce.wwu.edu/Resources/CEP/eJournal/v002n001/a008.shtml.

August, Diane, and Kenji Hakuta. 1997. *Improving Schooling for Language Minority Children*. Washington, DC: National Academy Press.

August, Diane, and Timothy Shanahan. 2006. *Developing Literacy in Second-Language Learners: Report of the National Literacy Panel on Language-Minority Children and Youth*. Mahwah, NJ: Lawrence Erlbaum Associates.

August, Diane, and Timothy Shanahan. 2010. "Effective English Literacy Instruction for English Language Learners." In *Improving Education for English Learners: Research-Based Approaches*, 209–49. Sacramento, CA: California Department of Education.

Baker, Colin. 2006. *Foundations of Bilingualism and Bilingual Education*. Clevedon, UK: Multilingual Matters.

Baker, Colin, and Sylvia P. Jones. 1998. *Encyclopedia of Bilingualism and Bilingual Education*. Clevedon, UK: Multilingual Matters.

Bakker, Joep, and Eddie Denessen. 2007. "The Concept of Parent Involvement. Some Theoretical and Empirical Considerations." *International Journal about Parents in Education* 1: 188–99.

Ballantyne, Keira G., Alicia R. Sanderman, and Jack Levy. 2008. "Educating English Language Learners: Building Teacher Capacity." Washington, DC: National

Clearinghouse for English Language Acquisition. www.ncela.gwu.edu/practice/mainstream_teachers.html.

Bartolomé, Lilia I. 1994. "Teaching Strategies: Their Possibilities and Limitations." In *Language and Learning: Educating Linguistically Diverse Students*, ed. Beverly McLeod, 199–223. New York: State University of New York Press.

Bartolomé, Lilia I. 2000. "Democratizing Bilingualism: The Role of Critical Teacher Education." In *Lifting Every Voice: Politics and Pedagogy of Bilingualism*, ed. Zeynep F. Beykont, 167–86. Cambridge, MA: Harvard Education Publishing Group.

Becker, Adeline. 2003. *Claiming Opportunities: A Handbook for Improving Education for English Language Learners through Comprehensive School Reform*. The Education Alliance. Brown University. www.alliance.brown.edu/pubs/claiming_opportunities/claimopp_1.pdf.

Bialystok, Ellen, Fergus I. Craik, and Jennifer Ryan. 2006. "Executive Control in a Modified Anti-Saccade Task: Effects of Aging and Bilingualism." *Journal of Experimental Psychology: Learning, Memory and Cognition* 32: 1341–54.

Britton, James. 1992. *Language and Learning: The Importance of Speech in Children's Development*. New York: Penguin Books.

Brooks-Gunn, Jeanne, and Greg J. Duncan. 1997. "The Effects of Poverty on Children." *The Future of Children: Children and Poverty* 7: 55–71.

Callahan, Rebecca. 2006. "The Intersection of Accountability and Language: Can Reading Intervention Replace English Language Development?" *Bilingual Research Journal* 30(1): 1–21.

Caldas, Stephen, and Nicole Boudreaux. 1999. "Poverty, Race, and Foreign Language Immersion: Predictors of Math and English Language Arts Performance." *Learning Languages* 4–15.

Campos, Jim S. 1995. "The Carpinteria Preschool Program: A Long-Term Effects Study." In *Meeting the Challenge of Linguistic and Cultural Diversity in Early Childhood Education*, ed. Eugene E. García and Barry McLaughlin, 34–48. New York: Teachers College Press.

Capps, Randy, Michael Fix, Julie Murray, Jason Ost, Jeffery Passel, and Shinta Herwantoro. 2005. *The New Demography of America's Schools: Immigration and the No Child Left Behind Act*. Washington, DC: The Urban Institute. www.urban.org/UploadedPDF/311230_new_demography.pdf.

Cárdenas-Hagan, Elsa, Coleen D. Carlson, and Sharolyn D. Pollard-Durodola. 2007. "The Cross-Linguistic Transfer of Early Literacy Skills: The Role of Initial L1 and

L2 Skills and Language of Instruction." *Language, Speech, and Hearing Services in Schools* 38: 249–59.

Cazden, Courtney B. 1988. *Classroom Discourse: The Language of Teaching and Learning.* Portsmouth, NH: Heinemann.

Contreras, Frances E. 2010. "The Role of High Stakes Testing and Accountability in Educating Latinos." In *Handbook of Latinos and Education: Theory, Research and Practice*, ed. Enrique G. Murillo, Sofia A. Villenas, Ruth Trinidad Galván, Juan Sánchez Muñoz Murillo, Corinne Martínez, and Margarita Machado-Casas, 194–209. New York, NY: Routledge.

Corder, Pit S. 1967. "The Significance of Learners' Errors." *International Review of Applied Linguistics* 5: 161–69.

Corson, David. 2001. *Language Diversity and Education.* Mahwah, NJ: Lawrence Erlbaum Associates.

Collier, Virginia P. 1995. "Acquiring a Second Language for School." *Directions in Language and Education* 4: 1–2.

Collier, Virginia P., and Wayne P. Thomas. 2009. *Educating English Learners for a Transformed World.* Albuquerque, NM: Fuente Press.

Coltrane, Bronwyn. 2002. "Team Teaching: Meeting the Needs of English Language Learners Through Collaboration." *Center for Applied Linguistics* 25: 6–7.

Cortés, Carlos E. 1986. "The Education of Language Minority Students: A Contextual Interaction Model." In *Beyond Language: Social and Cultural Factors in Schooling Language Minority Students*, ed. Carlos. E. Cortés, 3–33. Evaluation, Dissemination, and Assessment Center, Los Angeles: California State University.

Commins, Nancy L., and Ofelia B. Miramontes. 2005. *Linguistic Diversity and Teaching.* Mahwah, NJ: Lawrence Erlbaum Associates.

Crawford, James. 1992. *Hold Your Tongue: Bilingualism and the Politics of English Only.* New York: Addison-Wesley.

Crawford, James. 2001. *At War with Diversity.* Clevedon, UK: Multilingual Matters.

Cummins, James. 1979. "Linguistic Interdependence and the Educational Development of Bilingual Children." *Review of Educational Research* 49: 222–51.

Cummins, James. 2000. *Language, Power and Pedagogy: Bilingual Children in the Crossfire.* Clevedon, UK: Multilingual Matters.

Cummins, James. 2006. "Bilingual Development in Educational Contexts: Canadian Perspectives and Issues." Presented at the Language Acquisition and Bilingualism

Conference. Toronto, Canada. www.psych.yorku.ca/labconference/documents/Cummins.pdf.

Cummins, James. 2008. "BICS and CALP: Empirical and Theoretical Status of the Distinction." In *Encyclopedia of Language and Education. Volume 2: Literacy*, ed. Nancy H. Hornberger, 71–83. New York: Springer Science + Business Media LLC.

Cummins, James. 2008. "Teaching for Transfer: Challenging the Two Solitudes Assumption in Bilingual Education." In *Encyclopedia of Language and Education. Volume 5: Bilingual Education*, ed. Nancy H. Hornberger, 1528–38. New York: Springer Science + Business Media LLC.

Cummins, James. 2009. "Fundamental Psycholinguistic and Sociological Principles Underlying Educational Success for Linguistic Minority Students." In *Social Justice through Multilingual Education*, ed. Tove Skutnabb-Kangas, Robert Phillipson, Ajit K. Mohanty, and Minati Panda, 19–35. Bristol, UK: Multilingual Matters.

Darder, Antonia. 1997. "Creating the Conditions for Cultural Democracy in the Classroom." In *Crossing Cultural Borders: Education for Immigrant Families in America*, ed. Concha

Delgado-Gaitan, Concha, and Henry Trueba. 1991. *Crossing Cultural Borders: Education for Immigrant Families in America*. New York, NY: The Palmer Press.

Delfino, Aleman, Joseph F. Johnson, and Lynne Perez. 2009. "Winning Schools for ELLs." *Educational Leadership* 4: 66–69.

de los Reyes, Eileen, David Nieto, and Virginia Diez. 2008. *If Our Students Fail, We Fail. If They Succeed, We Succeed: Case Studies of Boston Schools Where Latino Students Succeed*. Mauricio Gaston Institute for Latino Community Development and Public Policy. www.gaston.umb.edu/articles/delosreyes_2008_Boston_Casestudies.pdf.

de Oliveira, Luciana C., and Steven Z. Athanases. 2007. "Graduates' Reports of Advocating for English Language Learners." *Journal of Teacher Education* 58: 202–15.

Dugger, Kathleen. 2007. Making Sense in Social Studies. www.readingquest.org/bkgd_sol.html.

Epstein, Joyce L., and Stephen B. Sheldon. 2006. Moving Forward: Ideas for Research on School, Family, and Community Partnerships. In *Handbook for Research in Education: Engaging Ideas and Enriching Inquiry*, ed. Clifton. F. Conrad and Ronald Serlin, 117–37. Thousand Oaks, CA: Sage Publications.

Epstein, Joyce L. 2001. *School, Family, and Community Partnerships: Preparing Educators and Improving Schools*. Boulder, CO: Westview.

Espinosa, Linda. 2007. "Second Language Acquisition in Early Childhood." In *Early Childhood Education*, ed. Rebecca New and Moncrieff Cochran, 72–79. Westport, CT: Greenwood Publishing Group.

Espinoza, Linda. 2008. "Challenging Common Myths about Young English Language Learners." *Foundation for Child Development Policy Brief, Advancing PK–3*, 8. New York: Foundation for Child Development.

Freeman, David, and Yvonne Freeman. 2006. *Teaching Reading and Writing in Spanish and English in Bilingual and Dual Language Classrooms*. Portsmouth, NH: Heinemann.

Freeman, David, and Yvonne Freeman. 2007. *English Language Learners: The Essential Guide*. New York: Scholastic.

Freire, Paolo. 2000. *Pedagogy of the Oppressed*. New York: Continuum International Publishing.

From Risk to Opportunity: Fulfilling the Educational Needs of Hispanic Americans in the 21st Century. 2003. The Final Report of the President's Advisory Commission on Educational Excellence for Hispanic Americans Commission Report. www.yesican .gov/paceea/finalreport.pdf.

Fry, Richard. 2008. *The Role of Schools in the English Language Learner Achievement Gap*. Pew Latino Center. pewhispanic.org/files/reports/89.pdf.

Gándara, Patricia, and Julie Maxwell-Jolly. 2005. "Critical Issues in the Development of the Teacher Corps for English Learners." In *Preparing Quality Teachers for English Language Learners*, ed. Hersh C. Waxman and Kip Tellez. Mahwah, NJ: Lawrence Erlbaum Associates.

Gándara, Patricia, and Megan Hopkins. 2010. *Forbidden Language: English Learners and Restrictive Language Policies*. New York: Teachers College Press.

García, Eugene. 2001. *Student Cultural Diversity: Understanding and Meeting the Challenge*. Boston: Houghton Mifflin.

García, Eugene E., Bryant T. Jensen, and Kent P. Scribner. 2009. "Supporting English Language Learners: The Demographic Imperative." *Educational Leadership* 66: 8–13.

García, Gilbert N. 2000. *What Is the Length of Time It Takes Limited English Proficient Students to Acquire English and Succeed in an All-English Classroom?* Research Brief. National Clearinghouse for Bilingual Education.

García, Mario T. 1991. *Mexican Americans: Leadership, Ideology, and Identity, 1930–1960*. New Haven, CT: Yale University Press.

García, Ofelia. 2009. *Bilingual Education in the 21st Century: A Global Perspective*. Oxford: Wiley/Blackwell.

Gay, Geneva. 2000. *Culturally Responsive Teaching: Theory, Research, & Practice*. New York: Teachers College Press.

Genesee, Fred, and Caroline Riches. 2006. "Literacy: Instructional Issues." In *Educating English Language Learners: A Synthesis of Research Evidence*, ed. Fred Genesee, Kathryn Lindholm-Leary, Bill Saunders, and Donna Christian, 109–75. New York: Cambridge University Press.

Genesee, Fred, Kathryn Lindholm-Leary, William Saunders, and Donna Christian. 2006. *Educating English Language Learners: A Synthesis of Research Evidence*. New York: Cambridge University Press.

Genesee, Fred, Johanne Paradis, and Martha B. Crago. 2004. *Dual Language Development and Disorders: A Handbook on Bilingualism and Second Language Learning*. Baltimore: Brookes Publishing.

Gifford, Bernard R., and Guadalupe Valdés. 2006. "The Linguistic Isolation of Hispanic Students in California's Public Schools: The Challenge of Reintegration." *Yearbook of the National Society for the Study of Education* 105: 125–54.

Goldenberg, Claude. 2008. "Teaching English Language Learners: What the Research Does and Does Not Say." *American Educator* 32: 42–44.

Goldenberg, Claude, and Rhoda Coleman. 2010. *Promoting Academic Achievement among English Learners: A Guide to the Research*. New York: Corwin.

Gottlieb, Margo. 1999. *The Language Proficiency Handbook: A Practitioner's Guide to Instructional Assessment*. Illinois State Board of Education, Assessment Division.

Graves, Michael F. 2006. *From the Vocabulary Book: Learning and Instruction*. New York: Teachers College Press.

Grosjean, François. 1982. *Life with Two Languages: An Introduction to Bilingualism*. Cambridge, MA: Harvard University Press.

Guiding Principles for Business and School Partnerships. The Council for Corporate and School Partnerships. www.corpschoolpartners.org/guiding_principles.html.

Hakuta, Kenji, Diane August, and Jennifer O'Day. 2009. *The American Recovery and Reinvestment Act: Recommendations for Addressing the Needs of English Language Learners*. ELL Working Group on ELL Policy. www.stanford.edu/~hakuta/ARRA/ELL%20 Stimulus%20Recommendations.pdf.

Hakuta, Kenji, Yuko Goto Butler, and Daria Witt. *How Long Does It Take English Language Learners to Attain Proficiency?* 2000. Policy Report 2000-1, Santa Barbara:

The University of California Linguistic Minority Research Institute. www.usc.edu/dept/education/CMMR/FullText/Hakuta_HOW_LONG_DOES_IT_TAKE.pdf.

Heath, Shirley B. 1983. *Ways with Words: Language, Life and Work in Communities and Classrooms.* Cambridge: Cambridge University Press.

Hornberger, Nancy H. 1994. "Continua of Biliteracy." In *Literacy Across Languages and Cultures*, ed. Bernardo M. Ferdman, Rosemarie Weber, and Arnulfo G. Ramírez, 103–39. New York: State University of New York Press.

Horwitz, Amanda R., Gabriela Uro, Ricki Price-Baugh, Candace Simon, Renata Uzzell, Sharon Lewis, and Michael Casserly. 2009. *Succeeding with English Language Learners: Lessons Learned from the Great City Schools.* The Council of the Great City Schools. www.cgcs.org/publications/ELL_Report09.pdf.

Jeynes, William H. 2005. "A Meta-Analysis of the Relation of Parental Involvement to Urban Elementary School Student Academic Achievement." *Urban Education* 40: 237–69.

Johnson, David W., Roger T. Johnson, and Edythe J. Holubec. 1993. *Circles of Learning: Cooperation in the Classroom.* Edina, MN: Interaction Book.

Joint Statement on the Teacher English Fluency Initiative in Arizona May 2010. www.tesol.org/s_tesol/bin.asp?CID=80&DID=13248&DOC=FILE.PDF.

Kagan, Spencer. 1992. *Cooperative Learning.* Capistrano, CA: Kagan Cooperative Learning.

Karabenick, Stuart A., and Phyllis A. Clemens Noda. 2004. "Professional Development Implications of Teachers' Beliefs and Attitudes Toward English Language Learners." *Bilingual Research Journal* 28(1): 55–75.

Karra, Maria. 2006. "Second Language Acquisition: Learners' Errors and Error Correction in Language Teaching." *Translation Theory, Translator Education.* www.proz.com/translation-articles/articles/633/.

Katz, A. (2001). Weaving Assessment into a Standards-Based Curriculum. *NABE News* 24(6): 13–15.

Kidder, Tracy. 1990. *Among School Children.* New York: Harper Perennial.

Kohler, Adriana, and Melissa Lazarín. 2007. *Latino Education in the United States.* Statistical Brief No. 8. National Council of La Raza.

Krashen, Stephen. 1981. *Second Language Acquisition and Second Language Learning.* Oxford: Pergamon Press.

Krashen, Stephen. 1982. *Principles and Practices in Second Language Acquisition.* New York: Pergamon Press.

Krashen, Stephen. 1993. *The Power of Reading: Insights from the Research.* Englewood, CO: Libraries Unlimited.

Krashen, Stephen. 1996. *Every Person a Reader: An Alternative to the California Task Force Report on Reading.* Culver City, CA: Language Education Associates.

Krashen, Stephen. 2003. "Three Roles of Reading for Minority-Language Children." In *English Learners: Reaching the Highest Level of English Literacy*, ed. Gilbert García, 55–70. Newark, DE: Pearson.

Krashen, Stephen, and Grace McField. 2005. "What Works? Reviewing the Latest Evidence on Bilingual Education." *Language Learner* 1(2): 7–10, 34.

Ladson-Billings, Gloria. 2008. "I Ain't Writin' Nuttin': Permissions to Fail and Demands to Succeed in Urban Classrooms." In *The Skin That We Speak: Thoughts on Language and Culture in the Classroom*, ed. Lisa Delpit and Joanne Kilgour Dowdy, 109–20. New York: New Press.

Lagemann, Ellen Condliffe. 2004. Bilingual Benefits Interdisciplinary Perspectives Conference, Harvard Divinity School, Harvard.

Lara-Alecio, Rafael, Martha Galloway, Beverly J. Irby, and Genevieve Brown. 2004. "An Analysis of Texas Superintendents' Bilingual/ESL Teacher Recruitment and Retention Practices." Presented at the annual meeting of the American Educational Research Association, 2004. http://ldn.tamu.edu/Archives/rrAERA04.pdf.

Lindholm-Leary, Kathryn, and G. Bosarto. 2006. "Academic Achievement." In *Educating English Language Learners: A Synthesis of Research Findings*, ed. Fred Genesee, Kathryn Lindholm-Leary, William M. Saunders, and Donna Christian, 176–211. Cambridge: Cambridge University Press.

Linquanti, Robert, Thomas B. Parrish, Amy Merickel, and María Perez. 2006. *Effects of the Implementation of Proposition 227 on the Education of English Learners, K–12. Findings from a Five-Year Evaluation: Final Report.* American Institutes for Research and WestEd. www.wested.org/cs/we/view/rs/804.

Long, Michael H. 1996. "Authenticity and Learning Potential in L2 Classroom Discourse." In *Language Classrooms of Tomorrow: Issues and Responses*, ed. G. M. Jacobs, 148–69. Singapore: SEAMEO Regional Language Centre.

López, María Pabón, and Gerardo López. 2010. *Persistent Inequalities: Contemporary Realities in the Education of Undocumented Latina/o Students.* New York: Routledge.

López, Michael L., Sandra Barrueco, and Jonathan Miles. 2006. *Latino Infants and Their Families: A National Perspective of Protective and Risk Factors for Development.* National Task Force on Early Childhood Education for Latinos Report. Tempe, AZ: Arizona State University.

Marshall, Megan L. 2003. *Examining School Climate: Defining Factors and Educational Influences.* Center for Research on School Safety, School Climate and Classroom Management. http://education.gsu.edu/schoolsafety/download%20files/wp%202002%20school%20climate.pdf.

Marzano, Robert J. 2003. *What Works in Schools: Translating Research into Action.* Alexandria, VA: Association for Supervision and Curriculum.

Marzano, Robert J. 2004. *Building Background Knowledge for Academic Achievement: Research on What Works in Schools.* Alexandria, VA: ASCD.

McLaughlin, Barry. 1992. "Myths and Misconceptions about Second Language Learning: What Every Teacher Needs to Unlearn." *Educational Practice Report*: 5. National Center for Research on Cultural Diversity and Second Language Learning.

Menken, Kate, and Beth Antuñez. 2001. *An Overview of the Preparation and Certification of Teachers Working with Limited English Proficient (LEP) Students.* Washington, DC: National Clearinghouse of Bilingual Education.

Meskill, Carla. 2005. "Infusing English Language Learner Issues Throughout Professional Educator Curricula: The Training All Teachers Project." *Teachers College Record* 107(4): 739–56.

Moll, Luis, Cathy Amanti, Deborah Neff, and Norma Gonzalez. 2001. "Funds of Knowledge for Teaching: Using a Qualitative Approach to Connect Homes and Classrooms." *Theory into Practice* 31: 132–41.

NASBE Study Group on Language and Learning. 2007. *E Pluribus Unum: English, Language Education, and America's Future.* Alexandria, VA: National Association of State Boards of Education.

National Task Force on Early Childhood Education for Latinos. 2007. *Para Nuestros Niños: Expanding and Improving Early Education for Latinos.* www.ecehispanic.org/work/expand_MainReport.pdf.

Nieto, Sonia. 2000. "Bringing Bilingual Education Out of the Basement, and Other Imperatives for Teacher Education." In *Lifting Every Voice: Pedagogy and Politics of Bilingualism*, ed. Zeynep F. Beykont, 187–207. Cambridge, MA: Harvard Education Publishing Group.

Nieto, Sonia. 2000. *Affirming Diversity: A Sociopolitical Context for Multicultural Education.* Boston: Allyn and Bacon/Longman.

Nieto, Sonia. 2007. "School Reform and Student Learning: A Multicultural Perspective." In *Multicultural Education: Issues and Perspectives*, ed. James A. Banks and Cherry A. McGee Banks, 425–43. Boston: Allyn and Bacon.

Nieto, Sonia, and Patty Bode. 2008. *Affirming Diversity: The Sociopolitical Context of Multicultural Education*. Boston: Allyn and Bacon.

Nieto, Sonia. 2010. *Language, Culture and Teaching: Critical Perspectives*. New York: Routledge.

Noddings, Nel. 2002. *Starting at Home: Caring and Social Policy*. Berkeley: University of California Press.

Pape, Stephen J., Barry J. Zimmerman, and Frank Pajares. 2002. "Becoming a Self-Regulated Learner." *Theory into Practice* 41: 62–63.

Predictable Books. 2009. Education Oasis. www.educationoasis.com/curriculum/Reading/resources/predicatable_books.htm.

Puente, Sylvia, and Reyna Hernandez. *Transforming Early Learning: Educational Equity for Young Latinos*. 2009. Latino Policy Forum. www.latinopolicyforum.org/assets/Transforming%20Early%20Learning%20FINAL.pdf.

Report from the National Comprehensive Center for Teacher Quality and Public Agenda. 2008. *Lessons Learned: New Teachers Talk About Their Jobs, Challenges and Long-Range Plans*. Issue 3. Teaching in Changing Times. www.publicagenda.org/files/pdf/lessons_learned_3.pdf.

Reeves, Janelle R. 2006. "Secondary Teacher Attitudes Toward Including English-Language Learners in Mainstream Classrooms." *Journal of Educational Research* 99: 131–42.

Reyes, Augustina. 2006. "Reculturing Principal as Leaders for Cultural and Linguistic Diversity." In *Preparing Quality Educators for English Language Learners: Research, Policies, and Practices*, ed. Kip Tellez and Hersh C. Waxman, 145–65. Mahwah, NJ: Lawrence Erlbaum Associates.

Rolstad, Kellie, Kate Mahoney, and Gene Glass. 2005. "The Big Picture: A Meta-Analysis of Program Effectiveness Research on English Language Learners." *Educational Policy* 19(4): 572–94.

Rothstein, Richard. 1998. "Bilingual Education: The Controversy." *Phi Delta Kappan* 78: 672–78.

San Miguel, Guadalupe, Jr., and Richard R. Valencia. 1998. "From the Treaty of Guadalupe Hidalgo to Hopwood: The Education Plight and Struggle of Mexican Americans in the Southwest." *Harvard Educational Review* 68: 353–412.

Slavin, Robert E., and Alan Cheung. 2003. *Effective Reading Programs for English Language Learners: A Best-Evidence Synthesis*. Baltimore, MD: Johns Hopkins University, Center for Research on the Education of Students Placed at Risk.

Shin, Fay, and Barry Gribbons. 1996. "Hispanic Parent Perceptions and Attitudes of Bilingual Education." *The Journal of Mexican American Educators* 6: 16–22.

Shin, Fay, and Simon Kim. 1998. "Korean Parent Perceptions and Attitudes of Bilingual Education." In *Current Issues in Asian and Pacific American Education*, ed. Russell Endo, Clara Park, John Tsuchida, and Alan Abbayani. Covina, CA: Pacific Asian Press.

Smiley, Patricia, and Trudy Salsberry. 2007. *Effective Schooling for English Language Learners: What Elementary Principals Should Know and Do*. Larchmont, NY: Eye on Education.

Snow, Catherine. 2002. *Reading for Understanding: Toward an R&D Program in Reading Comprehension*. Santa Monica, CA: RAND.

Soltero, Sonia W. 2003. "Debunking Urban Legends on Bilingual Education." *Diálogo*, 7(1), 20–24.

Soltero, Sonia W. 2004. *Dual Language: Teaching and Learning in Two Languages*. Boston: Allyn and Bacon/Longman.

Statement of NCTE Against Arizona Department of Education Ruling on Teacher Speech. June 2010. www.ncte.org/library/NCTEFiles/Involved/Action/NCTE positiononAZELLrules.pdf.

Suárez-Orozco, Carola, Marcelo Suárez-Orozco, and Irina Todorova. 2008. *Learning a New Land: Immigrant Students in American Society*. Cambridge, MA: Harvard University Press.

Suárez-Orozco, Carola, and Marcelo Suárez-Orozco. 2001. *Children of Immigration*. Cambridge, MA: Harvard University Press.

Swain, Merrill. 1985. "Communicative Competence: Some Roles of Comprehensible Input and Comprehensible Output in Its Development." In *Input in Second Language Acquisition*, ed. Susan M. Gass and Carolyn G. Madden, 235–56. Cambridge, MA: Newbury House Publishers.

Swanson, Christopher. 2008. *Cities in Crisis: A Special Analytic Report on High School Graduation*. Editorial Projects in Education (EPE) Research Center. www.edweek .org/media/citiesincrisis040108.pdf.

Tanenbaum, Courtney, and Lindsay Anderson. 2010. *Title III Accountability and District Improvement Efforts: A Closer Look*. ESEA Evaluation Brief: The English Language Acquisition, Language Enhancement, and Academic Achievement Act. American Institutes for Research.

Tharp, R. G. 1994. "Research Knowledge and Policy Issues in Cultural Diversity and Education." In *Language and Learning: Educating Linguistically Diverse Students*, ed. B. McLeod, 129–67. Albany: State University of New York Press.

The Education Alliance at Brown University. 2003. *Claiming Opportunities: A Handbook for Improving Education for English Language Learners Through Comprehensive School Reform*. Providence, RI: Brown University. www.alliance.brown.edu/pubs/claiming_opportunities/claimopp_all.pdf.

Thomas, Wayne P., Virginia P. Collier, and Martha Abbott. 1993. "Academic Achievement through Japanese, Spanish, or French: The First Two Years of Partial Immersion." *Modern Language Journal* 77: 170–80.

Trueba, Henry T. 1991. "The Role of Culture in Bilingual Instruction: Linking Linguistic and Cognitive Development to Cultural Knowledge." In *Bilingual Education: Focusschrift in Honor of Joshua A. Fishman on the Occasion of his 65th Birthday*, ed. Ofelia García, 43–55. Philadelphia: John Benjamins.

Trueba, Henry T. 1999. "The Education of Mexican Immigrant Children." In *Crossings: Mexican Immigration in Interdisciplinary Perspective*, ed. Marcelo M. Suárez-Orozco, 253–75. Cambridge, MA: Harvard University, David Rockefeller Center for Latin American Studies.

Tse, Lucy. 2001. *Why Don't They Learn English? Separating Fact from Fallacy in the U.S. Language Debate*. New York: Teachers College Press.

United States Department of Education. 2008. *The Biennial Report to Congress on the Implementation of the Title III State Formula Grant Program, School Years 2004–06*. Office of English Language Acquisition, Language Enhancement, and Academic Achievement for Limited English Proficient Students: Washington, DC. www.ed.gov/about/offices/list/oela/title3biennial0406.pdf.

United States Government Accountability Office. 2009. *Teacher Preparation: Report to the Chairman, Subcommittee on Higher Education, Lifelong Learning, and Competitiveness*. Committee on Education and Labor, House of Representatives. www.gao.gov/new.items/d09573.pdf.

Usdan, Michael, Barbara McLeod, and Mary Podmostko. 2000. *Leadership for Student Learning: Reinventing the Principalship: School Leadership for the 21st Century Initiative*. A Report of the Task Force on the Principalship. Institute for Educational Leadership. www.iel.org/programs/21st/reports/principal.pdf.

Valdés, Guadalupe. 2001. *Learning and Not Learning English: Latino Students in American Schools*. New York: Teachers College Press.

Valenzuela, Angela. 1999. *Subtractive Schooling: U.S. Mexican Youth and the Politics of Caring*. Albany: State University of New York Press.

Walqui, Aida. 2000. *Access and Engagement: Program Design and Instructional Approaches for Immigrant Students in Secondary School*. Washington, DC: Center for Applied Linguistics and Delta Systems Co. Inc.

Waring, Rob. 2002. "Basic Principles and Practices in Vocabulary Instruction." *The Language Teacher*, 26. www.jalt-publications.org/tlt/articles/2002/07/waring.

WIDA-www.wida.us/.

Williams, Debra. 2007. *Preschool Seats Go Begging in Poor Black Communities*. Catalyst-Chicago. www.catalyst-chicago.org/news/index.php?item=2260&cat=30.

Wong Fillmore, Lily, and Concepción Valadéz. 1986. "Teaching Bilingual Learners." In *Handbook of Research on Teaching*, ed. Merlin C. Wittrock, 648–85. New York: Macmillan.

Wong Fillmore, Lily. 2005. "When Learning a Second Language Means Losing the First." In *The New Immigration: An Interdisciplinary Reader*, ed. Marcelo M. Suárez-Orozco, Carola Suárez-Orozco, and Desiree B. Qin, 288–308. New York: Routledge.

Zahed-Babelan, Askarian, and Mahdi Moeni Kia. 2010. "Study of Teacher-Students Interaction in Teaching Process and Its Relation with Students' Achievement in Primary Schools." *The Social Sciences* 5: 55–59.

Zehler, Annette M., Howard L. Fleischman, Paul J. Hopstock, Todd G. Stephenson, Michelle L. Pendzick, and Saloni Sapru. 2003. *Descriptive Study of Services to LEP Students and LEP Students with Disabilities*. Volume I: Research Report. U.S. Department of Education, OELA. Arlington, VA: Development Associates Inc.

INDEX